Living
Legends

Sandy Thorne is a bush poet and Australia's favourite yarn spinner. She describes herself as the oldest jillaroo in the west and is also a former horse-breaker and bull-catcher. She is the author of *Bonzer* and *Old-Timers: Magnificent Stories from Mighty Australians*. Sandy has performed at countless festivals, concerts, conferences and other events as well as on TV and radio all over Australia, New Zealand and the US. She launched her first book, *I've Met Some Bloody Wags!*, in 1980 on *The Midday Show* by ripping the top off a stubby with her teeth. Her books have sold over 460 000 copies. Sandy lives on a station near Lightning Ridge in New South Wales.

sandythorne.com.au

SANDY THORNE

Living Legends

TRUE TALES OF EXTRAORDINARY OLD-TIMERS

MICHAEL JOSEPH
an imprint of
PENGUIN BOOKS

MICHAEL JOSEPH

Published by the Penguin Group
Penguin Group (Australia)
707 Collins Street, Melbourne, Victoria 3008, Australia
(a division of Penguin Australia Pty Ltd)
Penguin Group (USA) Inc.
375 Hudson Street, New York, New York 10014, USA
Penguin Group (Canada)
90 Eglinton Avenue East, Suite 700, Toronto, Canada ON M4P 2Y3
(a division of Penguin Canada Books Inc.)
Penguin Books Ltd
80 Strand, London WC2R 0RL England
Penguin Ireland
25 St Stephen's Green, Dublin 2, Ireland
(a division of Penguin Books Ltd)
Penguin Books India Pvt Ltd
11 Community Centre, Panchsheel Park, New Delhi – 110 017, India
Penguin Group (NZ)
67 Apollo Drive, Rosedale, Auckland 0632, New Zealand
(a division of Penguin New Zealand Pty Ltd)
Penguin Books (South Africa) (Pty) Ltd
Rosebank Office Park, Block D, 181 Jan Smuts Avenue, Parktown North,
Johannesburg, 2196, South Africa
Penguin (Beijing) Ltd
7F, Tower B, Jiaming Center, 27 East Third Ring Road North, Chaoyang District,
Beijing 100020, China

Penguin Books Ltd, Registered Offices: 80 Strand, London WC2R 0RL, England

First published by Penguin Group (Australia), 2014

1 3 5 7 9 10 8 6 4 2

Text copyright © Sandy Thorne, 2014

The moral right of the author has been asserted

Cover design by Nikki Townsend © Penguin Group (Australia)
Text design by Samantha Jayaweera © Penguin Group (Australia)
Author photograph by Kristin Williams, Lightning Ridge
All other photographs belong to the subjects of the stories
Illustration on page 1 by Click49/Shutterstock.com
Typeset in Sabon by Samantha Jayaweera
Printed and bound in Australia by Griffin Press, an Accredited ISO AS/NZS 14001
Environmental Management Systems printer

National Library of Australia Cataloguing-in-Publication data:

Thorne, Sandy, author.
Living legends : true tales of extraordinary old-timers /
Sandy Thorne.

9781921901379 (paperback)

Australia–Biography.
Australia–Biography–Anecdotes.

994.0922

penguin.com.au

Contents

To all our war veterans.
You made this country what it is
and we owe you so much.

Conversion Table

10 acres	4 hectares
8 inches	20 centimetres
1 foot	30 centimetres
10 miles	16 kilometres
10 shillings	1 dollar
6 pence	5 cents
4 farthings	1 cent
1 pound	2 dollars
4 gallons	18 litres
6 stone	38 kilograms

All conversions are approximate.
* Currency conversions are based on those used in 1966,
when decimal currency was introduced in Australia.

G'day. You are about to meet some wonderful people. People who all have a great story to tell. They'll make you laugh, make you cry, astonish you with their resilience and bravery – what they have endured – and endear themselves to you by the sheer fact that they have put more into life than they have received.

As you read their stories in the comfort of your chair, enjoy the many unusual and sometimes amazing adventures they have experienced during their long lives.

All have been through incidents that are fascinating, funny, frightening, just plain horrendous or absolutely hilarious! Some are ordinary people who have lived long, interesting lives, some are extraordinary individuals whose stories are often shocking or simply breathtaking.

From highly diverse backgrounds, they have one thing in common: they are all *young at heart*!

For example, Dot, still pretty at ninety-seven years old, laughs as she's pulling on her bowling shoes, telling you about the time she got shot in the face on her dairy farm. 'Dusty', a 94-year-old larrikin livewire, is revered in many circles for surviving thirty missions as a rear gunner on bombers in WW II, and still helps his community. Entertainer Terry, who's toured all over Australia singing and telling jokes for half a century, is still on stage and still lovin' livin' on laughs. Neville the naughty auctioneer and retired stock agent still raises eyebrows with his devilish wit at charity auctions. And then there's 'Winki', a bloody wag from Eulo whose yarns about her time as a bush nurse go back a hell of a long way, when hospital conditions were still positively Crimean! And that's just a few of the characters – variety is the spice of life, and of this book.

So make a big pot of tea or pitcher of daiquiris, settle back and enjoy reading the life stories of these lively, lovely people.

They've Seen It All

You can only marvel at the changes they have seen,
from bullockies and steam trains when they were young and keen,
to road trains, jets, computers and phones that have a brain,
the world they knew in simpler days can never be the same.

Children walked 3 miles to school, along the dusty tracks;
to clear the land or build a road, you swung a 5-pound axe.
The laundry was a full day's toil, the woodstove blazed all day;
once in a while there'd be a dance and everyone was gay*.

Their happiness in simple pleasures, to dance, sing or recite,
'round the campfire or piano, was a perfect Saturday night.
And when a lad would court a girl, with rosy maiden's blush,
they 'stepped out' till they were sure, with no unseemly rush.

Coarse language never reached the ears of the fairer sex;
men tipped their hats in the street in masculine respect.
They were all females' protectors, proud of being strong;
a firm handshake sealed a deal, a man's word was his bond.

Yes, you can only marvel at the changes they have seen;
since the Depression and World War II, how different life has been.
They could never have imagined when they were boys and girls
that it would be their generation who'd see two different worlds.

*happy (the original meaning)

1.

Bob Duncan

BULLDOZER ARTISTE, TRUCKIE, FIGHTER, BUFFALO
HUNTER, CROC WRESTLER, LOTTO WINNER
AND LIFESAVER

Like most bush blokes, Bob Duncan is a man of many talents. Perhaps the one that really shines more brightly than the others is his brilliance as a physician who can heal sick and injured motors and machines.

If they handed out Rhodes Scholarships to genius bush mechanics, Bob would be on the honour roll. This laidback, modest outback bloke can take on seemingly impossible problems with recalcitrant or unconscious engines of any size, in the most awkward of locations, and achieve the impossible. What he has done to keep machinery and trucks moving in the middle of nowhere is the stuff of legend.

When workshops, tools, machines and spare engines are way out of reach and other fellers would be calling on the radio for help, Bob refuses to give up, almost relishing the challenge. As he stares at the problem and quietly nuts out what he has to do to get out of this fine mess, he squats his wiry but powerful frame down in the dust, stockman-style, pushes his sweat-stained old hat back on his head, then slowly, thoughtfully, rolls a durry while chucking his brain up a cog or two. It's a perfect picture of the quintessential resourceful bushman that any artist or photographer would love to capture. As a master of improvisation, this great character who can fix just about anything has no equal. Magnates like Lindsay Fox or Twiggy Forrest would kill to have him on their staff.

He's a great feller to have a drink and a joke with, too, but watch him if he's drinking rum! After enough Bundys, this bantamweight will take on the biggest bloke in the pub if he senses an insult to him or a mate. Keep an eye on your missus or your sheila, too, for Bob is ambidextrous – a fighter *and* a lover! So how did he acquire all these skills? Where did this graduate from the Outback School of Hard Knocks hail from?

Born on 13 August 1939 in Richmond, Melbourne, the son of Charles, a civil engineer, and Gladys, a lovely lady, Bob was the second oldest of six children. At the time, Charles was designing the irrigation channels and other infrastructure for the Murrumbidgee Irrigation Scheme. They lived at North Melbourne, but moved when Bob was a baby, to Woods Point, Gippsland, at the head of the Goulburn River, where his father was the chief engineer for the Morning Star goldmine. During the terrible Black Friday bushfires that year, his mother had to run from danger, carrying him and holding his brother's hand, to the nearby creek, taking refuge in the water as the flames bore down on their home in the bush. Mother, baby and toddler not only survived the flames that flew through the trees above them, but miraculously, their house and pets did also. However, all the small buildings near the house were burnt to the ground. Nearby, two men were boiled to death in a ship's tank.

With the threat of Japanese invasion, their father had joined the army, was made a captain, and sent to New Guinea to hold the 'Yellow Peril' back and hunt them away from Australia. While he was away, the rest of the family moved temporarily to a farm at

Cudgewa at the foot of Mount Kosciuszko, owned by their grand-mother and their Uncle Allan, who was with the army in Egypt. After an ammo truck near Allan was blown up, he returned home with injuries that prevented him returning to life as a farmer, so he became a bootmaker. Bob vividly remembers two things from those years: helping his injured uncle cut wood and his mother and grand-mother's despair at the wartime rationing.

When his father returned from the war, they moved back to Woods Point, which was a place known for extremes of weather: snowfalls and bushfires. Despite being freezing in winter, it was a great place to grow up and enjoy a bush childhood with plenty of mates and plenty of simple country fun, like swimming in the creeks. They had to slog to school in the snow at times, but weighed against that discomfort was the fun of learning from their schoolteachers to ski on Mount Matlock. Bob vividly recalls his fear when he first took off downhill, gathering speed, and suddenly realised he didn't have a clue how to stop!

He loved being a constant help to his mother by collecting firewood and carting it home. He did many other chores for his three-pence a week pocket money, which he saved up to go to the movies, held in the old Cobb and Co station every three or four months. Charlie Chaplin's were his favourites and, later, The Three Stooges.

As they grew up, Bob and his older brother, Warren, would often go fishing in the Goulburn River. Bob recalls their mother's delight at all the trout they'd bring home. She never knew that their impres-sive hauls were due to the detonators her dear boys pinched from the mine to blow up the fishing holes! She would often have to break up fights between the brothers, but was in for a nasty shock one day when, after Warren had been flattened by Bob, the older brother got to his feet enraged and drove a pick through his sibling's foot, pinning it to the ground. Ouch! Their mother had to pull the pick out then carry Bob to the bush nurse. Another vivid memory is of being sick all the way to the Melbourne Show in his father's company car – a '39 Ford.

Even at primary school, Bob was a ladies' man. With a typical cheeky grin, blue eyes twinkling, he declares he still remembers *all* his girlfriends from Woods Point! When he was aged twelve, he told his father that a preacher from Mansfield was coming to christen any children who hadn't been and that he needed to know what religion they were. For a joke, his father told him to say they were 'Calathumpian', which he did, to the delight of the congregation. The dark spot of his otherwise happy childhood was the fact his dad was always extra hard on him and, sadly, Bob always felt he didn't like him. His father's weapon of choice when giving a belting was his leather razor strop. Bob's hands and bum were also well used to the feel of the teacher's cane. When he was fourteen, he decided he was sick of being flogged. He began rubbing rosin from pine trees into his hands to get them hard. After being caught pinching a ciggie from the teacher's packet, and receiving six 'cuts' on each hand, he suddenly let drive and flattened the teacher, then raced home and chopped his father's razor strop into pieces. Thus ended Bob's formal education. He was off to work, and mighty happy about that!

On his first day working for Gold Mines Australia (now called WMC) in the Morning Star mine, his father, who by then was manager, thought he'd give Bob a fright when he went down the shaft in a cage for the first time. A steam winder sent the two cages up and down a 2000-foot drop in a 5-metre-wide vertical shaft, and Bob was sent flying down as fast as it would go, on his own in the pitch darkness. He swears his handprints would still be on the bar across the steel cage!

Already used to physical work, he was tasked to be the carpenter's offsider, cutting and shaping, then fitting all the different pieces of timber required in the mine: collars, beams, stays, supports, etc. – an important and exacting job. On leaving the mine each day, the men had to empty their pockets and lunchboxes in front of the security manager, then go through the turnstiles in the nude to the showers. Bob's pay was 4 pounds, 12 shillings and sixpence a fortnight for twelve eight-hour days underground. He paid 2 pounds of it to his mother for board. When he decided he just couldn't work for his father any longer, he moved to Sydney to his Aunty Edna's at Mascot and got a job at Allen's Sweets at Rosebery, carting boxes of Minties and other lollies all over the factory, plus sweeping. After being hospitalised for appendicitis, he returned to work before feeling fully recovered – fearful of losing his job – and the cranky foreman sacked him because he was too weak to swing the broom to his liking. The foreman at his next job in a billycan factory was an even bigger bastard. When Bob decided he couldn't take his attitude any longer, he lost his temper and belted him up into a heap, leaving piles of dented billycans hell west and crooked! He'd also had a gutful of Aunty Edna by then, so he packed up, left the cranky old bitch, and headed for the first live-in job on a farm he could get, milking cows and doing other farm chores at Colac. The boss there was a good bloke, but it was cold, miserable weather and he saved every penny he could for six months, to go to the Northern Territory.

He was prepared to have another go at working for his father, who by then was managing the Northern Hercules goldmine at Pine Creek, 64 miles from Katherine. This time he would be working with, and apprenticed to, his brother-in-law, Cliff, who ran the mine's workshop and was a good bloke. Cliff taught him to fix all types of machinery and vehicles and it became obvious soon after his arrival that Bob was just a natural. He drove the mine's truck the 35 miles into Pine Creek every week to pick up supplies, including the fuel, from the train from Darwin. His lack of a driving licence didn't seem to bother anybody. He and Cliff enjoyed fishing for barramundi in the Mary River, both the legitimate way and occasionally with the help of explosives.

As well as quickly picking up an ability to drive all sorts of vehicles, Bob also found he was a natural horseman. He'd palled up with Clark Taylor, the son of a local cattleman, and on days off would go out to Goodparla Station, which was made up of 1700 square miles of Arnhem Land. There he quickly learnt how to ride, muster, shoot and hunt. It was exciting fun for a teenager, helping to catch brumbies and scrub bulls, shooting buffaloes and huge wild pigs from horseback, and going croc hunting at night. The bigger crocs were skinned, the smaller ones kept to be stuffed. It was 'hairy' wrestling the crocs to the boat at night, but Bob had the advantage of being half mad, as many young blokes in the Top End are. One night a croc, about 4 metres long, that his mate Clark had shot, started sinking. Bob flew out into the water to get a rope around it and manoeuvred it across to the boat, when suddenly it came back to life! Bob wasn't game to let go and his mate was laughing so much that he was no help. Fortunately the monster succumbed again and Bob lived to tell the tale.

The Aboriginal stockmen took a shine to Bob and showed him how to track the wild bulls, brumbies and buffaloes, and where to look for them. Bob earned the admiration of these men by being willing to get on any of the brumbies that looked like they could become a stockhorse, and getting back on again and again each time he was thrown. Soon he was riding them out of the yards with the best of them. The boss paid him 2 shillings and sixpence for every horse he rode out, the breaking-in process being extremely basic – rough as guts, in fact. That was handy extra dough along with what he made from croc skins and 'stuffers'. It wasn't a life for the faint-hearted, being on a Territory station back then. When he once had to run for the jeep to get his .38 Colt revolver, with a mad scrubber cow chasing him, the blokes all laughed as if it was a great joke. 'By cripes, that Bobby can run! 'N' he's a bloody good shot, too, 'ey!' they told the boss later. Bob was also a 'deadeye Dick' with his Martini .303, and later with his Swedish .306, a heavier rifle with an army sniper's scope.

He loved the time he spent on the station during the years he was in that area, but he also enjoyed his job in the workshop, where he learnt more and more about motors and machines, and how to operate a dozer.

He stayed at Pine Creek until the mine shut down when he was nineteen years old. All that time he didn't drink – apart from one incident – but he was to well and truly make up for that later on. The legal drinking age was twenty-one, but at eighteen he had been introduced to alcohol while staying at a mate's place in Darwin to have some flying lessons. They were celebrating the fact that Bob, after just a few lessons in a Tiger Moth, had flown solo for the first time. He'd met a pretty nurse and was supposed to take her out to dinner that night, but several bottles of Buffalo Bitter killed enough brain cells to cause him to forget about his date. She didn't forgive him, so that should have put him off grog for good, but the big thirst of the Territory eventually got to him.

A memory of his years at Pine Creek that always makes him laugh is of the policeman's face when Bob asked for a driver's licence on his seventeenth birthday. He'd been driving into town in the truck for a couple of years by then. The policeman said, 'What! You little bastard! You haven't got a licence to drive *anything*?' When Bob replied 'Nup', the copper just shook his head, laughed, and gave him an E class licence, which entitled him to drive everything from a road train to a car.

When the mine closed, his father went to Darwin and set up a business with a partner, Dr Keith Hudson, exporting live buffaloes to Timor. Unfortunately it didn't prove viable, so he went to Western Australia as an engineer, building power stations from his base at Esperance. Meanwhile, Bob had settled in to life in Darwin, which was a wild old town in the late '50s. He'd put his age up to get a job driving a taxi, and knew everybody. He earned a reputation for not being a bloke to trifle with or to attempt evading a fare from. One drunk female who refused to pay the 10-shillings fare to Parap threatened to smash the windscreen with a rock if he didn't drive off, so he soon pushed her arse over head and retrieved the 10-shillings note out of her purse. Many lively and humorous incidents occurred during this time, but one which stands out in Bob's memory happened when he was taking two highly intoxicated gay men, who were having a big argument in the cab, back to a passenger ship docked at the wharf. When one paid the fare of 5 shillings, the other one walked around to Bob's window and gave him another 5 bob, saying, 'I won't have that dirty slut pay *my* fare!'

The Greek man who owned Bob's taxi and five others lost his entire fleet of cars one night gambling against some Chinese men in a game played with dominoes. Bob had been there with him and had to stay awake all night as they played. That was the end of his cabbie career, because the Chinese put on their own drivers. Free as a bird again, Bob had a bit of a blowout at the famous Don Hotel and discovered rum and Coke. He thought they were good tucker, and when closing time was announced, ordered twelve. Refusing to leave until he'd thrown them all down, he soon found himself spending the rest of the night as a guest of Her Majesty. He was to enjoy the lock-up 'bed and breakfast experience' quite often during his knockabout life in the bush. Then it was off to Groote Eylandt, where manganese, used to harden steel, was mined, to earn a big quid operating scrapers, dozers, etc. Conditions were tough, camped in tents, but the fishing was great, and every three months he had three weeks off to play merry hell in lively, almost-anything-goes Darwin.

His next job was working for the Commonwealth Department of Works as a bulldozer operator, constructing beef roads. The base was at Katherine but a lot of time was spent out in bush camps. Katherine remains Bob's favourite place in Australia. He loved jumping the 20-metre drop off the railway bridge into the river, swimming at Jim Jim Falls, and fishing for barra at the Gorge, using his favourite tackle: dynamite. He also enjoyed the job and the good company. The cook at the Katherine base, Mick Campbell, was a good bloke and a good mate. Bob introduced him to his mother, who had left his father. They got on well and eventually married. When they were at the base, the men were issued with special coins to spend on stubbies of beer at the wet mess. They had 'NT Beef Roads' written on the back, and the word 'Stub-loon' on the front. The Territory thirst was hard to quench, but this was a way of limiting how much they could drink every night. One night after hunting crocs for extra money, Bob pulled into the Katherine Hotel with a big thirst, but the pub was so chock-a-block, he couldn't fight his way to the bar. So he went out to his truck, retrieved a bag containing eight 'stuffers' (small crocs less than a metre long), and tipped them out among the crowd. The patrons immediately scattered, hell west and crooked, while the stuffers snapped at everything they could see. Fortunately the publican, Pat Kirby, could see the joke and gave Bob a beer.

On the beef-roads job, he taught himself to drive the grader, which was a far more challenging skill than bulldozing trees out of the way. It's difficult to get the road perfectly level and to know where to put the dirt. He helped construct beef roads to Top Springs, Timber Creek and Borroloola – areas of great isolation. One day a tree came down on his dozer, smashed the canopy and bent the fuel tank. Despite a head injury, he managed to call up the flying doctor, who told him what to use from the medical kit he carried, which had everything numbered. Rather than call for the doctor to fly there to stitch his head up, he stitched it up himself with the aid of his ute's rear-vision mirror. A few rums would have been handy but he had none. His stitching skills were called in again not long after, when he sustained a quite severe leg injury. This time he bound it up and waited till he could get back to camp and have a few grogs first. He had a few beers with his workmates then set to work with needle and thread, having a few good swigs from his 'tallie' between stitches. He'd just finished his gruesome, painful task when one of the blokes, who'd had a considerable amount of grog, suddenly went troppo. This was a fairly normal occurrence in the Territory, especially when the wet was approaching and the humidity almost unbearable. The sight of Bob stitching his own leg up must have sent him over the edge. He went to his donga, got his .303 and took a shot at Bob. He missed, but hit Bob's bottle of beer. That was almost enough to send Bob off his rocker also. As the ratbag ran off carrying his three-o, Bob took off after him, spun him around and gave him a hell of a hiding, which put him into Slumberland until they were able to send him off to the funny farm, tied up in the back of a ute.

Working on the road from Daly Waters to Borroloola, the gang would all go to the Daly pub for the weekend and play up like second-hand motorbikes. Bob had got onto some extra cash by collecting dingo scalps. Worth a guinea (21 shillings) each, they were lawfully legal tender when taken to a town. On Bob's first trip to Daly pub, the publican wouldn't cash a cheque for him to quench his thirst, so he went out to his truck, brought twenty scalps in and dropped them on the bar. The publican had to accept them as legal tender and from then on he and Bob got on just fine.

One day Bob was helping the mechanic fix a water tanker near Daly Waters when the head of the big hammer he was using flew off and hit him in the face, breaking his nose, smashing his front teeth and splitting his lip. The mechanic drove him to Katherine, 157 miles away, to get help. As there were three pubs on the way, they were legless when they arrived at the hospital many hours later. The cranky matron was not impressed, and didn't give Bob a local anaesthetic when she stitched his lip up. Fortunately he was still anaesthetised by alcohol when the doctor then straightened his nose, which was way off centre, by brutally screwing it around to where it should have been, as if Bob was a plastic mannequin. The next day, he returned to have the stumps of all four front teeth pulled out by Dr Moo, a Chinese man who later became an excellent eye doctor, tutored by Flynn of The Inland. Bob eventually had dentures made, and those dentures were to have a very adventurous life! In the meantime, how could Dr Moo's attractive assistant, Yvonne, not be drawn to this smashed-up, dishevelled, hungover patient as he helped Dr Moo haul his teeth out while managing to wink at her at the same time? After a whirlwind courtship (he was pretty toey), Bob married Yvonne, aged eighteen, and they flew to her home state of Western Australia. His three years with the Department of Works were up and they had a policy of flying their men to any city (for either a holiday or to start a new life), after every three years of service. He was only twenty-one, but had packed a lot of living into the years since he'd flattened his Grade Eight teacher and left school.

In Perth, Bob soon secured employment with Bell Brothers, a big earthmoving company that sent him to the Kimberley to work on dozers, building a beef road from Napier Downs to Mount House. While a cutting was being dynamited through Inglis Gap, Bob was clearing a stretch from Silent Grove to a place called March Fly Glen, which turned out to be appropriately named. If you haven't been bitten by a march fly, try to imagine the stinging power of a thousand mossies hitting you with one agonising 'ZAP!' He had to wear overalls, gloves and a veil while bulldozing there.

Yvonne came from that region and lived with her mother in Derby while Bob was away with the crew. When they'd been married for six months, he came home unexpectedly and saw her walking hand-in-hand with another bloke, who of course was soon flat on his back seeing stars and wondering what had hit him. Bob gave Yvonne's dainty arse a good kick in the direction of her mother's house, then said, 'Adios. See you in the divorce court.' Broken-hearted in the knowledge Yvonne had been two-timing him for quite a while, he headed back to the Territory in his Plymouth to get right away from her. Thus began a monumental bender in Katherine, until his mum and Mick conspired with the supervisor from the old outfit he worked for, the Department of Works, to shanghai him while dead drunk, to get him away from his watering hole. He woke up in the back of a Land Rover at a road-making camp between Timber

Creek and Top Springs – in the middle of nowhere. Bob drove doz-ers and graders in that area for the next couple of years and became famous locally for his totally insane stunt of swimming the croco-dile-infested Victoria River, drunk and sober, to get to the Vic pub, then swimming back again to the side where his camp was located.

When that job was completed, he went to the Kununurra Ord River Diversion Scheme, just across the Western Australian border, where Thiess Bros were building the channels. Beer at the wet mess there cost 10 shillings a jug and a thirsty Bob chugged a lot of jugs, happy to pay the shilling deposit on their return, and foregoing the plastic glasses. He worked with a good crew and when an argument was settled by a fist fight, all was forgiven next day and it was back onto the machines, black eyes and grazed knuckles and cheekbones accepted as normal.

The next big job Thiess had on was putting down an open-cut mine, 650 feet deep, at Mount Isa, and Bob camped at their Star Gully camp. Again, conditions were hot and harsh, but he was used to that, as the other operators were, and they just got stuck into get-ting the job done. Most people would only be in Mount Isa to earn big money, and Bob was earning 60 pounds a week plus 3 pounds 'lead bonus'. All his crew were highly experienced, good workers and good operators but for some reason the younger of the Thiess Bros, who were contracted to Mount Isa Mines, engaged a 'time and motion' expert to monitor their staff with a stopwatch. On his report, the whole crew were sacked. Their union closed down the entire mine and young Thiess went to the pub to reinstate them. Bob was no pinko, but the mass sacking on the advice of some 'hare-brained academic dill' had been wrong.

Mount Isa locals back then liked to skite it was 'the world's big-gest city' because its main street, Camooweal Street, ran 117 miles to its 'outer suburb', Camooweal. The Isa was a rough, tough, fairly wild place back then. Typical of mining towns, women were outnumbered by six to one, so there were plenty of fist fights over them. Bob drank at Boyd's pub, where blood as well as beer was often splashed over the tiles. He occasionally enjoyed the hospitality of Her Majesty there, but was disgusted with the running of the lockup at 'Mosquito Hill', where no Aeroguard was supplied for him and his fellow guests.

After the Isa job was finished, he was sent with his crew to build a road from Dajarra to Boulia. During their first blowout at the salubrious Dajarra pub, Bob was barred for knocking a bloke out who'd picked on his little mate. From then on, he had to stay out on the verandah and his mates would ferry beers out to him. The next job offered a change: it was back over the border again into the Territory, carting freight between Darwin and Alice, driving a B Model Mack – a trip that usually took twenty-one hours. Once, when he picked up a female on the outskirts of Darwin and they 'honeymooned' all the way to the Alice, the same distance took three days! She left Bob with a 'souvenir' that wasn't much fun at all. It took twelve needles in his bum to return a certain part of his anatomy to normal, that was 'lit up like a Christmas tree'!

Alice Springs also provided Bob with what *only he* would describe as his 'funniest night in a lock-up'. He'd taken on fighting three Aboriginal blokes in a pub, and an Irish copper 'with a sense of humour' (according to Bob) locked them all in the one cell. They had a 'great old time' for about an hour until the Irish sergeant thought Bob had had enough fun, and put him in a separate cell. The next day, he fined Bob 10 shillings and the Aboriginal fellers, who'd started it, a pound each. He told them all that the next time they wanted to fight, to go outside the town boundary. In a fight,

Bob's secret weapon was the fact he's a 'southpaw' (left-hander), which nearly always takes an opponent by surprise.

He then found himself in charge of a gang of Thursday Islanders, tying down concrete on a wharf near Cairns. He'd only been on the job a few days when the foreman said something to one of the Islanders that Bob considered was insulting. He grabbed him and hurled him in the shark and croc-infested water. The foreman survived but Bob's job didn't.

In 1968, Bob answered his sister's invitation to visit her for a holiday at Lightning Ridge in New South Wales, home of the world's best-quality black opal. His brother-in-law took him mining, and when Bob found some stones straight away, he was hooked. Like many visitors from all over the world, he loved the atmosphere of the town, which was friendly yet still very Wild West. The place was full of characters, so he fitted in perfectly. He set up a camp in the bush 4 miles out of town and proceeded to do what a lot of opal miners don't manage: he made a living from the stones he dug up. It was the old-fashioned pick and shovel style of mining, shifting a lot of dirt between each opal, but he found enough to keep him going. The two best stones he found were valued at $15 000 and $10 000. He also did mechanical work for people, but mining came first.

In 1972 he married Dot, a nice lady who worked at the Community Health Centre. It was hard for a wild bloke like Bob to have a quiet wedding. As Dot walked down the aisle of the Bush Church, the electric organ, which was playing *Here Comes the Bride*, suddenly carked it in a huge puff of smoke. Bob's admiring gaze and quiet smile turned into a wide-eyed exclamation of 'SHIT!', but he didn't take it as an omen and was happy to at least attempt to settle down with Dot. He'd bought a house and had taken on the responsibility of raising her four children. With a heart like a lion, he also agreed to raise two more who Dot wanted to foster, and built extra rooms for them. With all those mouths to feed, reality had set in regarding the likelihood of doing a big starve now and then, in between finding opals, so he bought himself a business. The local carrier had passed away and he purchased his Mercedes truck, carting wool from district stations and backloading goods – mainly heavy machinery – from Brisbane, Sydney and Newcastle, where the wool sales were held. Bales of wool weigh approximately 180 kilos, and nowadays wool carriers use a forklift, but Bob loaded them the hard, old-fashioned way, using bale hooks and brawn. It was exhausting, as was the lack of sleep, doing three trips a week. He slaved like that for five years, until the doctor told him if he didn't ease up, he would cark it. Miraculously, he found someone to buy the business, which by then included a tipper, a 32-metre tipping trailer, a smaller Nissan truck and a UD CWA45.

If anyone said to him these days that they were going to buy a truck and become a carrier, he would tell them to go and see a psychiatrist. The happiest day of his life was seeing 'the arse end of those trucks and trailers leaving my yard for good'. No more working for the taxation and transport departments, and the tyre, fuel, spare parts and insurance companies! Then there were the people who wouldn't pay their bills. He was tempted to shame them in the local paper. (He still might!)

As an owner-driver, his mechanical ability had been vital to his survival. The most major 'operation' he performed on the UD should be included in the annals of amazing feats involving a vehicle. After he broke down on the north side of Lithgow, with 120 bales of wool, a bloke in a big new Mack pulled up to see if he could help. When Bob told him he was okay, that he was going to clean out his injector pump that he'd put on a tarp beside the truck, the bloke said, 'That's impossible. I'll take it to a workshop in Lithgow for you.' Bob assured him it wasn't f**kin' impossible, and as the bloke drove off shaking his head at the perceived stupidity, proceeded to use the compressed air stored for his brakes to painstakingly blow out the injectors and injector pump. This job would normally be done in a pressurised room, and all parts put together in a container covered in diesel. As usual, Dr Bob's surgery, conducted under primitive conditions, was successful, and the patient roared off to get its load to the Newcastle wool sales.

He was also greatly skilled at dodging 'scalies' – officials who check the weight of loads on road vehicles – when carting some weird piece of mining machinery that was too high or too heavy for their liking. However, sometimes his triumphant grin would be somewhat dimmed, particularly the night he bought a burger at Coonabarabran, and didn't have time to eat it *before* driving off, which is always a wise thing to do. Wrestling it into his hungry gob, he found his teeth were sort of 'bogged', and because he was buggered and cranky, he roared, 'Bugger the bloody hamburger!' and chucked it out the window. Unfortunately, his teeth were still stuck in the cheeseburger.

Life on the road always has many memorable moments! The most unusual load he carted was thirteen camels, four drafthorses, six mules, ten donkeys, thirty chooks and one ferret, from Cobar, for Collarenebri identity Mick James.

After he sold the trucking business, he operated machines for a local contractor and enjoyed a break from the punishing regime and stress he'd been through for five years. He was always in demand to repair dozers and other machinery for opal miners and graziers.

In 1994, Dot died suddenly of a heart attack at a barbecue for her son's twenty-first. Fortunately all her children were grown up by then. In his grief, Bob wanted to get away from Lightning Ridge, where everything that reminded him of his happy days with her made him sad. He took the offer of a job as service manager for a company with trucks and heavy machinery, putting the sewerage on at Nords Wharf on Lake Macquarie near Swansea. It was a great place to live and he enjoyed fishing from his tinny, never dreaming what was about to happen to him. In 1996, Bob, who'd worked so hard all his life, won Lotto. He then made a bloody big mistake – he didn't keep it a secret. He agreed to the publicity-seeking news-agent's request to be interviewed by the *Newcastle Herald* about his life. His picture was on the front page under the headline 'Crocodile Bob Wins Lotto', and the story described how the former buffalo and croc shooter, truckie and dozer driver, was now rich. His prize was $166 666.66 and he threw the biggest party Nords Wharf had ever seen, hiring the hall and a disco, and laying on grog and tucker for everyone from miles around.

Then he went back to the Ridge to enjoy his retirement and continue to search for opals when he felt like it. His winnings would have bought him the flashest air-conditioned brick house in the Ridge, but he was happy with his bush mining camp and spent $40 000 making it more comfy. Naturally it wasn't long before he had a new girlfriend, whom he took on a $20 000 holiday. She then drove off in his new flash car and Bob hasn't seen her, or the car, since.

Bob is a kind man and is simply far too generous. He fell for every hard-luck story put on him by 'friends' and others close to him. They soon cleaned him out, 'borrowing' but never repaying. He heard every excuse under the sun for a fair while, then gradually realised he had been too easy going with the 'loans'. He now wishes he'd never won the money, because it's associated in his mind with greed, deceit and disappointment. If he could turn back the clock, he would tell absolutely *no one* about his win.

To escape those determined to suck every last dollar out of him, he moved to Gunnedah to help his daughter and son-in-law with their successful business, HE Silos, building and delivering silos in the rich farming district. Like all people who leave the Ridge, he kept going back now and then, and finally returned to his mining camp on the opal fields for good, after four years away. In April 2010, he became a hero after saving the life of a local woman, Donna Synnderdahl. Donna was a friend who used to do her washing at Bob's place, as her nearby camp had no power. She had put her washing on and returned home for something and never came back. This was out of character and Bob looked for her everywhere.

Bob went to the police telling them something must be wrong, but they dismissed his concerns, saying she'd probably gone to a party. Bob continued to search and to plead with the police to help him, for three long and trying days. Finally, on the fourth day, he managed to convince them that she must have met with foul play, or fallen down a shaft that wasn't covered, as they are supposed to be by law. At last, a big search was organised. All this time – from Friday afternoon till Monday afternoon – Donna had been lying injured, wondering if she'd ever be found, after tripping and falling 20 metres down an uncovered mineshaft, just 200 metres from her camp. What had saved her from more serious damage than the facial cuts, abrasions and internal injuries she suffered, was the fact that due to water running into the mine over time, and running gravel into it, the shaft had a slippery-dip slope that had prevented the sort of injuries she would have received from a head-first drop.

It's hard to imagine that someone lying there in the dark, injured, for that length of time, would be able to cling to hope, but Donna knew in her heart that her kind and reliable friend Bob would keep looking for her. She owes her life to him. She is owed compensation, but has never been able to receive any, which is disgraceful.

Bob helps many people in the Ridge, as he has done all his life, in many parts of Australia. He's the man everyone calls when they're in strife with their machinery – especially older dozers, trucks, graders – you name it! They just won't let him 'retire'. He mightn't have much money left but he has many friends. One of them was fishing way up near Burketown recently and when he mentioned to another fisherman he was from the Ridge, the bloke asked if he knew a feller called Bob Duncan. He proceeded to enlighten Bob's mate about how mad Bob was in his younger days, when he used to swim across the croc-infested McArthur and Victoria rivers – even when they were in flood – to get a beer! He's been in lock-ups from Dubbo to Derby, he's had more fights than feeds, been chased by many an irate husband, but Bob has had more than his share of fun as well, and swears he wouldn't change a damn thing . . . except keeping his Lotto win to himself!

2.

William 'Dusty' Miller

WW II SURVIVOR EXTRAORDINAIRE

If you know of Dusty Miller's background when you meet him, you are mightily tempted to rub his arm for good luck, because he is one of the luckiest men you'll ever meet.

To survive thirty raids over Germany in World War II, in Lancaster bombers that were hit with flak or sustained other damage on every raid, is amazing enough, but Dusty really beat the odds by surviving those missions in the most diabolically dangerous position of all: rear gunner. Anyone knowing anything about wartime aircraft would, on hearing that a friend or relative had been made a rear gunner, automatically say 'God help him!' There wouldn't be a more dangerous job, apart, perhaps, from being the offsider of a novice knife-thrower . . . Maybe Hitler's food-taster was an equally dodgy insurance risk.

Jammed in a claustrophobic perspex bubble attached to the fuselage, in clear vision of the fighter planes that mostly came up from behind the bombers, rear gunners were in the most vulnerable position of the aircraft – the first target young Hans, Heinz or Klaus would aim for. As well, there was simply no room to wear a parachute. There was only room for the man and his four rifles.

So it was his .303s against the young German's 20-millimetre cannon. Therefore it was fairly important, in that little perspex bubble, to be alert. He had 180-degree vision and could see upwards just 'a bit', so the fighter pilot pretty much had the advantage. Two young men who didn't even know each other would be shooting at each other, and one or both would die . . . the futility of war. One of the Lancaster's escort fighters might, with luck, take the Messerschmidt out before its pilot could do his job. Either result meant a flood of mother's tears – hearts broken that would never mend.

On making it to their target, they then flew through great storms of murderous flak from the hundreds of anti-aircraft guns that had been waiting to greet them with their missiles of death. On every operation there was damage, and the young pilot – possibly still a teenager – at the controls would be fighting with all his skill to get the massive, wounded aircraft turned for home, and then 'carry' her, with God's grace, over the Channel to England, while all on board prayed she could somehow land safely, knowing there were bits blown off or engines on fire.

That Dusty lived to return home to his family is one of the miracles of war. Seven decades on, the memories of what he endured are still sharp. Mention of the mates he lost still chokes him up, but he came back and just got on with making the most of life, as most of his fellow-survivors did. He had signed up at seventeen years of age, and spent five years putting his life on the line for Australia and the Empire.

Our young nation was just starting to recover from World War I when Dusty arrived at Albion Private Hospital, Brisbane, in 1923, as one of five children (four boys and a sister). He went to Wooloowin

Primary School. He remembers his mother was always very busy and was a tougher disciplinarian than his father, who was an excellent musician. His dad worked at Palings Music Store and also rode his horse to farms to tune pianos for 7 shillings and sixpence apiece. Dusty remembers a strict Christian upbringing and his father saying, 'You children may open your mouths but don't let any noise come out,' when adults were talking. While he was growing up, there was no money for luxuries and certainly not for any store-bought treats. Even tea was considered a luxury and was not given to children. Consequently he has hardly ever had any desire to drink tea. Belts had to be pulled in even tighter during the poverty years of the Depression, which most children today could not begin to imagine. Sometimes there wouldn't even be – literally – a spare penny for him to go to cubs on a Saturday.

In 1930, the family moved to Toowoomba, where his father bought a music store in Ruthven Street, selling instruments and gramophone records. At the old Empire Theatre he used to organise a regular concert called, in those un-PC days, *The Nigger Minstrel Show*. He conducted choirs, including the Christian Endeavour Choir Group, which featured, on one memorable occasion, a thousand voices. He also rode a horse to tune pianos on properties all over the Darling Downs. Because the music store was large and deep, as was the one next to it, Woolworths bought both properties and his father moved to a shop further up Ruthven Street. Young William didn't inherit his father's musical capabilities but his older sister played their piano.

By the time he'd reached his teens, they had moved back to Brisbane. A memory that stands out was breaking his leg at Sandgate saltwater baths while skylarking as thirteen-year-old boys normally do. His mate yanked him into the pool and his leg became hooked between the railing and the side of the pool, breaking it badly and putting him on crutches for a long time. To add to his woes, he then broke an arm!

From State Commercial High in George Street, Brisbane, he left after Junior (Intermediate) to go to work, which was normal then. His first job was as an office boy for Bankers and Traders, a fire and general insurance firm in the finance area of Eagle Street. (The firm is nowadays represented by the 'B' in QBE.) The big attraction was the big pay: 16 shillings a week. He paid his mother 10 shillings board and his weekly tram ticket cost 2 shillings and threepence. After two years learning many skills and acquiring a lot of information about buildings and insuring them, he was sent out of the headquarters to inspect and measure up buildings, then discuss insurance needs with the owners and recommend appropriate amounts. At last, at seventeen years old, he was able to use a company car to drive around during work hours. When he'd started, he'd walk to the Stamp Duty office in George Street to get policies stamped, but since his promotion he'd become the envy of lads his age, at the wheel of a '38 Chev, motoring all over Brisbane. On weekends, he played tennis and cricket, and went to Caloundra by train and bus to enjoy the beach.

When Britain declared war on Germany, William knew in his heart he must go to fight for the Empire. Young Australians felt great patriotism for the King and our motherland back then. He chose to join the RAAF but was told when he tried to enlist that he needed his parents' signed permission because he was under eighteen. They were not happy and wanted him to wait till he was older, but he pointed out that if they signed the papers, he would definitely be accepted into the RAAF, whereas down the track, if he had to wait, there was a chance he'd be drafted into the army – and even worse, to his mind, he might end up in the infantry. Memories of what soldiers in the army endured during World War I and their wholesale bloody slaughter were still fresh in everyone's minds, so his parents reluctantly signed. Every family in Australia had lost a father, son, uncle or cousin just two decades earlier. That veterans signed up again for World War II is quite astonishing, whereas it's easy to imagine teenage boys like William were simply raring to go to battle for King and country and to 'teach those Germans to jolly-well behave'.

He was soon learning drill, fitness, discipline and military history at the three-month Initial Training School at Sandgate (near the south end of the Hornibrook Bridge), and left after three months with the classification AC (aircraftsman) 2 – 'the lowest form of life in the RAAF', according to William. Then it was off to Wireless Training School at Maryborough, where he learnt morse code, then south to a gunnery and bombing course at Evans Head RAAF base. They trained in Fairey Battles, an ancient aircraft, firing Vickers GO's (gas-operated guns) from WW I. He emerged as an LAC (leading aircraftsman, equivalent to a lance corporal in the army), which sent his pay soaring with an additional sixpence a day!

The next phase of William's great adventure was sailing from Brisbane heading for the UK, where the RAAF recruits were needed to assist Britain's RAF. The ship they were transported on, a Dutch freighter, was only escorted for two days, then they had to be alert for signs of enemy ships and planes. What a thrill it would have been for all those naive young Australian boys to then sail into San Francisco. They then travelled across the US, making lots of stops on a troop train that was luxurious compared with those in Australia, with clean sheets every night for a start! They camped for a few weeks at an army camp 40 miles out of Boston, then boarded

the *Queen Elizabeth* for the UK. It had just been finished at the ship-
yards in Scotland when war broke out, so was fitted out in the US
for use by troops instead of as a cruise ship. When they left on her
to cross the Atlantic for England, they were unescorted as no naval
ship could match the new ship's speed. The Captain was therefore
changing course every few minutes for protection from subs.

The English crew soon gave William the nickname 'Dusty',
because his surname was Miller and everything that's milled (wheat,
timber, etc.) creates dust. No more 'William' from then on. Dusty
was one of a group on board of Australian airmen trained in aircraft
recognition who volunteered to look out for planes. His 'spot' was
the port side of the bridge and he used the English Captain's huge
binoculars. A junior officer came out and said graciously to him,
'The Captain's compliments. He has asked me to ask you: would
you please refrain from whistling?' (This old superstition from the
days of sailing ships sprang from the belief that when you are whistling you are chasing away the wind.)

When they arrived in England, they were taken to Lincolnshire
in the Midlands, mustered into groups of pilots, observers and wireless operator/gunners (known as WAGS), and sent to the OTU
(Operations Training Unit). Some aircrews, like the one Dusty
was placed with, had a wireless operator as well as their gunners,
and when their skills were tested, it was found that Dusty's shooting skills were slightly better than the bloke who was made wireless
operator. Hence he was given the dubious distinction of taking up
the rear gunner's possie. Not exactly a cushy appointment. He was
now part of 9th Squadron. There were eighty-seven bomber squadrons in England, forty-seven of which were based at Lincolnshire
because the land was flat.

During training, he spent as much time as possible in the flight simulator, which was fitted out as a Tiger Moth. He would have loved to be a pilot, but because of his natural ability as a gunner, was given that position. He was confident that he would be capable of at least keeping the plane in the air should the pilot be dead or injured during battle, but was not given that chance as the rear gunner position is the least feasible from which to reach the cockpit. Later in the war, after his thirty raids were over and he was miraculously still alive, he tried again to become a pilot, but because it was thought the war wouldn't last much longer, his application was knocked back.

It was in the aircrew's own interest to keep fit and not put on weight. During training, they practised bailing out from a big tower. It must have been a 'surprise' to find out that the pilot was the only crew member who had room on board to wear his parachute! Another unwelcome piece of info would have been the reality that on every trip, a plane was hit somewhere. The ground staff would repair damage as fast as humanly possible and were considered part of the team. They'd ask the flight crew when they returned, 'Where did we go?' Targets were usually a secret till after take-off. Aircrew, who had a white flash on their caps, often shouted their ground crew beers and a meal, even though it was a known fact that when women in the pubs asked ground staff what the white flash on some of the caps stood for, they'd reply, 'Stay away from those blokes – they've got VD.'

They trained in Wellington bombers at Silverstone air base, which is now famous as a motor racing track. When Silverstone crops up in conversation with Pommies about famous racing drivers, Dusty loves to shock people by saying, 'I've crashed there twice.' His first crash there occurred during a training exercise when a motor caught fire and the Wellington crash-landed in a tremendous fireball. Because he was at the rear of the plane, Dusty managed to wind his turret open and throw himself out backwards, which is like throwing yourself off the roof of a house – one that's moving. He recovered from his injuries and was the only one to survive the crash. The Wellington had fabric skin kept on the framework by glue, known as dope, that was highly inflammable. There were 3000 built – mostly in the UK – between 1936 and '45, and they were initially used for training only, but later for raids, when aircraft builders could barely keep up with replacing crashed planes. They carried more bombs – including the 4000-pound 'Cookie' – than the American-built B-17 Flying Fortress. As well as being armour-plated, the B-17 was also burdened with the weight of thirteen guns and their ammo, plus crew, thus its take-off weight was enormous. In a bit of light-hearted wartime banter between aircrews, Dusty's squadron would sing this little ditty very loudly at the wet mess when the American B-17 crews walked in: 'We fly, fly, fly in Fortress-es at thir-ty-thou-sand feet . . . But! . . . [quieter, with a cheeky grin] We've only got a teeny-weeny bomb!'

Once mustered into squadrons, which consisted of 30 seven-man crews, the discipline was still strict, but there was no saluting among members, so in Dusty's words, 'All BS was dropped, resulting in closer and better camaraderie.' It's interesting to note that Lord Nuffield, who owned the company that produced Morris cars, gave every aircrew member based in the UK 6 extra shillings a day while on leave – which was ten days for every six operations (ops) – so they could really enjoy themselves, or at the least, enjoy a few beers and a meal on him.

There were many squadrons from the US and Canada, as well as Australia and all over Britain. There were even some Irish Liberals who'd joined the RAF, but when they went home on leave they made sure they were in civvies! Dusty's mother's family had come from Scotland, and when his aircrew included a Scot with a very heavy accent, he had to take on the role of interpreter. His pay when he joined up was 16 shillings a day; the poor old Pommies received 10 shillings.

His second crash in a Wellington happened during a gunnery exercise in which eleven men were on board. Again a motor caught fire, and the pilot managed to land then helped the crew out of the hatch above him, one by one. It was an ankle-busting jump to the tarmac. The pilot was yelling to them, 'Don't run too far and lay flat!' Ammo and bits of the plane, which had caught fire by then, were flying everywhere. They were all, including the pilot, who left 'his ship' last, miraculously lucky to survive, although some were injured.

The Wellingtons normally had a crew of five. The pilot and the bomb aimer were trained as observers, the wireless operator and gunners were trained for both jobs, but the wireless operator normally stayed with the wireless. The bomb aimer also looked after the nose turret with two Browning .303s. The rear gunner had four of these guns, which fired at once – but when a fighter pilot was shooting at him with his 20-millimetre cannon, it was a very uneven contest.

Dusty was happier when re-mustered to Lancasters, which were best for the job as they could take more punishment. They could limp home with three engines out of action, depending on what other damage the plane had. Inflight, they were all hooked up by intercom. The tremendous noise of the Rolls-Royce Merlins was deafening without earphones. There was no air-conditioning or heating and the slipstream buffeting Dusty's turret would have him frozen in –30 to –35 degrees Fahrenheit, even in his special suit that had heating elements through it. He wore four pairs of gloves, which he'd have to peel off if he had a gun stoppage. Even when the heated suit was working, he'd turn it off as they flew closer to the target, to stay ultra-sharp. It was an average eight- to nine-hour round trip each operation, so they all took 'wakey-wakey' pills before leaving. His squadron did the greatest number of raids over Berlin, which was the most feared target. It had by far the most searchlights, including the dreaded blue lights that were more easily controlled to keep their bright glow on a plane that was trying to get away from it. Despite the frantic efforts of the pilots caught in their trap, few planes escaped from them.

The crew of seven included an older engineer who'd worked as ground crew, positioned up with the pilot, reading all gauges and helping with the undercarriage. There was a mid-upper gunner half-way down the fuselage, who could see out the top, searching for fighters above them. Then there was Dusty in his little rear 'bubble', well aware when he climbed into it that many rear gunners ended up literally being hosed out of it.

Through the perspex he saw many Allied aircraft shot down by the tremendous concentration of anti-aircraft guns from the ground. (I dared not ask him to tell me his feelings when he saw this happen, due to the obvious sorrowful emotion in his voice. It's horrendous enough for those of us who weren't there to even imagine that appalling sight.) Those who survived and returned to base after each raid or op were put through an Intelligence debrief, answering questions like, 'Where are the fighters more concentrated?' and 'Where was the flak the thickest?' To which the reply often was, 'It was so thick above our target, you could walk on it.' (Anti-aircraft shells explode into many pieces of deadly shrapnel.) Then the crew would undergo 'the cure' to settle their nerves before going to bed:

get drunk, smoke a hundred cigs and start thinking about preparing mentally for the next day. Meanwhile, the ground crew were slaving to repair the damaged aircraft as fast as they possibly could.

Motors were frequently beyond patching up, so it was arranged for US engineers to fit the Lancasters with Packard Merlin engines. A Packard is a beautiful motor, but it's not a Rolls-Royce, and their main failing was their tendency to throw pistons. During the war, 7000 of these engines were built in Canada. The aircraft were then ferried to the UK by ferry pilots, some of whom were female. One lady was licensed to fly twenty-eight different planes – a notable achievement.

The squadrons were under the constant and worrying threat of dire punishment for exhibiting a 'lack of moral fibre' if they ever turned back without 'a bloody good reason!' for not completing their mission. In hindsight, Dusty believes this was very unfair and very wrong – disgusting even – and probably caused unnecessary losses.

Before they took off on a raid, they enjoyed a really good meal – possibly their last. There was rationing in Australia, but not as stringent as in the UK. Butter and bacon were each rationed in Australia at 8 ounces per person a week; in England it was 2 ounces of butter and 1 ounce of bacon.

One of the most heart-stopping incidents of his war service occurred, strangely enough, on the airfield at Silverstone, in his favourite plane, *Oboe*. All the squadron's crews, and many others about to take part in an op, were all in their planes, checking everything – motors, radio, intercom, etc., when suddenly there was a *big* bang and everyone almost needed fresh underwear. 'Cookie', the 4000-pound bomb, had fallen out of her bomb bay because some dill hadn't closed the doors properly. She was lying on the grass below her travelling companions: 45 000 pounds of smaller bombs, high explosives and incendiaries. Everyone's hearts had stopped beating and their breath had frozen. A few choice phrases, such as 'Goodness gracious me!' and 'Oh what a jolly nuisance!' were then heard, and the armament section were summonsed in a polite manner to put the 'big girl' back in her place, and to 'shut the jolly door properly this time, chaps!' By then, they were half an hour late for their allotted take-off.

Away they went, with – no doubt – a few grey hairs, headed over the North Sea at 10 000 feet. Above that height oxygen is vital, as the air is 'rare'. The crew would put their masks on at take-off in case things became hairy and they forgot to put them on in the heat of the moment. Then a second setback hit them: the intercom failed to work. This was absolutely disastrous as it was impossible for them to operate successfully without communication. The crew would always use the same few words to communicate their ultra-brief instructions, replies and information, so that if it was crackly, they could hopefully still pick them up and understand. Desperately, the wireless operator continued to fiddle with it until he was able to talk intermittently, between crackling. This was still a highly dangerous situation, but no one on board wanted to be accused of having a 'lack of moral fibre'. They pressed on, then at 15 000 feet, the portside motor caught fire. Dusty remembers thinking at that stage, *Now we're in trouble.*

The engineer hit the appropriate button and thankfully the fire went out. Without that engine working, the pilot had to fly lower. With the tremendous weight on board the Lancaster, it couldn't climb higher over Germany, so they were in a 'sitting duck' position, heading for the target and the anti-aircraft guns and curtain of flak. The best height for a Lancaster to drop its bombs is 20 000 feet (the

B-17's is 30 000 feet), but this was now impossible to achieve.

To make matters worse, the motor that was out controlled many things, including rotating the rear turret and allowing its guns to fire, and running the oxygen to the crew. The skipper decided this was definitely a case for turning back and so it was 'Home, James, and don't spare the horses'. Their bombs and a lot of fuel had to be dropped into the North Sea to enable them to land the crippled plane. Afterwards, on terra firma, they were able to joke that they were living up to the 9th Squadron's motto: 'There's always bloody something!'

Not a word of criticism was said to the *Oboe* crew, which had an excellent reputation of both above-average accuracy (photos were automatically taken when they dropped their bombs) and fuel efficiency. Their engineer was highly skilful in using less power than most other crews, using just enough revs for the situation, and averaged 200 gallons an hour of fuel, as against 240 gallons used by most of the other crews. Some of the other pilots and engineers complained their planes were just not performing well, but in reality they were abusing the motors to get home faster.

Although crews were briefed to fly higher after dropping their bombs to get above the reach of the 'ack-ack', Dusty's crew tended not to take *Oboe* up too high, as the headwinds were strongest further up, especially heading home, west to east.

His crew were having a bit of a blowout at the Green Dragon pub in Hertfordshire once, and they 'borrowed' the pub's sign, which featured a splendid painting of a fire-breathing dragon. They got an erk (ground crew member) to copy it onto the fuselage of *Oboe*, where it looked absolutely fabulous. When they returned the sign, the publican was so pleased he shouted them free grog all night. As the only Aussie left in his crew, it was an ordeal for Dusty to force the weak Pommy beer down, so he usually drank black and tan Guinness, which at least had a bit of a kick. The drawback was that it took about five minutes to pull one properly. Scotch was hard to get as the Yanks bought it all. Singalongs at the pub were a great way for them to forget their troubles, for a while at least. Some of Dusty's crew always took their musical instruments and consequently received free beer all night.

Each Lancaster squadron's 'tour of duty' was thirty ops, whereas the Pathfinder squadrons did forty-five. Of thirty crews that had started with Dusty's, his was the only one to complete their full run. They had survived where so many had been shot down in flames. They were justifiably extremely proud of their impressive record of accuracy. Because of that record, they were invited to join the Pathfinders, after twenty-three trips, in going for the Pathfinders' total of forty-five but after a lot of thought, Dusty's crew decided that would be pushing their amazing luck too far. The pressure that mounted as they headed towards their total of thirty was something that had to be conquered – an almost-unimaginable challenge. Lion-hearted young men they were, who'd seen their lion-hearted friends spiralling towards earth or crashing on the airfield, time after time.

Just under 60 000 young men were killed in the bomber squadrons that flew out from Britain. A memorial to them was erected three years ago in a London park, and the Australian government invited eighteen ex-WW II bomber crewmen to go, with reimbursement for their expenses. It was later discovered the Canadian government sent *hundreds* of their veterans across to it. (Unfortunately, Dusty was too unwell at the time to travel.)

The raid on Nuremburg on 30 and 31 March 1944 – widely described as the most calamitous operation of WW II – is the subject of a ninety-minute documentary being made for its seventieth anniversary. Dusty has replied to an invitation by Timeline Productions in New York, to be part of the film. He will be one of the last who can tell firsthand of the night 795 bombers took off from airfields all over England and how ninety-five did not return.

There were many times during Dusty's thirty ops that he faced death in the face, but perhaps the closest he came occurred after being hit, while airborne, by one of their own planes. When the squadrons were heading out, planes were continually buffeted by the slipstreams of aircraft up front, making it dangerously difficult to see them. On 24 February 1944, Dusty's plane was heading to a raid over Schweinfurt. After take-off they'd headed south and were still over England when suddenly another plane on the starboard side clipped them, rendering their fin and rudder useless and wiping out aerials. The mid-gunner had seen it happen, but couldn't identify the plane. Although Dusty's turret was scraped, he miraculously survived the collision. With an aircraft that was difficult to control, their pilot nevertheless elected to fly on and do their job. Somehow he kept it on course to the target, then back to England.

With the fin and rudder worse than useless, it was a titanic challenge to his skill to land the wounded *Oboe*. Added to his problems was the fact that there were normally between twenty and thirty planes trying to land all at once, in the dark, and on top of that was the fact he couldn't send or receive radio instructions. He had no choice but to take potluck and went down, knowing he faced a tremendous battle to keep it on the runway, and pull up before it ended. It took till the very end to pull up. The relief of the pilot and crew was indescribable. Dusty was out first, and he saw the Commanding Officer (CO) racing over to them in a jeep. 'What the hell are you doing? Why didn't you call up?' he yelled.

'We were hit on the starboard side,' Dusty yelled back, and after one quick, eyebrow-raising look at the damage, the CO radioed for a tractor to come and tow the plane away. The next day, the Armoury Sergeant told Dusty the shocking news that of the four bolts that normally held his turret onto the fuselage, there was only one left. Yet again, it simply was not his day to go.

The pilot was recognised for his exceptional skill and ability by having a green endorsement put in his logbook. Green meant 'done bloody good!', while red meant the opposite. After the war, the RAF organised for as many aircrew as possible to fly over Germany to both see the country by daylight and to bring POWs home – mainly in Wellingtons. The most impressive sight his crew saw was the massive cathedral in Cologne still standing, barely damaged, with everything around it flattened for miles. That astounding vision certainly gave them food for thought.

Back in Australia, his family had been shocked and upset by a story in the Brisbane *Courier-Mail*, which intimated that he was missing in action. It was a confusing report and it was actually another flight sergeant, who'd received the same decorations as Dusty and was mentioned earlier in the text, who was missing.

His crew had made a pact at the start of their tour, that none of them would marry until it was over. He'd had his eye on an attractive English girl named Lorna, who was in the Women's Land Army, and found out at a dance that she'd had her eye on him. They had met when he'd visited a farm where she was working. He'd taken a mate there who was also a rear gunner and who just happened to be in the crew of the legendary Guy Gibson, who led the Dambusters. They were both hoping to buy eggs, which were absolutely precious at the time.

He and Lorna subsequently enjoyed going to dances together when he was off duty. After peace was declared in Europe, he was still on active reserve for seven years as a flight lieutenant. In February '45, the couple was married in the Methodist Church in Chesterfield, Derbyshire. Although 'his' war finished in May, the pair were unable to sail for Australia until October, due to a shortage of ships. The RAF had commandeered accommodation for officers at the Strand and the Metropole hotels in Brighton. It was a cushy start to their married life, but considering what he had endured, and after the difficult, dirty toil on farms that Lorna, who was tiny, had contributed to the war effort, they both certainly deserved a bit of comfort and a seaside break.

While living in comparative luxury at the Metropole, Dusty got a good laugh from an example of the 'pukka' British attitude to being an officer – a class distinction that was still very much in evidence. Unlike English officers, Australian junior officers of his rank did not have 'batmen' who acted as valets, polishing their shoes and brass, laying out their clothes, bringing their shaving water, getting them cups of tea, etc. English officers were used to such treatment, being mostly from the upper classes. When they moved into the hotel, the Australians were highly amused to be informed that due to shortage of personnel because of the war, they would have to share a batman between four officers. However, to compensate for this, they would be given an extra 2 shillings a day, as a hard-living allowance! That gave the Aussies a huge laugh.

After Dusty's wedding day, the second-proudest day of his life was at Buckingham Palace, where he was presented with the Distinguished Flying Medal (DFM) by King George VI – the bloke he'd signed up to give a hand to five years earlier. The King said to him, 'It's been a long time,' in reference to the wait after being nominated for the medal. Dusty replied, 'Yes, Your Majesty, too long.' The King gave him a warm smile. His invitation, sent from St James's Palace, had allowed him to take two people along, so he'd taken his proud bride and her equally proud sister. His DFM took pride of place alongside his eight other medals, which included the '39–45 Star and Air Crew Europe medal and bar. Both these awards indicated he had been on active service since early in the war.

When they arrived back in Australia, he went back to his old firm, Bankers and Traders, who found a job for him in Townsville. Upwardly mobile, he accepted a better position with National and General Insurance, a subsidiary of the National Bank. He was soon in the position of North Queensland manager, with four branches, thirty-five staff and a big salary; life was very good. He and Lorna had four beautiful daughters and lived in what was one of the most idyllic places in the world – Magnetic Island (until the world discovered it!). Dusty commuted to work by ferry – a wonderful way to start and finish the day.

A business associate had advised him that to really get on in life, he needed to start investing in real estate. With his connections in banking, it was comparatively easy for him to get started with a rental house on the mainland. In fact, he secured both the house and the loan on a handshake. A man's word was his bond then and a handshake sealed a deal. With access to staff interest rates, he continued to acquire other properties as he could afford them. A friend happened to be a director of Mount Isa Mines and introduced him to trading in shares. His first advice was to buy shares in Adelaide Steamship, which were just a few pence. A while later, an unhappy Dusty phoned him to have a bit of a whinge that the share price had dropped. He was given the reply, 'Buy more, you mug!' They rose to 15 pounds a share.

He had also taken his predecessor's advice to join a bowls club in order to make and keep business contacts. Although he thought he was a bit young to play the game, he found he really enjoyed it and has played bowls for relaxation and in competition ever since. He also joined Legacy, to help war widows and their children, and as in his new sport of lawn bowls, was to rise to the top locally, becoming Townsville President. His region covered a massive area, from Cardwell to Bowen, west to Winton, Mount Isa and Camooweal.

In the 1950s, Dusty felt the war widow's houses were disgraceful and neglected, and was determined to do something about it. He found out that Legacy Brisbane Water, in New South Wales, had built a block of units and he obtained a copy of the plans. Then he went to the mayor of Townsville, Angus Smith, who was a top bloke, to see if the council would help with land. Angus had been on the same rookie's course in the war as Dusty, but had gone to the Middle East. He gave Legacy two adjoining blocks of land at the rental of 1 pound per year, and told Dusty, 'The city's architects are yours for this project.' Dusty then investigated federal and state government grants. The project received 4000 pounds from the former and the state made it possible to furnish the units completely. Due to Dusty's lobbying, the sixteen 1-bedroom brick units and community hall were built and furnished at the most reasonable price possible, and he was very proud of that achievement. War widows were interviewed to determine who was most eligible and in need, and their rent was set at 5 pounds a week.

Men of Dusty's age group found it hard to handle the sight of young men with long hair, which became the fashion during the '60s. Dusty particularly hated to see flowing locks on young men on his staff. He decided the only way to get them to trim their hair was to compromise, so he called them all in and said he realised they were following the latest fashion but he would not tolerate untidiness and their hair looked unkempt. He offered this deal: 'I'll meet you halfway. I'll grow sideburns if you'll trim your hair so it looks neat.' They took him up on it. He didn't like his sideburns but every other bloke was wearing them then.

His house at Magnetic Island went from being a weekender to a big comfortable home. But in 1971 the merciless Cyclone Althea managed to wreck it. Dusty had been invited to a function that week, but declined as it was storm season and he sensed a big one was brewing. When the winds escalated at 7 p.m., he phoned his office manager and said, 'I don't think I'm going to make it to work tomorrow.' He knew they would be bound to be receiving a lot of insurance claims, but he still did not expect quite the level of ferocity of Althea. He and Lorna sheltered under their solid dining table, surrounded with mattresses. Their terrified Airedale and poodle crawled in to join them. As they heard their neighbour's house breaking up, they could only wonder how long theirs would last and if they were going to survive. Debris started smashing their windows, their walls were shaking, and then the roof lifted and blew away. It was a long, frightening night under that table, hanging onto the mattresses for dear life. The dogs had run out and were found hiding under the house next day.

In the morning, they could see that not only was their house wrecked, but many treasured belongings were lost or ruined, including Dusty's precious wartime logbooks, but at least the couple was alive and uninjured. Thirty inches of rain had fallen during the cyclone.

Dusty was able to get to his office by speedboat the next day. The only power in town was for the hospital. When he walked into his building, all six phones were ringing. He picked one up and it was the general manager from Sydney, Mr Mann, who asked, 'How much is this going to cost us?' Dusty was disgusted that he was obviously only thinking about money, not the human cost of the cyclone. However, Mr Mann rang back shortly afterwards, having obviously seen reports on the news that altered his thoughts from 'strictly business' to a humane attitude, and he instructed Dusty, 'Don't be tough on people when they put their claims in.' Dusty asked him to send up a team of loss assessors to assist the one he had on staff. He'd noticed that the old-fashioned high-pitched roofs mostly survived during every cyclone. Althea was the biggest of the four he'd been through.

He was so busy he'd hardly had time to think about organising his own house to be levelled and rebuilt. The Legacy ladies heard his house was ruined and one of them who was on holidays in Brisbane phoned him to offer he and Lorna the use of her house in Belgian Gardens. (It's interesting to note here that the suburb's name was changed from German Gardens during WW I.)

It was completely out of character for Dusty to become involved with racehorses – generally a perfect way to send yourself broke – but a solicitor friend convinced him it would be a ton of fun to join his syndicate, with two other pals who were buying a well-bred filly. They had plenty of joy during the next few years, having been lucky enough to pick a winner with the purchase of Darkest. She won eleven out of fifteen races, so started at 9-to-1 odds-on favourite in Townsville's biggest race, The Cluden Plate. She won the race, before retiring to stud. Their second horse, Super Cavalier, was equally successful, winning the richest provincial race, the North Queensland Cup, after winning the Cairns Christmas Cup by eleven lengths. He was sent to Brisbane and was just pipped at the post by the famous star of the turf at that time, Refulgence. As well as the solicitor and

Dusty, there were two other well-respected businessmen and a barrister in their group, but when their successes kept rolling in, they
were dubbed 'the Asian Syndicate' (after a well-known crime gang)
and the name stuck, so they could only laugh it off.

In 1972, Dusty's mother became very ill, so they moved to
Brisbane to be near her. He tried retiring but became bored and went
into selling real estate housing packages at Arana Hills, with great
success. He sold five in one day, off the plan, and enjoyed meeting
the people and helping them with all sorts of advice from his own
experience with owning and inspecting houses and with insurance.
When accused of being 'lucky', he'd reply, 'I work on my luck.'

When the development was sold out, he and Lorna carefully
planned a six-month trip to Europe, to begin in 1974 with the
Munich Olympics. Their son-in-law and his father who owned two
pubs at Waitara, Sydney – the Blue Gum and the Sawdust – invited
them to spend a couple of months helping out in one of the pubs
and spend time with their grandchildren before they left. They
accepted and just missed the '74 floods that swamped Brisbane.
Dusty enjoyed learning how to run the big, busy pub, and when
they returned from their long holiday, he agreed to run it for six
months so their daughter and son-in-law could go on a holiday. 'It'll
round off my worldly experience,' Dusty joked with everyone. Their
next adventure was a long around-Australia trip. For a test-run,
they took their caravan to Port Douglas, where the park fees were
7 shillings and sixpence per night.

Dusty's current car, a smart diesel Peugeot, is the first car he's
owned since 1955 that doesn't have a towbar. Yes, at ninety years
old, he's still driving and still doesn't need glasses or a hearing aid.
He's also still playing competition bowls, involved with Legacy,
going to the gym four times a week, out to dinner with friends at

least twice a week and volunteering as a Justice of the Peace once a week at Coolum Library – his calendar makes your head spin. He's glad he chose Yandina, behind the Sunshine Coast, as his retirement spot in 1982, because 'it's a lovely little country town with terrific people'. He and Lorna, who, sadly, passed away in 2012, built their dream house on an acre of lawn and garden, which Dusty keeps as neat as a park in her memory. They enjoyed doing everything together for sixty-eight years.

A life member of Yandina Bowls Club, he's been their secretary since the year he arrived. He spent thirty-five years as an umpire at every level from club to international and teaching nearly 300 bowlers to be umpires. His Award for Meritorious Service came after ten years on the State Committee of the Royal Queensland Bowls Association (now Bowls Queensland). After surviving four heart 'events' and major open heart surgery, he joined the National Heart Support Group, visiting heart patients to give them advice and hope, until it was made defunct through the stupidity of a past federal government.

In his role at the library as volunteer JP, he witnesses many documents, and enjoys helping people with all the documents that are required by bureaucrats these days for many things. He can't give legal advice in that role, but is happy to tell anyone who'll listen that anyone middle-aged or older who hasn't signed an enduring power of attorney document and an Advanced Health Directive (AHD) has 'rocks in their head'. Dusty is a spot-on bloke who has great credibility. 'An AHD has it in writing that if things go badly with your health, e.g. after a stroke or serious accident, *your wishes* are that you don't want to be left a vegetable. The AHD form should accompany anyone going into hospital and can be downloaded or obtained from a newsagency.'

As well as his busy schedule that keeps him active, he has lots of young friends who keep him young at heart. What a privilege it is to meet and spend time with this wonderful Australian, to whom we all owe so much. Thank you, Dusty!

3.

'Winki' Higgins

BUSH NURSE AND BLOODY WAG!

'Winki' Higgins is a one-off, a once-met never-forgotten true character. After delivering the last of many hundreds of babies she helped into the world during her long career, her complete honesty and incorrigible sense of humour saw her fill out on the appropriate paperwork: 'Place of birth: Rubbish Tip, Pt Hedland.' (The father was a dog-catcher who lived in a caravan at the local tip.)

After signing on for a stint at Darwin Hospital in the mid-1960s, her Northern Territory background helped her to see the funny side of what was the first of many parties she was invited to. 'When I arrived, there was a sign outside the nurses' quarters that said: "Party on tonight. 15 females wanted." A group of us went along and it was held in the bush outside town. The blokes were wild but acting like gentlemen. Seeing only a keg of beer, I asked if there was anything to eat, and the reply was, "Yeah, plenty to eat, love. See them big lumps over there in the long grass. We dropped three buffaloes there this arvo. Yez can have as many steaks as yez can eat."'

Having a yarn with Winki is as good as a tonic. When she relates stories like the above, her frequent laugh is loud and contagious. Imagine a cheeky little pixie with big twinkling eyes, a huge larrikin

grin, an animated face and a pukka accent that really belongs on the
stage, and you have Winki Higgins, the outback girl who lives on an
island.

Well, most of the time she does. When the pull of the bush gets
too strong, she leaves Macleay Island in Moreton Bay, in South-
East Queensland, and heads for her hideaway at Eulo, west of
Cunnamulla. Winki has a spiritual and ancestral connection with
that region. Her father, John – better known as Jack Higgins – drew
his first property there in a ballot held for returned soldiers from
World War I. It was situated on the Paroo River and he named it
Boobera. He cleared his land – the hard way – by day, and studied surveying by correspondence at night. The latter entailed six
years of perseverance with pure maths. During the war, he'd been
an engineer.

He was determined and intelligent, and tough enough to do well
out in that marginal country and acquire a second property in the
safer district of Chinchilla. An open-minded forward thinker, he
employed a woman to manage the second property – most unusual
for that time. He escaped the effects of the Depression while putting
his surveying qualification to good use in Malaya, mapping out railway lines for the British Government.

By the time he married Winki's mother, Sydney socialite Mavis
Ivy Wendt, in the early 1930s, he'd been asked to use his engineering
and other skills to set up a goldmine at Tennant Creek in partnership with her brother-in-law. The man who was to become Winki's
favourite uncle, Uncle Dolf (Rudolf) Schmidt, had been prospect-
ing there in between running his large Northern Territory cattle
stations, Alroy Downs and Rockhampton Downs. Dolf was a member of a big family descended from German farmers, who did well
wherever they pioneered in their chosen adopted country. His base

had been the Cunnamulla district. (The Schmidt dynasty's story has been chronicled recently in two fascinating volumes: *An Eye to the Sky*.) Dolf's success led to him being appointed the Pastoral Superintendent of the English-owned Australian Agricultural Company. You have to wonder if Dolf and his many cousins, when on their way to fight in World War I, dwelled on the thought that they could possibly end up shooting at distant relatives. His generation considered themselves thoroughly Australian, but perhaps the thought was there . . .

The goldmine was named Peko, after Dolf's little dog that accompanied him everywhere, which had been named after pekoe tea. He and Winki's father later found first-rate copper there and floated the company. Mavis left the comforts and hectic social life she was used to in a posh Sydney suburb, for a hut with no electricity and a dirt (antbed) floor. She took one look at it and ordered her new husband, who was used to roughing it, to 'do something about it', which he did, but she still had to cope with conditions that were awfully difficult. The noise of the stamper battery, for instance, drove her mad. It's quite amazing that she coped with the extreme heat, isolation and lack of any comforts. Even the little township of Tennant Creek didn't have electricity – everyone out there just had to cope without it. When Mavis described the place to relatives in Sydney, Winki often heard her say, 'It's totally uncivilised – no one speaks the King's English or plays bridge.'

Somehow she endured her first pregnancy through the desert summer. Winki was due in March 1936. In the stifling February heat, her mother headed for Sydney, a tremendous journey – first by car over the rough dirt road to Alice Springs, then to Adelaide on the old Ghan train, which contained a flagon of warm water (due to the outside heat) on a rack, with a glass for the comfort of *all* the passengers, then another train to Melbourne. Her aunt there, who was quite a character, insisted she was to travel no further and began practising racing her car to the hospital. Mavis christened her baby daughter Alroy, after her best friend. Before getting the nickname that stuck throughout her life, she was known to all around the goldmine as 'Insect' or 'Frog', because those animals were her constant, and only, playmates. But before arriving as a baby at her dusty, noisy home, she first had to fly from Adelaide to Alice in a Guinea Airways Hawker de Havilland. As the fledgling airline's youngest-ever passenger, her photo appeared in the Adelaide *Advertiser* under the caption 'Alroy Didn't Cry'.

Winki's dad doted on her. He would contact Radio Australia and order them to play her favourite nursery rhymes and songs, especially 'Wee Willi Winkie'. Her mother hated the hardships of her life out there, but stuck with the man she married, as women did back then. However, he never complained when she did something a little extravagant to break the monotony, like ordering lobsters to be flown in from Brisbane, when he was happy eating kangaroo tail. After Winki's arrival he employed a companion help who fortunately lived up to that job description and made life a little more bearable. As Winki grew up, her dad – a boxing instructor in World War I – taught her how to box and to defend herself when she inevitably went off to boarding school and out into the wide world. Her mother had an Aboriginal domestic, a nice lady called Lulu, brought over from Alroy Downs station, and Lulu's daughter took over the role as Winki's playmate to replace her collection of insects and frogs. She clearly remembers the floods of '39 – fortunately their house was on two levels by then.

When World War II started, her mother, who was president of the Tennant Creek CWA, organised her ladies to put on big morning teas for the troop convoys passing through. They set beautiful spreads out under trees, with mossie net doilies keeping the flies off everything. A group of soldiers came back and with the army's blessing, built a proper hall for the CWA.

Winki was fascinated with a German man, Karl, who was employed to do general maintenance, around their home and the mine. She loved to listen and watch while her mother helped him improve his smattering of English. Now and then he'd disappear into the desert on his bicycle, which her parents put down to 'being a little eccentric'. As he was a good worker and a pleasant fellow, her father tried to protect him from being taken to an 'alien camp', when World War II began, but eventually Karl was hauled off. With labour impossible to get as the war escalated, the Peko mine had to be mothballed. After the war, the federal government sent her father back to reopen the mine. Some old buildings had been bulldozed and in the wreckage of Karl's hut, they found maps of every mine in the Northern Territory and many properties – quite puzzling.

In the early 1950s, Winki's mother, who still loved the bright lights of Sydney, had achieved her ambition of buying a house in the city. One day, Karl suddenly turned up at her door, and they enjoyed a cup of tea and a good old chat. He shocked her by admitting he had been a spy who mapped properties and mines. On those occasions he'd ridden off on his bicycle, it was to hand over maps and other information to a Japanese plane's crew that was supposed to land in the desert and collect them from him.

When the mine had to be closed in 1941, her father – too old to enlist in the military – went to Sydney and got a house and a job at Double Bay as an engineer, building planes for the war effort, but the 'workers' constantly whinging and going on strike drove him mad. He contacted Winki's Uncle Dolf and asked him to find a good property for them to buy in partnership and he would run it. Thus Winki's childhood was spent first in the desert, then Double Bay, then the first-class, wool-producing, Mitchell-grass plains of Cryon Station, near Walgett in north-west New South Wales. She was a well-travelled little girl. She loved life on Cryon, riding her pony behind the sheep, watching the tremendous activities in the 22-stand woolshed, with its steam engine chugging and puffing away, and going pig hunting with her father. After a brief interlude of luxury in Sydney, her poor mother was back to coping without electricity – how she hated the hardships of the bush! When she could escape back to Sydney, she caught the uncomfortable and slow North-West mail train (known to all as 'I'll Walk Beside You') from Cryon's siding. The steam train sometimes caused the paddocks to catch on fire as it passed through, and it would be 'all hands to the hessian bags'.

Soldiers coming home on leave or returning to fight slept on the floors of the carriages. A terrible story from the war regarding Winki's family was the sad scenario of her mother's sister, Aunty Lillian Schmidt, keeping her house in the Sydney suburb of Killara for years after it was over, in the faint hope that her airman son, Alan, missing in action after a clandestine mission over Burma, would miraculously walk through the door. Alan and his plane were never found.

One time, Mavis went on a trip to Sydney and arrived back in the west with a surprise for Winki – a little playmate, her brother, Winton. As the children grew up, their mother conducted correspondence schooling through the Blackfriars organisation. She was hard-pushed to get her offspring inside for lessons when there was sheep work or pig-chasing on. Winki rode her pony to collect and deliver their correspondence papers to and from the railway siding – any excuse to get on him! Once, when she had to send a poem away with her lessons, she would have caused a few laughs at Blackfriars HQ, with this little gem taught to her by her character of a mother (who had attended St Margaret's school, Ascot, Brisbane):

Mary had a little lamb, a fluffy little mascot.
She cut its throat and sold its coat and bought some flats at Ascot.

For pocket money, Winki and Winton would ride around with hessian bags, collecting wool from dead – usually flyblown – sheep. Even though they did extremely well out of the legendary 'pound for a pound' wool boom of the 1950s, their father, who was very strict, decided if his children wanted spending money, they had to work hard at a horrible job to earn it. This character-building exercise would stand Winki in good stead later in life, when she encountered the horrible jobs a nurse just *has* to do.

One day, Mavis received a letter from Blackfriars commenting that Winton 'wasn't doing his slopes [in his writing] properly'. On her next shopping trip to Sydney, she went out to the Blackfriars headquarters and said to the teacher who'd complained, 'I've come here to discuss your letter about my son's slopes. Do you have any idea what a country wife and mother has to do on the land?' She then proceeded to enlighten him about life without electricity, and coping with droughts, fires and plagues. During this diatribe, the teacher was speechless. Eventually, he promised, 'I shall never complain about your son's slopes again.' Winton later went to Barker College, became a successful barrister, then a senior lecturer and professor at Macquarie University.

At age twelve, Winki reluctantly left on the train for the Sydney Church of England Girls' Grammar School branch (SCEGGS) in

Moss Vale in the Southern Tablelands of New South Wales, where she played up a treat for nearly two years, until 'they chucked me out!' Then she was sent to Kambala in Sydney's Rose Bay. She loved it there, decided to knuckle down and study, and won a commonwealth scholarship to go on to uni. Like all boarding schools in the 1950s, the food was absolutely *not* to die for. Winki remembers seeing a girl from Mungindi hoeing into her dessert bowl for a spoonful of lemon sago, only to dig up a plug! Because there was a direct DC3 flight between Sydney and western Queensland back then, many parents out there, including relatives of Winki's mother, sent their children to Sydney, rather than Brisbane, schools. Thus, Winki maintained connections with her western Queensland relatives while at school.

The school's nurse was an elderly ex-World War I sister named Matron Walker, who doled out their weekly doses of Cascara to prevent the stodgy food binding them up. Several of the girls would sneak their dose to Winki, who'd bolt it all down and somehow survive. Matron Walker told her stories of war experiences, one of which Winki could never forget. She said when she was in England she heard a drummer leading a group of marching soldiers one day. On asking a doctor where they were going, she was told they were being marched into a forest nearby to be shot, as they had returned from the Western Front with an incurable VD, known as the 'French Disease'.

Perhaps that was the story that inspired Winki to become an avid student of military history. During a history leaving exam in 1953, she wrote the story the matron had told her in thirty-six pages of foolscap in three hours, receiving an 'A' for effort, as well as the content. The impressive grade made up for her sore hand.

While she was at Kambala, her father and Uncle Dolf sold Cryon

Station. Her father bought 5000 acres at Sutton Forest, near Moss Vale, and developed it, using his surveying skills, which he had always used on the land and to help neighbours out. He called the development 'Cryon Park', but, unfortunately, had a stroke halfway through the development. He had also developed another goldmine, named the Northern Star, back at Tennant Creek. His long-suffering wife accompanied him out there. Winton begged to be allowed to leave Barker and attend school at Tennant Creek, as he loved life in the region. They had a house in town and a hut 28 miles out at the mine, where the gold was made into ingots. Winki's father once asked her mother, who was his bookkeeper, to take the gold – which he packed in the back of their ute and covered with a tarp – into town and hide it in a safe place, as there was no bank. For protection, he gave her his Luger pistol, which she hoped she would never have to use. The next time he went into town and climbed into bed in their house, he said, 'My feet are freezing.' She had packed the gold along the foot of the bed, the safest place she could think of.

Perhaps Jack Higgins's cold feet inspired him to ask Dolf to organise for the English, Scottish and Australian (ES & A) Bank to start a branch at Tennant Creek. They built a Sidney Williams hut, with antbed floor, and rented it to the bank for 10 shillings a week. The manager slept in the partitioned-off back section and obtained his drinking water from a 44-gallon drum. It was surely the least-desirable posting the ES & A could offer some unsuspecting, possibly unpopular, employee. However, the first deposit by Dolf Schmidt and Jack Higgins was 4500 pounds sterling worth of gold bars – worth around $1.25 million now.

'Unfortunately, although Dad and Uncle Dolf were exceptionally smart men, they were too trusting, and certain well-known people in Australian society ripped them off after they floated Peko,'

Winki explains. 'Being thoroughly decent, completely honest country men, they expected that the men they dealt with had the same standards. However, they went on to continue their successful lives.'

Winki loved going back to Tennant Creek from Sydney for the school holidays – an epic journey both ways. The planes always flew at night because hot-air pockets made daytime flights very uncomfortable. She missed her adventures there when her mother bought a house at Gordon in Sydney, and because she'd finished high school, enrolled her at Macquarie Business College. The bush girl hated it, but stuck it out, and received her diploma. As she'd suspected, she also hated office jobs, surrounded by 'old women in their thirties'. City blokes didn't appeal to her, either – they were too pale and soft compared with country fellows, so she decided she would try to get a job as a station bookkeeper. The thought of going to the bachelor and spinsters balls out west and meeting handsome, bronzed jackaroos was very exciting. She soon discovered she didn't have enough experience to get a station bookkeeper's job, and her best friend, a nurse at Royal North Shore Hospital, was encouraging her to 'give it a try' and join the profession. Winki just missed out on a vacancy at St Martin's Private Hospital, at Clayfield, Brisbane, but got a start at Royal Prince Alfred (RPA) in Sydney's Camperdown, where she discovered she loved nursing, despite the harsh, regimented conditions.

'The matron was a terrifying dragon, an ex-World War II sister, as most matrons were then,' says Winki. 'You could pick them by their distinctive veils with the Rising Sun badge on it. The quarters were old wartime huts, the food was dreadful, and the starched uniforms were constricting. The buildings and their facilities were positively Crimean – not much flasher than in Florence

Nightingale's day – but the hygiene standards had improved since then. Everything in the wards had to be scrubbed spotlessly clean with White Lily, and every ward had to be tidy, to the most stringent military standard, when the dragon made her inspections. Even the ashtrays on every bedside table had to be tidy!

'The 1950s was an era of prudery. Lady Mulvey, on visiting the gynaecological wing, gasped at the sight of a new painting on the wall of a reclining nude, and immediately took it down. She was a gynaecologist and obstetrician in an era when female doctors were rare, and even rarer in that field,' she says.

'Of course, it was always a challenge for blokes to try and break into the nurses' quarters. One day I noticed two strange, unattractive nurses in a hallway. I soon noticed they had black hairs sticking out of their stockings, and sure enough, big, unmistakeable Adam's apples. Turned out they were Sydney Uni students carrying out a 'dare' on Commemoration Day. They didn't get past the cranky sisters, who guarded our virginity like Alsatians. I worked out how to sneak out, then back in again after our curfew, using a nail file. Once I was caught and 'gated' for a week. On another memorable day, my mad mate held her ciggie lighter up to the sprinklers. In no time the quarters were crawling with big handsome firefighters, who took the false alarm in good spirit. One of them said, "At last we've made it in here!"

'I also remember a particular doctor who had no bedside manner whatsoever with the patients. He asked a very ill man one day how he was feeling, to which the poor old bloke replied, "I feel cold, doctor." Imagine how he felt when the doctor said as he walked off, "You're going to be feeling a lot colder soon."

'The code for asking, when going on shift, if anyone had died, was "How many red crosses last night?" There were several deaths a night in the medical ward, but it's amazing more patients didn't die after their operations, because there were no recovery rooms then – nurses took them straight from theatre, armed with a gag and vomit bowl. One terrible night, the lifts stopped working and the orderlies had to sling the dead bodies over their shoulders and carry them down the stairs to the morgue. Laying out bodies was something you just had to do, but it was still a traumatic experience for teenage girls – no wonder we partied like mad! At RPA, the wards held thirty to forty patients and, in busy times, extras were placed down the middle of the wards on stretchers. RPA was probably the last hospital in the world – but definitely in Australia – that used hurricane lamps for night rounds, with newspaper wrapped around them. Other hospitals used torches. Ether was used for cleaning the walls, and one night the vapour combined with fumes from the lamp caused a fire, which resulted in a patient, who had tried to help put it out, being burnt to death. Next morning's headline on page one of the *Sydney Morning Herald* was: "RPA Still Uses Crimean-era Lamps!" It took a death to get rid of them. It'd be impossible for today's nurses to understand what nursing was like back then.

'When I began researching military medical history, naturally I first turned to the story of Florence Nightingale, who had saved many lives during the Crimean war, by promoting fresh air, drainage and hygiene in the wards. Florence went on to reorganise all British hospitals, using a strange, but successful strategy to promote her beliefs. She stayed in bed, so the politicians had to come to her. They did so, and she was able to convince them to implement changes in British hospitals. Isn't that amazing? I was hooked on history after reading that!'

After four years' training, Winki wanted to specialise in midwifery and went to Crown Street Women's Hospital, where an average 6000 babies a year were born. While she was training, a couple of born-again Christian nurses used to berate her for going out having a good time whenever she could instead of studying. When they'd start up, Winki would sing dirty ditties at the top of her voice. Eventually she passed her exams with honours, leaving the God-botherers – as she called them – floundering in her wake.

She had to do a stint in the adoption nursery at Crown Street. It was a distressing experience to see the girls giving birth and going through all that pain with a pillow put under their chin, so they wouldn't get a chance to see their baby. To Winki, an even more distressing thing to witness, unless it was medically necessary, was the new procedure of inducing births. What she saw caused her to resign from midwifery.

It was time for her to go bush again. An ad she read caught her eye and imagination. Darwin Hospital, in the mid-'60s, was a new and different experience – an even bigger adventure than Winki had known, for sure. Darwin's population was 15 500 people and many, if not all of them, were characters. One doctor was so short-sighted and absent-minded that she used to hop in other people's cars and drive off. She'd walk out to the hospital carpark, squinting, and any vehicle that vaguely resembled hers became her transport. Naturally, nothing was locked in Darwin then. Eventually the police got so sick of catching her driving the cars reported 'stolen', they gave her a number plate, and fixed it to the dashboard of her car so there could be no more mistakes.

Then came three years for Winki in an opposite climate and environment at Hay Hospital in the Riverina region of New South Wales, where the winters are frosty. Her time spent at Hay was full of fun and wonderful friendships. Any nursing sister is on her feet all day, but at Hay, where there was a shortage of women, she was danced off her feet every weekend as well. At last she had fulfilled her dream of attending all the bachelors balls (as the B & S's were called then), meeting handsome and charming jackaroos and stud managers. However, one of them broke her heart . . . severely.

Hay was full of characters, and the two most outstanding in her memory were a brother and sister who lived at the cemetery and were the gravediggers. They would take turns to visit any patient on their 'last legs' and measure them up to gauge how big a hole they'd have to dig. The sister was a little 'different' to other people. She would hide behind a headstone when anyone visited the war graves for those who died in the old POW camp that had been stationed in the town during WW II. Perhaps she still associated visitors with 'the enemy'. When she went to town, she would wear a school uniform with a pleated skirt. Like her brother, she was an excellent plumber, and always did the plumbing jobs at the hospital. When she was a patient once, and there was a problem with the plumbing (the hospital's, not hers!), she was able to direct her brother and his offsider exactly where to look for the problem and how to fix it.

Then there was the old stockman who worked on a big famous station not far out of Hay, and spent every one of his annual holidays at his holiday cottage . . . in Hay. He'd take his car down off blocks, and drive around Hay during his hols, but only around the town. He never drove over the bridge to see 'the other side of the world': South Hay. Then he'd go back to the station for the next eleven months.

Winki delivered the seventeenth child of one poor woman in town. The woman was given a tube of spermicide by a sympathetic and no doubt appalled doctor (so there wouldn't be a Number Eighteen), but unfortunately she used a tube of Bostik contact cement instead. She had to go to the hospital to have the Bostik removed. The downside of living in a small town is that everyone knows everyone's business. From then on the poor lady was known as 'Mrs Bostik'. Then there was the time Winki, who was Sister-in-Charge at the time, rang the doctor to say a patient was about to deliver twins. His response was: 'You deliver them. Carry on, Sister.'

'No, they're premature – you deliver them,' she replied. He drove in and, immediately after the birth, pulled off his gloves and strode towards the exit door. Winki called out, 'Come back! There's a third baby!' (The couple already had six children.) When the third, 6-pound bub was delivered, Winki phoned the father. 'Congratulations! You've got triplets!' she announced, and then heard a *clunk* as the phone dropped. After settling mother and babies down, Winki had to ring the pub, where the father of nine had gone to launch himself into a monumental bender.

Although she loved working at Hay, her broken heart was too much to cope with in the district where 'he' resided, so she took off overseas for a year. First to America, where it fascinated her to see the Confederate flags flying everywhere in the southern states, a hundred years after the Civil War. Then it was on to the mother country: the United Kingdom. In Wales, she enthusiastically joined the locals in their pub pastimes of singing, plus drinking jugs of half-whisky, half-beer, then having a ping-pong competition, with hilarious results. In Berlin, the Wall with its tank traps and dreadful history was depressing, but not quite as overwhelming as a local chap who fell madly in love with her. She had enjoyed his company but was definitely not interested in marriage. Eventually, to fend him off – after he'd declared he would follow her to Australia – she asked him if he was circumcised. When he replied, 'No, I am not Jewish!', she told him that all uncircumcised men entering Australia were circumcised at the wharf before they were allowed into the country. That cooled his ardour.

She returned to Oz just in time to help her mother pack up her house in Gordon, Sydney, and make the big move to set up a new home on the Nerang River at Budds Beach, the Gold Coast. (This house was to survive the 1974 floods because, remembering the '39 floods at Tennant Creek, her mother was smart enough to choose a block on high ground). Winki worked at the Glen Pacific Private Hospital at the Gold Coast, which had been a soldier R & R base during World War II. Because she was extremely competent at the admin side of nursing, she was encouraged to apply for the top job in the Uniting Church's Blue Nurses organisation. She made the final shortlist, but when asked at her interview by the panel of clerics if she attended church, her flippant reply of 'Weddings, christenings and funerals!', probably cost her the job. Because she was worried about a perceived threat to Australia from Indonesia at the time, she was keen to join the Army Reserve, partly to go to all their cocktail parties, partly to serve at the frontline if the need arose. However, because she was short-sighted, she was told she'd have to serve at a military hospital nowhere near the frontline. The female colonel interviewing her asked if she'd consider joining the full-time army, but Winki distinctly felt the Colonel had a 'peculiar' interest in her, which put her right off.

She then became what was known as a 'Tourist Sister', being posted all over Australia. She loved the more remote places such as Port Hedland in Western Australia. A big attraction there was the great fishing. On her first fishing trip, Winki was the only customer on board who wasn't seasick, so she and the skipper had twenty-six lunches to choose from! A horribly sick Scotsman, who had been begging to get off the boat, was left clinging to a buoy until they returned for him hours later. Her last task there was delivering the dog-catcher's baby at the rubbish tip.

She then became a relieving Flying Sister in remote areas of Western Australia, and a great admirer of the multi-tasking skills of Robin Miller, who was head Royal Flying Doctor pilot in the state at the time. The daughter of Mary Durack, Robin, who wrote the book *Flying Nurse*, actually managed to deliver a baby while flying her Wackett aircraft from Wyndham. She couldn't put it on auto-pilot because of the thermals, so she somehow flew the plane while leaning over her seat to assist the birth. Winki regarded knowing this marvellous heroine as a great privilege. There's a Wackett plane statue at Jandakot, Perth, as her memorial.

A friend encouraged Winki to join the Australian Navy, which appealed to her – they had smarter uniforms than the other services, or anywhere else, for one thing. Nursing sisters graduated from training as an officer, and going to sea would certainly be 'something radically different' for Winki. Away she went to Canberra for her interview. Typically, she partied with friends until 3 a.m. the night before, but managed to scrub up all right next morning – enough to impress the grim-faced Commander of the navy's nursing services, and hardened panel of navy captains, who were staring up and down at her. She was sent to HMAS Creswell, a naval training facility at Jervis Bay, in 1980, for the Direct Entry Officer's course, which certainly sorted out the wheat from the chaff. There were challenging disaster exercises, where she experienced the thrill of being winched from the waves into a helicopter, while wearing the size-ten sandshoes and huge overalls she'd been issued with. ('The crutch of mine was at my knees,' she says.) Once when she was floundering about in the water in these outsized garments, waiting to be 'rescued', she said to one of her mates who she knew was terrified of sharks, 'Whatever you do, don't pee in the water – the ammonia attracts sharks.' What a diabolical thing to do to a fellow female! Winki also enjoyed the parties that were on every night.

At HMAS Penguin, near Mosman in Sydney, she thoroughly enjoyed the new challenges of the full-on training in nuclear, biological and chemical defence. This included learning (from experience) to endure teargas and, best of all, to use 9-millimetre handguns and self-loading rifles, where the skills she learnt during childhood shooting lessons with her father were called upon. Being on a simulated sinking ship was an exercise that involved being immersed in water up to her neck, then escaping out through a porthole headfirst, off Balmoral Beach, which entertained the sunbathers immensely. A cousin of her mother's was a VIP who arranged for Winki to fulfil her dream of going to sea on a submarine, HMAS *Otway*, from the navy base at Neutral Bay. Five miles off The Heads, the sub went down to 160 feet, where Winki enjoyed filet mignon for lunch with the officers. She also enjoyed her fascinating conversation with a leading seaman who explained the mysteries of sonar, pointing out that every ship has a signature sound, and can be heard from 22 000 metres away. After the trip, Winki wrote a report for the navy, recommending dietary changes – more fibre and veggies – for submarine staff, to reduce the hazard of constipation due to lack of exercise.

When the VIP cuz was attending the stiffly formal graduation function not long after, he amazed Winki's superior officers by calling out delightedly, 'Winki, darling! You look marvellous in that uniform! Come and have a chinwag!'

She was posted as the sole nursing officer at HMAS Nirimba, an apprentice training establishment near Richmond, which she enjoyed for a couple of years. She also embraced her next posting at HMAS Penguin, where naval staff received first-class medical and surgical treatment. After six and a half years' service, she resigned to go bush again, but joined the Naval Reserve and was called back to serve during the Gulf war.

After leaving the regular navy, the call of the outback saw her travelling again as a 'Tourist Sister', gadding about the countryside during the 1990s, working in many bush towns, including Quilpie, Proserpine, Mossman, St George, Moree, Collarenebri, Esperance and Broome. Probably her favourite posting of her long career was as a bush nurse at Tibooburra in far north-west New South Wales, where she was on call twenty-four hours a day, but loved it. The people there, who put up with such tremendous hardships but never lose their sense of humour, were 'her kinda people'. One local wag, who'd been hired to install new loos in the hospital, perched a white porcelain 'throne' on top of the striking rock formations that are the entrance to this isolated little town, to give visitors a laugh as they drove in. When Winki could get away for a break at the Gold Coast, her 'half-way stop' was at Eulo, where her father had started himself off on the hard road to prosperity, after surviving the gunfire of the Great War (the one that was supposed to end all wars!). She felt a great affinity with the country around Eulo.

And so it was only natural for her to buy her 'little piece of outback paradise' there, where she retreats to every chance she gets. She last nursed in 2007, at seventy-one years of age. Winki Higgins certainly has plenty of great memories to dwell upon while she savours the peace and quiet of the outback – the patients she's helped, the many characters she's worked with and the challenges she's met and overcome during a long and excellent career. When you meet her and hear her yarns, punctuated with her huge laugh, you can't help thinking, 'What a gal!'

4.

Roy Mawer

VIETNAM VETERAN, NATIONAL CHAMPION, WORLD-
RECORD-HOLDER WATERSKIER AND WILD MAN

There's a hell of a lot more to waterski racing than being towed along behind a boat and having buckets of fun, which is the general misconception. When national champion waterskier Roy Mawer (the surname is pronounced 'more') is about to start in a race, the normally laughing and joking larrikin says very, very seriously to the boat's driver and observer, 'These are my signals. Now don't forget: my life is in your hands.'

Yes, waterski racing is *that* serious. At 160 kilometres per hour, you simply cannot fall off. The water is like concrete. You don't want to even think about the injuries you will suffer – that's if you survive the fall. A broken neck is highly likely; ripping your shoulder joint is almost certain. The latter leaves your arm hanging like a lump of meat – a permanently useless appendage. It's fairly commonly seen at top-level ski-racing events. The dreaded affliction is known among competitors as 'dead arm'.

Most competitors these days are, to a certain degree, protected when racing by tougher and tighter rules than when Roy began in the '70s, and it's unlikely that they train on lots of beer and compete after 'a few', as he and his contemporaries once did. But ute-loads of beer didn't hold him back from rising to the top of his sport and becoming a successful businessman on the way. He'd already soared like Cazaly over the hurdle of being called up to fight in Vietnam when he turned twenty years old. Roy Mawer is one of those people who scrambles back from life's cruel blows and upsets, onward and upward, and has as much fun as humanly possible along the way. Focused on being successful, both at work and at play, Roy perfected getting the balance of leisure and work right, long before the phrase 'time management' became popular. Perhaps having that perfect balance in life was reflected in his daring skills on the water?

He's the youngest 'old-timer' to be in this book, but like many returned servicemen, he's packed a lot into his life. It could be assumed that someone like Roy, who's seen his mates falling around him in a welter of screams and carnage, who's experienced indescribable fear and sorrow, would, having survived, go a little harder than ordinary people to have as much fun and do as many thrilling things as he could manage, as though life could end any day. But Roy has always grabbed every day in both hands and got the most out of it. He's been known to play up a bit at night too. Wherever that cute-as, cheeky-bugger Roy boy is, there's fun, laughter, guitars, singing and the warmth of camaraderie.

To many young blokes, being called up as a 'nasho' (national serviceman) was being given the rough end of the pineapple. But young Roy already knew all about that. Born at Bulli in 1948, he worked from when he was a toddler on his dad's pineapple farm near Gympie, Queensland. His father was a World War II veteran and had bought the farm with a soldier settler's loan from the government. The poor man had five little mouths to feed on a very meagre income. Returned men should not have had to battle the way he, and many of them, did to survive. Pineapple farming was backbreaking work. By the time Roy was five, he was rounding up cows on the dairy farm they'd moved to at beautiful Eungella, west of Mackay. On winter mornings, his father would 'coax' him out of bed with his stockwhip to get help with the milking. Like all kids on dairies, Roy would defrost his feet in fresh, warm 'meadow cakes' (cowpats). His earliest memory of attending the local one-teacher school was getting a big smack from the teacher, Mr Ready, for pulling his pants down in front of the girls. That was a shock because he only wanted to show off his brand-new undies he was so proud of! (Well, that was *his* story . . .)

The family struggled to make a living. Encroaching lantana bush, almost impossible to control then, bit into their small profit. Apart from taking up more and more grazing land, it also poisoned the cows that were unwise enough to try it. Life on the farm was hard. There was no power. Roy's few toys were homemade, as were all the clothes he, his sister and three brothers wore. Eventually the lantana made it impossible to continue and they left it to take over completely, selling their cows and moving to Cairns, where his dad, who had been in the Australian Navy, had got a job fuelling ships at the naval oil fuel installation.

Then aged six, Roy remembers the great excitement of moving to the big smoke. Cairns was then a town of 28 000 people. He started Grade Two at Machans Beach School and soon had many friends. The only blot on the horizon was that he wasn't allowed to go to the swimming lessons at the beach because he could already swim! On hot summer days, stuck in the classroom doing schoolwork, he wished he'd been smart enough to pretend that he couldn't. In 1956 they moved to Nelson Street in the Cairns suburb of Bungalow, and were soon feeling their house almost moving off its stumps in a big cyclone. When the school was closed and children sent home to shelter, the wind from the sea was so strong, pushing him along on his bike, that he passed cars – his little feet couldn't keep up with the pedals. During the night, his dad woke everyone in the house to come and help him. Sheets of tin from the migrant centre across the road had smashed four big, old windows in his home and he needed their mattresses to fill the holes, and their help to hold them there. That was a long, frightening night. The next day, the kids heard, to their dismay, that their school had survived, although the assembly hall was flattened.

They could see that the corrugated tin roof on the migrant centre had peeled off and was all over the place. Roy and his mates were scrambling to collect it all before school, to sell to the scrap-metal dealer. They called themselves the 'Nelson Street Gang' and built a great cubby and a treehouse in the surrounding bushland from the sheets the dealer didn't want. The gang used to regularly have fights with both the local Aboriginal kids and those from the migrant centre – mostly Italian. This warfare could get a little serious. The Aboriginal kids once fired burning arrows into the long dry grass to send Roy's gang fleeing from their treehouse, the flames chasing them. The Italian kids once tied the slowest of Roy's mob up to a stake, which had kindling set under it ready to light, then sent a runner to Roy's gang to demand twenty Phantom comics to release him. Someone's grandma stepped in and made them let the poor boy go. Roy chased the gang leader all the way to the migrant centre, where the boy's mum came out to save her precious son from harm. Roy had his shanghai slung around his neck, the rubber part at the front, the wooden fork (made from a guava tree) hanging behind, which she grabbed and jerked, pulling it as far as she could, then let go. Boy that hurt! He was almost choked as well. Italy: one. Aussies: nil.

Another part of growing up in the 1950s was saving up to go to the local show. Roy collected and sold scrap metal and bottles each year to get his desired total of 2 quid (about $4 today) to splurge on the great once-a-year day.

No family seemed to have any money to spare then. No one was flash but life was good in a place like Cairns – a wonderful town to grow up. Even if your parents could afford shoes, they weren't needed in that northern climate. Roy's dad made him a bike from assorted bits and pieces from the dump and, as was normal then, his mum made all his clothes. You weren't embarrassed about having a crappy-looking bike and homemade clothes, because every kid was in the same boat.

When he was fourteen, his family were enjoying one of their regular camping weekends at Four Mile Beach, Port Douglas, where they had tons of fun that cost nothing. Roy was invited to have a go at waterskiing. When he was about to attempt take-off, he was stung on the back by a dreaded box jellyfish, the venom of which is often fatal. He couldn't help screaming at the unbearable pain. A lady nearby was about to try and rub sand on his back when his parents, running down to him with a bottle of metho, yelled at her to get away from him. If she had squashed the tentacle stuck there, the sacs of poison would have been broken. The tremendous pain subsided during the next couple of hours and he was ready to have another go at waterskiing, despite a very sore back. The scars lasted for years. It had been a less-than-perfect introduction to what was to become an all-consuming passion.

In Grade Eight he applied for a printer's apprenticeship, but as he was 'vertically challenged', was told he needed to 'go away and grow up', as he'd need to be a lot stronger to handle the lead plates. Disappointed, he enrolled at Cairns High School, where he regularly received glowing-red bum cheeks courtesy of a cane expertly wielded by Principal Crosswell, who was dubbed 'Deadly' by the boys. Although bright at schoolwork, Roy thought the best part of secondary school was playing footy. He remembers how proud he felt playing representative rugby league for Cairns.

On holidays he earned good money picking up spuds, which was the worst job ever, but it was a job. He'd hitch a ride to Dimbulah and walk into a farm and ask, 'Got any work, mate?' The next holidays he picked tobacco, which was also a terrible job, but not as backbreaking as collecting spuds. He'd start at 4 a.m. after a cup of tea, run stretchers along the rows by the lights of the tractor, then at sun-up he'd begin picking any leaves that were starting to go brown, plus break off suckers, until breakfast time. Then he'd pick till lunch, rest till three, pick till dark, then, after dinner, string all the leaves up in the drying barn, with two leaves to a stick. He slept in a shed and was paid 2 pounds a day – good money, but well-earned by such a young feller. 'You were expected to work fast and you just had to get used to having an aching back,' he says. 'I was finally able to buy myself some nice clothes and still save money.'

When Roy finished intermediate school, he got an apprenticeship as a panelbeater. 'Every kid in my class received apprenticeships,' he explains. 'My boss was impressed with the fact I had a natural talent for repairing dents properly. I enjoyed fixing them as perfectly as they could be done – the old-fashioned way. I liked learning the trade and the skills that went with it and, probably for that reason, and because I tried my best, I was good at the job. I also liked earning that pay packet every week. I gave Mum 2 pounds' board out of my 5 pounds a week. Being able to pay my own way, independent of my parents, made me feel good.

'The metal in car bodies was much thicker then. Hammering dents out neatly was not easy. I took pride in making smashed cars look like new again, so when 'bog' putty first came out, I felt it was like cheating. You mixed it with water and it took ages to get it to the right texture. Some repair shops used lead before bog was invented. The bog was easy to use to fill dents and, in some dodgy shops, cover rust – then it was filed off. Nowadays you can squirt bog out of a tube. My boss, who everyone called Tight-arse Tenni, had a primitive method of straightening bent chassis using big square logs and heavy chains that took hours and miles of patience to set up properly. Now there are machines to straighten out bent chassis. I'll never forget an old Italian bloke who brought his big Chrysler Royal back in, saying it hadn't been straightened out properly. When Tight-arse asked him what he meant by that, he replied, "Because-a she's-a cray-fishing!" It took a while before the penny dropped that he meant the car was "crabbing"!'

Roy was one of the last tradesmen to do a five-year – instead of a three-year – apprenticeship. (Tradesmen Australia-wide served a five-year apprenticeship up till the mid-'60s.) During that time he and his brother bought and rebuilt a smashed-up Holden FC, which his brother had to drive everywhere, as Roy was too young to get a licence. They then acquired a beautiful big American car, a De Soto, and thought they were Elvis and Buddy Holly, cruising around in that! Roy also bought a boat – a speedboat, naturally! – with a mate who taught him how to ski on lakes Eacham, Barrine and Tinaroo on the Atherton Tablelands. In no time flat, Roy was testing his limits and having a go at single skiing, then barefoot skiing, which isn't as easy as it looks. When you step out of your ski onto that water, travelling at speed, most people go 'base over apex' time after time, till they get it right . . . if they ever get it right. Roy picked the knack up much faster than most and absolutely relished the challenge required to master the skill. Being slim and short, he had an ideal build for barefoot skiing. Being closer to the water helps and being lean allows you to flex more.

Like most normal, young, male adrenalin junkies, he'd also ful-filled a dream of owning a motorbike. With his handsome face and huge personality, he was a regular chick-magnet and life couldn't have been better!

Then, in 1967, before his twentieth birthday, he lost the lottery. His number came up to be conscripted. He had just seven weeks of his apprenticeship to serve before he was a qualified tradesman and had planned on opening his own business. At work, when he finally plucked up courage to open the letter in his pocket and read his fate, he dropped the hammer he was using and walked out. Tight-arse yelled, 'Where are you going?'

Roy replied, 'I've been called up. I'm going to drink piss until I have to go.'

Tight-arse tried to reason with him. 'You've only got seven weeks to go. Don't throw this away.'

'I don't give a f**k!' Roy replied. 'I'm probably going to get shot so I'm going to have a good time before I have to go to the army.' Which he did. It was one long party, during which he drove his cars, motorbikes and boat even faster than he'd ever dared, and drank and danced more wildly than he ever had, which included, of course, lots of 'horizontal folk dancing' (his fave) with many girls, and breaking several hearts. He told the girl he was keenest on, who was crazy about him, to find someone else. During this long, debauched send-off to himself, he deliberately squandered all the money he'd saved to set himself up in his own business. He was going to Vietnam and he was living like he wasn't ever going to come back. The casualty lists on the front page of the *Courier-Mail* of young fellers his age who'd been wounded or worse, spurred him on to greater excess. Who could blame him? It wasn't a cowardly fear of facing up to bullets – it was a teenager's attitude: play up like merry hell while you can!

While he was over there, he used to laugh at blokes who were saving their pay. 'What're ya saving money for? Spend it now! Have as much fun while you're on leave as you can, 'cause it might be your last chance!'

When he had his army medical at Singleton, they measured his height twice. He *just* qualified, the minimum for nashos being 5 foot 2 inches, and had to have specially tailored battledress. Roy's lack of height has never worried him. It didn't even matter to him when girls were taller than him, nor when he was the shortest on the parade ground and his best mate was the tallest. His first pay, for sixty hours of service, was half the tradesman's wage that he would have been receiving if he hadn't been called up. He was also less than thrilled when he learnt that cushy jobs went to non-tradies and tradies were put into infantry. The reasoning being that because the latter had stuck out five-year apprenticeships, they had at least a modicum of discipline – the oil that infantry platoons run on. Roy knew enough by then to know that he had no choice.

When they went to the Jungle Warfare Training Centre at Canungra, the Commanding Officer greeted Roy and his fellow nashos with, 'I'm God, but you may call me Sir. Welcome to four weeks of pure bastardisation!'

Roy was put into the small-arms division and sent to train for several months with the 2nd Battalion, Royal Australian Regiment, in Townsville, before leaving for Vietnam. By then, he'd sold everything he owned and had continued to gamble and party like there was no tomorrow, until he'd been through every cent.

They landed in Saigon, then flew in a Caribou to the Australian Task Force Base at Nui Dat. His platoon had trained with the latest anti-tank weapons, but because of a government cock-up, they weren't allowed to use them in Vietnam and couldn't obtain ammo for them anyway. So they had to quickly learn how to use a 90-millimetre weapon like an old bazooka, which, despite its size, was called a recoilless rifle. They were also able to use 106-millimetre recoilless rifles, but they were so heavy they had to be carted about on the back of a Land Rover, which wasn't very practical. The 106 was about 6 inches in diameter and its ammunition splintered into millions of darts that shredded scrub and stripped trees bare. Roy has a great photo of himself over there in the jungle, carrying an M60, a monster weapon that's almost bigger than he is. He remembers carrying that big baby for many miles over rough tracks in the humid jungle.

'The M60 was my favourite weapon. It fired a hundred rounds a minute, every fifth round being a tracer. Speaking of weapons, the army tried to make sure our dicks didn't drop off when we'd been on leave. Before we went in to Vung Tau, out came the army-issue "white mice",' he says, in reference to condoms, which were jokingly described as 'sleeping bags for white mice'. 'It's hard for a civilian to even imagine how crazy we all went during those couple of days off.'

Another standout memory – one he has no fondness for whatsoever – is of the ration packs that he's certain had about as much nutrition as his socks. When the platoon members were out 'in the field', they'd wear the same uniform for a week and, if they were lucky, then receive a fresh drop from a helicopter. He'd learnt all the infantry secrets of looking after your feet and your boots. Infantry platoons spend more time in the field than others, and Roy was a forward scout. Then he was 'promoted' to being gunner. It was a well-known fact that if the enemy spotted a gunner, they aimed for them first and then moved on to the signaller.

One of his duties was protecting the dog handlers. For this task, he carried his best mate, his SLR (Self-Loading Rifle), which was heavier than the new ArmaLites, but packed a heftier 'punch'. The tracking dogs that were trained to follow the scent of the enemy knew they were about to work when their harnesses were placed on them. Most were black labradors (although some were crossed with kelpies), which were trained to follow the scent of the enemy, after one – or evidence of one, such as a footprint – had been sighted. Sadly, none of these dogs were allowed to come back to Australia.

Roy says that mines were the scariest thing in Vietnam. He was close by when one of his platoon stepped on one, with terrible results. Roy was out of range of the shrapnel, but half his platoon suffered terrible injuries, including missing legs. It was a scene he could never forget. That wasn't the full extent of the horror. When one of his mates stepped on the mine, no one knew if the platoon was in among others. Because of the acute danger of stepping on another, the survivors couldn't just rush about tying tourniquets and so on. Mine detectors were needed to find a safe path to the injured. During this incident, two of the most badly wounded were the blokes carrying the mine detectors . . . and the detectors were lying out of reach. One had lost a leg, while the other had smashed legs. So the rescue took time, and a lot of courage. Roy cleared a pad for the choppers to land.

In the book *Flashbacks*, written many years later by Peter Haran and Robert Kearney, who invited veterans to submit their stories, Wilf Matusch, who was evacuated that day, wrote, 'As the chopper lifted off, I could see "Shorty" Mawer standing there, looking up at us.' Also on that chopper was the Commanding Officer of the platoon, John Alcock, with shrapnel in his brain and an eyeball hanging. He was lucky enough to survive his injuries due to the skill of surgeons at a nearby US military hospital. John has since helped many veterans get disability pensions.

When the last of the injured had been flown out, Roy couldn't help thinking, *This war is so bloody stupid. Why don't they call it off?* He thought of those young blokes whose lives would never be the same, getting around with one or both legs missing, or trying to get over other injuries, and it hit him what a terrible waste the whole thing was. What the hell were they there for? What on earth were they achieving, or what could they achieve? Bloody nothing. He'd been there long enough by then to have worked that out.

When his year was over, the army wanted him to stay on as a lance corporal, but he gave that a miss. It was a nasty experience to come back to the ignorant, hurtful and enraging remarks from the public who didn't understand and from former mates who didn't go. Roy decided that much of the latter's aggressive attitude was driven by their guilt, whereas the public's hostility was influenced by the media. 'Worst of all was the condescending, even scathing attitude of many World War II vets,' he says. 'They thought we had been through nothing compared to what they'd experienced, and even went so far as to call us "pogos" – a very insulting army term for "blanket counters" or storemen. We had faced up to bullets and mines, we had seen mates shot or blown to bits, but they did not seem to care about that, or embrace us as fellow soldiers who'd fought and known the fear and horror and deprivation that goes with being in a war, because they regarded Vietnam as "a piddly little war". We could never point out to them that at least they knew who their enemy was, whereas we had the added danger of often being in a situation where you could easily mistake the Viet Cong as allies and pay a big price for that mistake. The way we were often treated at RSL clubs was both shocking and hurtful. Thank God that's all in the past now, but at the time, we were subjected to horrible experiences we didn't deserve.'

Roy felt there was a void in his life. He had given a year of his life and put it on the line for his country, yet he was ostracised in many circles. He tried to be positive and thought that maybe he could do something to help other veterans who were feeling the same way. So he organised a gathering of Vietnam vets at a hall west of Cairns, which was a great success. They got roaring drunk together, laughed, sang, and generally let off all the steam that had been building up since the magnificent big Hercules brought them back to Australia. Roy passed the hat around to raise money to put the next lunch on. This group developed into the Cairns branch of the Vietnam Veterans Association. Roy has always helped other veterans who aren't travelling too well, to seek professional help, or other support and guidance from the many caring veterans in their network. It's only in recent years that those worst affected by their experiences on the battlefield have been recognised by relevant government bodies, thanks to the never-ending campaign waged by men like Roy.

'When I joined the Vietnam Veterans Motorcycle Club, it was obvious when we all went out on rides together, enjoying our machines and the scenery, then having a great old chinwag over lunch and a couple of beers, that that was far more beneficial to those of us who were struggling with bad memories – or with anger about the long-term results of injuries, for example – than any time spent on a psychiatrist's couch.'

Shortly after Roy's return from Vietnam, he met and married Lena. Naturally, they were both overjoyed when their baby was born. Although a little early, the baby arrived safely and was given an injection that all premature babies received. Suddenly the baby was fighting for its tiny life and rushed to the intensive care unit (ICU). The nurse had given the wrong injection. Roy and Lena were unaware for a long time that this had happened. As he sat there numb with shock and fear in the horrific place that is the ICU , Roy overheard the doctor say to a nurse who was tending to his baby, 'There's a more important one over there.' He may have meant that the other baby had more chance at living, but his choice of words was poor and cruel, and was imprinted in Roy's brain forever.

Tragically, Roy and Lena lost their baby. Doctors covered up the true cause of death, suggesting that the baby had had no chance of survival because something Roy had been in contact with in Vietnam, like Agent Orange, must have obliterated his chance of siring a healthy child. That information was a double whammy on top of the baby's sudden death, and shocked and distressed him to the core. They eventually found out that the nurse had (accidentally) killed their baby, but in those days, no one took on a hospital in a litigation suit.

Feeling like he was drowning in this downpour of devastating emotions, he somehow found the strength to lift himself up and become the positive Roy he'd once been. *How can I get above this?* he asked himself. Since he'd come back from Vietnam, he'd had two years back at his old workplace, Tenni's Smash Repair Shop. During that time, one of his workmates had started urging him to go into partnership in their own shop. After some deep thought, he decided to take up his mate's offer and to throw himself into making the business a success.

Because he'd blown his nest egg before he went to Vietnam, and squandered every dollar since going there on having a good time, he had to borrow money from his dad to help start up Palm Panel Works. Thankfully, the business went so well that Roy was able to proudly pay his dad back within a year. By the time he owned the business outright, he had realised what he wanted to do to really make the most of his life. Instead of knocking himself out to rake in as much money as possible, he decided he would use his business to finance his freedom. His desired lifestyle was spending a lot of time on the water. He had taken up waterskiing again, and just loved being out in his boat, not just at the lakes and dams, but also out on the ocean, where the skiing challenges were greater. Plus, the Great Barrier Reef was at his door, waiting to be explored.

To take full advantage of living in such a blessed location, he needed more free time, and was prepared to make less money and enjoy himself more. He decided he would give his employees more responsibility and work if they wanted it, and would repay them for giving him his freedom, with good incentives. Many businesspeople he knew were too busy making money to really savour life with their wives and children. 'Times are tougher nowadays, and margins are smaller than when I first started filling up my cash register, but back then I knew a lot of people who were hell-bent on collecting money, and they still haven't woken up,' Roy says. 'Don't collect money. A hundred dollar note is just a piece of paper like a serviette until you buy something with it. Would you collect serviettes?

If you already have a house, a boat, a car, good food, what more do you want? What is the point of buying the flashest house you can, if you're then tied down, aren't really happy, aren't enjoying life? Why not be content with a decent, comfortable house without a massive mortgage, and enjoy yourself more? That's my philosophy and it's worked for me. If I'd had the money blinkers on, I wouldn't have been able to train for racing here and compete all over the country. I'd have thought, *I'd love to do that but I can't because I'm tied down five days a week.* Instead, I untied myself.'

Watching the Cairns to Green Island ski race one day, he heard the winner, John Middleton, say, 'When are one of you blokes going to beat me?' Roy then set to work building himself a racing ski. He didn't realise that it was the wrong shape and made from the wrong timber. When he lined up to start against the experienced blokes when the next year's race was on, he took off in front but lost his balance due to his crappy ski. John Middleton, who'd already won the first two Green Island races, won again. The next year, 1977, Roy built a better ski and started winning. That was no fluke – he continued to build better skis with special bindings that made his foot part of the ski, and won more and more races. Along the way, he helped form the Cairns and District Powerboat and Ski Club.

Roy was chuffed to be invited to race in Darwin. Trans Australian Airlines (TAA) offered him free flights if he wore a TAA t-shirt and carried a TAA flag. That was to be the first of many invitations to race interstate. He can never forget the massive thrill when he won his first Australian title in Perth in 1985. In his age group, Roy Mawer was the ski champion of Australia! That was when he discovered the phenomenon of the groupies: the star-struck females who hang around and throw themselves at stars of all sports. Poor Roy became exhausted from fighting them off with sticks! He also won the National Champion title in his age division in '89, '91 and '92, then retired from that competition to give other blokes a go.

During the late '70s and '80s, he won the Bridge to Bridge in Sydney – the biggest race in the world – thirteen years in a row. Occasionally during this era, he'd win a cash prize up to a thousand dollars, but mostly the prize was a trophy. Everyone was in it for the adrenalin rush of flying over the water at 100 miles per hour behind a 580-cubic-inch motor. Roy had the advantage of his build, which allowed him to be closer to the water, to be more flexible and to keep the ski in position on rough water, where his body virtually became a shock absorber. Immediately after take-off, the ski racer holds both handles behind their back with one hand and hangs onto the rope in front. The driver can't gun it until the racer has done this, so they must do it instantly. If you tried to ski at great speed holding the handles in front, you wouldn't last too long. Roy trained on planks – ordinary planks from the hardware shop – to improve his balance and technique for ocean racing and to strengthen himself even further to manage the formidable combination of swell and chop. Most people go arse over head the first time they ski on the ocean. At the top level, ocean ski racing is equivalent to Formula One motor racing in terms of the amount of concentration and fitness required to not kill yourself.

Roy once saw a race boat's crew come to grief during a race when the steering broke. In a split second, the observer was thrown out and was an ambulance case. The driver ended up with his head jammed between the seat and fuel tank, and had to be hauled out of his helmet. During another unforgettable race, over a choppy ocean off Darwin, Roy was flying along at 100 miles per hour when his observer let him down by not watching his signals to slow down.

When Roy fell, the impact tore off his life jacket. He survived, but took a long time to recover. The observer banned himself from holding that position of great trust ever again. Roy's most traumatic incident was seeing his brother's foot almost get sliced in half by a propeller when the boat stalled at the start of a race on Lake Tinaroo. They rushed him in a car to meet the ambo and, miraculously, there was a surgeon on duty at Atherton Hospital. By coincidence, Roy had been to school with him. The foot was saved and healed well.

Roy's wife, Lena, was also a deadly skier and was not only the first woman to complete the race from Fitzroy Island to Green Island to Double Island to Cairns, but also set a new record.

In 1974, Lena had produced another healthy baby, who they named Wayne. With his genetics, how could the little feller not become a champion too? Winning his first race at six years of age, he went on to become a great World Champion, trained by his dad. During Wayne's build-up to top-level ocean racing, which requires not just superb fitness, strength and balance, but also the ability to mentally hurdle the pain barrier, Roy decided one day that it was time for his son – not quite a teenager – to learn how to do that. Roy was in a boat, flying along as if in a race, towing Wayne to and from Green Island in a rough chop. When Wayne started signalling to slow down, Roy kept the pace up. When he finally stopped at Cairns, Wayne yelled angrily, 'Why didn't you slow down, Dad? I was in pain!'

Roy replied, 'Where was the pain? It was in your head. I'm going to teach you to get that pain out of your head and to only think about winning.' His usually ultra-polite, much-loved son then called him a name that was so bad ('F**khead!'), and so unexpected, that all the ski-club people gasped in shock, then roared laughing.

Wayne went on to impress his father and everyone else by

breaking through the pain barrier and becoming World Champion three times, and also World Wakeboard Champion twice. He fulfilled his father's dreams. Roy hadn't been able to go beyond being five-times Champion of Australia and competing overseas, because he started too late, but he has had the satisfaction of beating World Champions over here. He has also held the Cairns–Cooktown record since 1978.

When he and Lena's marriage finished, they remained friends and Roy continued to train their son in ski races and to mentor him through life. In a story that a movie scriptwriter would just love to steal, Roy's dad came around to his house after he'd found out he and Lena had separated and absolutely castigated Roy for not working harder on keeping the marriage going, pointing out how long his had lasted, through thick and thin. Roy's reflex was to attack. He said, 'Dad, the whole time I was growing up I heard you fighting and arguing with Mum at night about not getting any sex. You don't know what was going on in my marriage, so pull your head in about "sticking together no matter what". I'm doing something about my life that you should have done years ago.' Roy can't help grinning when he delivers the punchline of this story: 'The next day, Dad turned up on my doorstep again with his suitcase. He'd gone home, thought about what I'd said, packed his clothes and left Mum!

'Dad finally got his freedom from a marriage obviously not made in heaven and started to really enjoy life again. I bet Mum was dancing around the house too! Dad eventually bought another house for himself. We got on well while he was baching with me. He was ex-navy and told me that when he died, he wanted to be buried at sea.

'Believe me, when he dropped off his perch, that took a *lot* of organising. I arranged for a suitable boat and the funeral director said he researched the proper method of preparation, how the can-vas shroud should be made, etcetera. But when I tearfully launched Dad into the sea, he bobbed back up to the surface instead of sink-ing. Bloody hell, what a bummer! I had to get the gaff and pull him back in. The funeral director obviously felt a bit stupid, and sug-gested maybe he'd packed too much dry ice around the old man, so we had to open up the shroud, pull out as much of the dry ice as we could, then have another go. To make certain he wouldn't bob up again, I sacrificed my scuba-diving weight belt, putting it in with Dad before closing the shroud; then, successfully, thank goodness, we consigned him to Davy Jones's locker. Dad would've had a good old laugh at that!'

Roy has trained several skiers, including three other World Champions and, typically, has never charged for his time and exper-tise. Also typically, he modestly puts the success of his protégés down to the fact he trains them in water where resident saltwater crocs give them all the encouragement they need . . . not to fall off!

In 1997, he took Wayne to a famous US event, a 62-mile race from Long Beach to Catalina Island and back, which Wayne won. When they returned the following year, Roy was invited to have a go at a race for men over fifty called The Experts. As he knew the driver assigned to him was, comparatively speaking, a novice, he worked out a strategy for him to follow. He put some numbers on the dash and told him to only beat them, that they were the only starters Roy was concerned about. He'd also said, 'Whatever you do, *don't miss the bloody start!*' Unfortunately, that was exactly what happened, leaving Roy stuck behind a wall of boats, in conditions as choppy as buggery. He still managed to beat the field home, showing the crowd that without a doubt, the 'old man' was just as determined to win as his champion son. He had always hammered into Wayne and all his racing pupils the mantra: 'Remember the six p's! Prior preparation prevents piss-poor performance!'

Roy's pride is evident when he shows the great photo of Wayne in action winning the Diamond Race in Belgium. The photo is featured on the posters that are put up worldwide to promote the race each year. It's the most dangerous of the three major international races. Always held in Belgium, it's run along a canal, less than 100 metres wide, which means that with over thirty starters, the boats, which average 1500 horsepower, are at times very close together. This extremely difficult situation can, and does sometimes, result in a boat hitting the cement wall or a skier being hit by a boat. A driver and an observer were killed one year. At each turn, only three boats can fit in the canal and the inside boat's driver has to be very, very good to negotiate the bend safely. There's at least 50 metres of rope to get around it. Naturally, the boats and skiers behind the leaders slam over a lot of chop. It's a thrilling spectacle for the many thousands of people who line the canal banks. They get splashed, but they can see the fearsome concentration in some competitors' eyes as they go into the turns.

In 1986, Roy decided to help promote Cairns as a tourist destination, by attempting a Guinness World Record for the greatest number of skiers behind a boat. He organised 110 of the best skiers in Australia to converge and be towed on single skis by the *Reef King*, which takes tourists to Green Island. It took tremendous organisation. The navy gave him considerable help to make it happen. The feasibility was all to do with the speed of take-off and the weight of the skiers. With the help of North Queensland Engineers and Agents, Roy was able to ascertain that the *Reef King* had

7 tonnes of pull. When the 110 skiers all arrived in Cairns, he hammered it into them that they must do exactly what he told them to do and how important it was that they got it right first time. The crowd who turned up to watch took up a mile of foreshore. On the big day, the event was a great success, seen around the world on news and current affairs shows. Roy was a hero. His second wife, Joanne, whom he'd married in 1980, and their two pretty daughters, Jessica and Phoebe, were extremely proud. As well as being champions at dancing, the girls were also successful competitive skiers. When Phoebe took off barefooting like a professional, aged just eight, Roy proudly said to everyone present, 'Look at that! She's better than JC – he could only *walk* on water!'

In 1987, the Welcome March was a healing time for Vietnam veterans. To resounding cheers, they could hold their heads up with pride at last, drinking in the warmth and apology from the gigantic crowds that turned out to right those terrible wrongs. Best of all were the amends made wholeheartedly by the World War II vets. Roy had always felt a twinge of embarrassment when putting on his medals on Anzac Day, but not any more. The value of what they represented was finally recognised. Roy was chuffed to be invited onto the board of the Cairns RSL. At one meeting, the members were asked if anyone was prepared to host a Vietnamese student in their home for a year, as a goodwill gesture. Roy was first to put his hand up. He had already been on a trip back to Vietnam with fellow veteran Jim Armstrong, to visit old sites and 'put their demons at rest'. They were told that many soldiers from the South Vietnamese army, who'd been Australia's allies, were taken away after the fall of Saigon, to be 'reprogrammed', and were never seen again.

Several years later, Roy took Joanne on a holiday to Vietnam, and made a point of phoning the student he'd housed, who was named Wha, to see how she was getting on. Wha was tremendously excited and insisted they go immediately to her place at Vung Tau and stay with her family, where he and Joanne were treated like royalty. While having a chat with her Uncle Thu, who seemed like a lovely bloke, Roy's eyebrows shot up when he discovered that he had fought with the North Vietnamese army. That was a 'bit of a surprise', to put it mildly! When Roy said (with a grin) to Thu that maybe they'd been shooting at each other way back then, Thu laughed and said, 'Yeah, you Aussies shot me all right!' Taking off his shirt, he showed Roy his bullet scars. Spontaneously, Roy invited him to Cairns to be his houseguest and guest of the RSL on a goodwill mission. 'Vo Xuan Thu's visit was a huge success,' says Roy. 'He was living evidence that in the war, he was a soldier following orders from his army superiors, just like we were back then.'

Roy Mawer, you are not only a champion in sport, you are simply one hell of a man!

5.

Danny Frahm

THE MAN WHO CAN'T STOP GALLOPING

Have you ever jumped out of a plane with a parachute that wouldn't open? As a little kid, did you try to fly by flinging yourself off the branch of a tree while madly flapping your arms? Well, if you've never fallen off a galloping racehorse, let me tell you, the result is somewhere between those two scenarios.

I was to discover real pain when I began riding lively thoroughbreds that occasionally turned me into Queensland's first astronaut. Hence, I have the greatest admiration for jockeys – amazing athletes with more guts than a bar full of wharfies.

Former jockey Danny Frahm has big mobs of courage . . . plus, stitches, plates, bolts and screws in all limbs – his metallic mementoes of one of the most dangerous careers on the planet.

Now, if you're over sixty and need a few squirts of WD-40 on your joints to get mobile, you'll appreciate just how astonishing it is that Danny was riding in races up until two years ago at sixty-four years of age. Just the thought of coming off a horse that's going 80 k's per hour and hitting the ground makes most of us wince. After you reach your mid-thirties, you just don't bounce any more. That fact, coupled with the possibility of having a pack of very large and heavy animals wearing steel shoes galloping over the top of you as you lie there unconscious or gasping, makes the long career of Danny Frahm even more admirable and amazing.

If you haven't ridden a fit thoroughbred full of oats and rarin' to go, just try to imagine sitting astride a keg of dynamite that could explode at any second. Racehorses are naturally nervous animals. Most get pre-race 'jitters' and become a real handful, and there are rogues, ratbags and nasty types among them . . . just like people. During forty-eight years Danny spent perched up on a thin piece of leather posing as a 'saddle', with two long thin strips of leather the only thing between him and a ride in the ambo, he experienced horses rearing over backwards with him, rolling over him, falling with him, trying to pulverise him in the barriers – everything that a horse can do to a person – several times. But to a jockey, broken bones are just part of the job; you put yourself out in the spelling paddock for a while, then saddle up again.

Nuts, bolts and screws hold jockeys' limbs together, just as their nerve and toughness help them mentally overcome their accidents, no matter how horrific, to get back on board and racing as soon as humanly possible. After five decades in this risky business, most would think about retiring, but Danny kept racing because he loves it, and he loves horses. It took a broken neck – his third, but more serious than the others – to finally stop him. For insurance reasons, he is now restricted to riding track work (exercising and preparing horses for their next race). This is a laughable situation, for track work can be just as dangerous as racing, especially on green youngsters. Based at Moree in northern New South Wales, Danny has taken up training horses, and few would be better qualified. At sixty-six, he's also breaking in racehorses, with the keen eye and patience that's helped him guide over 1500 winners through the field to lead them all past the post.

When you meet this likeable bloke who was a champion for many years, you see a fit, young-looking horseman in jeans and a big akubra, with a gorgeous blonde wife who plainly adores him, and you find it very hard to believe that when he started riding in races in Brisbane, Bob Menzies was still the Prime Minister, Dwight Eisenhower was President of the USA (before JFK), Bart Cummings was still five years off winning his first Melbourne Cup, and Tulloch was just starting to make a comeback. Now *that's* incredible!

Danny's inbuilt love of horses had him begging his parents for a pony from when he could put his first sentence together. He could see the horses on the dairy farm next door at Virginia, a northern Brisbane suburb, back when all sorts of farms existed just a few miles from the city centre. The family had moved south from Bowen, home of the world's best mangoes. Sadly for Danny, his parents weren't interested in horses. He had to keep begging them for ten years before they finally gave in and bought his first pony, which he taught himself to ride. Danny made his dream of becoming a jockey happen with an attitude common among successful people: he saw an opportunity and pursued it until he got what he wanted. In 1960, he wrote a letter to prominent trainer Harry Hatten, who was so impressed with it, and with Danny when he met him, that he offered him an apprenticeship at his Hendra stables. His previous apprentice had been killed in a track-work accident.

Harry was a country bloke from Charleville – tough but fair. Danny impressed him with not only his willingness to learn everything about racing, but also with his tremendous enthusiasm doing stable chores – an energy generated by dedication, which has never slackened. His pay for the long, hard hours he put in was a princely pound a week, and he had half a day off every second Sunday. Apprentices received 30 shillings for riding in a race. Danny's opinion of his first boss is, 'He worked just as hard as I did and he was a good man.'

He once saw a racehorse kick Harry with both barrels. He'd held his hands up to protect his face and a hoof broke every bone in one hand. He told Danny to saddle up the lead pony for him, then he got on and, holding his injured hand clear, rode with the lad to the racecourse to observe the track work as usual. Finally, after what would have been a tremendously painful morning, he went to the doctor. A typically tough bushie!

It was a great thrill for Harry and everyone concerned when, aged just fourteen, Danny won his first race at Gympie. He was especially chuffed as his parents had driven up there to watch. His mount was appropriately named Come Lucky. His first metropolitan win followed soon after, on Glen Ivor at Bundamba. Danny knew then that he would ride many more winners for his boss.

Being from the west, Harry Hatten had a connection with Eromanga graziers and racing enthusiasts Walter Schaffer and his wife, who were kind enough to give his young apprentice a chance by allowing him to ride three of their first-class horses in races. The fact Danny worked them and they responded well to him helped them to make this extremely generous and potentially risky decision. Danny repaid their faith by riding Smokey Rose, Prunda and Dusty Boote to many clear and decisive victories, and he was written up in the *Courier-Mail* regularly as a 'promising apprentice', and then as a 'prominent apprentice'. His first win on Smokey Rose was by seven lengths. It was an unforgettable triumph for a teenage boy to beat the great George Moore (who rode the favourite), when he

rode Dusty Boote to win the Brisbane Handicap, and to win several races on Prunda, a champion which had been ridden to victory
twice previously by another international star, the Queen's jockey
Lester Piggott.

Racing was tremendously popular and drew packed crowds in
those pre-television days when it was the only form of legal gambling. A noticeable feature of every photo taken of Danny riding
winners at the three metropolitan tracks is that the people in the
enclosure, opposite the finishing post, are all men. Women did not
hold any prominent positions in racing then. All the men wore suits
and pork-pie hats, resembling a crowd of detectives. Jockeys rode
with their stirrup leathers much longer then. Danny recalls Irish
hoop Gavin Duffy being ordered by stewards to put his stirrups
down.

Many jockeys hated riding at Albion Park (now restricted to
trotting), because if you weren't out in front, you had sand in your
face from go to whoa. Not pleasant, especially back when goggles
weren't allowed. When sanity prevailed and jockeys were allowed
to wear them, they wore three or four sets and would take them off
one at a time after each pair became opaque. Horses either loved
or hated the sand as well. Danny regarded Albion as his favourite
track and would put his face behind the horse's neck to protect himself. Famous jockey George Moore once stated, 'Until a jockey has
ridden at The Creek (as Albion Park was once known), he's not a
jockey.'

Before one race started there, the owner of Danny's mount,
Gerda's Pride, which was starting at 33-to-1, promised him that if
he won he would buy him a car. Danny, who had just turned seventeen, won the race, and the owner, typical of many racing people
who took advantage of a kid, merely shouted him a meal.

Before the prevalence of private floats, he'd ride to the races, leading two other horses, being extremely careful when crossing the slippery, dangerous tram tracks. Apprenticeships continued until jockeys were twenty-one years old, an age Danny considers should have remained the rule because they were far more mature to handle their winnings, which were banked for them in a safe account until they finished. After shifting to Ron Conquest's stable, he continued to win but yearned to ride in the country, having occasionally enjoyed the different experience and atmosphere at tracks like Gympie. He was also sick of constantly having to starve himself. At country meetings then, a rider's weight had to be at least 7 stone 10 pounds, which was 7 pounds more than in the city, so Danny could also live a normal life there as far as meals were concerned. (The minimum weight has gone up 10 kilos since his apprenticeship.)

His final year was spent with Mick O'Shea at Goondiwindi (or Gundy, as the locals call it), where Danny felt much happier away from the hustle and bustle. From Gundy he was riding in races both sides of the border and making a name for himself. It was a golden era of country racing. He'd given reporters plenty to write about with his first win for Mick, taking the '67 Moree Cup on a 25-to-1 'roughie' named Road Crag, who had four legs but only one eye.

After winning the Inverell Cup in fine style, he was invited to join the stable of the Smith brothers, based at Barraba and Gunnedah in north-east New South Wales, with the pick of their thirty horses in work being the main incentive to lure him down there. Ernie Smith – one of the brothers – found him accommodation at Barraba and strongly advised him to buy an electric blanket! Thus began a tremendously successful partnership for the next seventeen years, with Danny becoming the top jockey of the north and north-west regions of New South Wales, riding between eighty and ninety winners a year, including all the major cup races – Armidale, Tamworth, Moree, Glen Innes, etc. – several times. It was not unusual for him to win three or four races at a meeting and he once rode every winner at Warialda. His favourite horse during that era was River Ridge, which he rode to victory thirty times, including in the prestigious Lightning Handicap in Brisbane, 1975. Another favourite mount Danny also rode to thirty wins was Jimalong. 'While River Ridge was a speed machine, Jimalong used his brain and I swear he knew where the winning post was. He just *wanted* to win,' he says.

This was definitely Danny's golden era. He won the Jockeys' Premiership no fewer than eight times and constantly received offers to move to other stables, including one in Hong Kong. He always declined. Apart from loyalty to the Smiths, who were good blokes, Danny liked the pace of life at Barraba, a quiet town where the biggest excitement, apart from the races, was catching a fish in the river. Big cities like Hong Kong were not his cup of tea and, besides, *Why move when you're doing well?* he thought to himself whenever these offers were made. When he won at Randwick in Sydney on a smart bush horse, Lady Bendina, he couldn't get back to Barraba fast enough. Didn't even stay the night in the Big Smoke.

He attended a jockey's meeting down there around this time, and city-based riders were saying they should be paid more than country riders at country meetings. Legendary hoop Jack Thompson stood up and said they had it the wrong way 'round!

Throughout Danny's early career, his mother filled ten scrapbooks with clippings about her talented son she was so proud of. The terms 'ridden beautifully', 'perfectly ridden' and 'rode a perfectly judged race' appear over and over to describe his performances. A good-looking young man with a wholesome, almost angelic face, Danny was always described in the press as a gentleman, and was very popular with the race crowds. He was modest, honest and could be relied upon by everyone there – punters, trainers, owners and stewards – to always be striving to win. He took his responsibilities to the public and to the horse's connections very seriously. Famous race caller Johnny Tapp was quoted in a racing magazine as saying, 'If Danny is on any horse with a realistic chance, he will have the horse in the right place at the right time.'

During this happy and fulfilling seventeen years, Danny's great mate and fierce rival on the track was Leon Fox, who Danny describes as a brilliant, polished, world-class rider. Leon once won two races in one day on the same horse, Gold Fiddle. Testament to the sacrifices made by many jockeys is the fact that Leon, who was tall, would have nothing to eat after Wednesday night before riding in races on Saturday, and have saunas every day. Sadly, this affected his health eventually. Danny would run so that he could enjoy good, healthy meals, and he sometimes played rugby. Unlike sweating in a sauna, running would keep his weight under control out in the fresh air. He liked running so much that he once ran the 40 kilometres from Barraba to Manilla for a bet, and when he got there, felt like turning around and running back home.

During such a long career, there were many outstanding moments. He caused an absolute sensation – and a never-to-be-forgotten drama – in a race at Tamworth in 1980, by winning it riding bareback, hanging onto his saddle. He had somehow kept his balance like this during the entire length of the straight, after his girth slipped and his saddle moved back towards the rump of his mount Housemaster, a magnificent dapple-grey. Housemaster must have wanted to win as much as Danny did, because normally a horse would drop its head and buck when anything gets near its flanks. Knowing that if the saddle carrying his lead bags somehow fell off, he could not be the winner, Danny had clung to it with one hand, with the reins in the other, all that way – a truly amazing feat that brought him a standing ovation on returning to the enclosure. Repeatedly described by racing journalists during the previous twenty years as a jockey who always gives a horse every chance to win, he certainly lived up to that reputation that day. One journalist present asked him if he intended to join a circus! Another seasoned racing reporter wrote: 'It was the gamest display I have ever seen.'

One of Danny's favourite sayings that every jockey can relate to is, 'You never get tired of riding winners.' Apart from the thrill of winning, Danny loved the great characters who gravitated to the racing scene. One standout he recalls is a trainer called Arthur Gore, a real wag who, after a few beers, called everyone – male or female – 'Shirley'. He couldn't be bothered straining his brain to remember names – it was much easier to just call people Shirley.

Times change and all good things come to a close, for various reasons. Danny was shattered when his brother Ron was killed in an accident in 1983, and went to spend time with his family in North Queensland, helping out on his cousin's farm at Bowen for a while. It was a healing time for him. Then another door opened. He took up a long-standing offer from New Caledonian trainer Gaby de Vair, to fly to the French province and try island life for a change. Immediately taking to the relaxed lifestyle, he enjoyed great success, winning thirty-six races from fifty-three rides, including the prestigious Coupe Clarke Cup, and returned for the following four seasons.

In 1985 he again enjoyed a spell doing something different: mustering Brahman cows in North Queensland. The attraction was not the humpy livestock, but a girl whose father owned a station at Corfield. While there he enjoyed riding in the races at places like Townsville, Hughenden, Richmond and Prairie. He was fascinated by the famed Min Min lights, which he describes as being 'like a cluster of spotlights', that occur when the heat from the ground rises to meet the cool night air. Unlike his fascination with the ever-dancing, ever-evasive Min Min lights, his romance fizzled out, but when he returned to New Caledonia for the start of the next season, the quiet, good-looking Queenslander was bowled over by the sight of a beautiful, blonde French girl, Mireille, a kindergarten director whose family owned racehorses.

Thus began another wonderfully successful partnership. Since their marriage at Tamworth twenty-five years ago, Mireille has helped Danny maintain his health and strength through good nutrition, which enabled him to continue racing long after most of his peers had retired from the track. He is convinced his wife's carefully planned meals have also enabled him to bounce back quickly from his injuries.

Following his five seasons in New Caledonia, Danny was happy to take up the offer to ride for Leon Fox's father and was back winning races at his old stamping ground.

During the 1989 Inverell Cup – a race he had won several times – another of those incredible, unforgettable moments occurred. Ten out of the sixteen starters fell – a 'snowball' catastrophe. Danny tried to jump the fallen horse in front of him, but his horse's hooves clipped those of the other horse, and he flew over his mount's head. However, luck was with him that day. He was the only jockey in the pile-up who didn't need hospitalisation. The film of the race is horrifying, with horses crashing to the track and jockeys flying up in the air, landing among the thundering field. That disastrous event is only rivalled by a Maiden Steeplechase at Riccarton, New

Zealand, a couple of years ago, in which five of the six starters fell, and one of the fallen jockeys – no doubt concussed – remounted the wrong horse! The only starter not to fall, Nana, was the winner, with What's His Name declared second by 128 lengths! The horse that had been remounted by the wrong jockey made it over the finish line, but was disqualified.

One day on a heavy track at Quirindi, Danny's horse suddenly, without any warning, collapsed, landing on him, breaking his collarbone – *very* painful – and a few ribs. He felt a pain like being stabbed, and didn't realise it was a rib piercing a kidney. Being used to pain, he intended to ride at another meeting the following day, but during that next morning, while riding track work, he had ridden three horses, putting up with the discomfort, when he started sweating profusely and shaking. He allowed himself to be dragged off to the doctor, who discovered an abscess on his kidney and promptly yanked the kidney out.

In 1993 a horse bucked out of the barrier then went over the top of him. Rising above the aches and pains, he rode in two more races that day and rode a winner the next day. That night he tried to kill the pain with a hot bath, with no success, and allowed Mireille to take him to the hospital for an X-ray, but the machine wasn't working. He felt worse next morning but rode track work, then went to a race meeting and rode in two races. Again Mireille took him for an X-ray and they waited to see what it revealed. The nurse, who knew him well from previous falls, appeared with a wheelchair saying, 'This is for you. Your neck's broken.' The same doctor who'd removed his kidney put him in a neck brace for twelve months with orders to stay off horses and let his injury heal. To keep earning a dollar, Danny and Mireille moved to Coffs Harbour, where they owned a unit, and bought a laundromat, which they ran with Mireille's mum.

Back in the saddle, back riding winners, plus the many horses that couldn't win – due to lack of fitness, being outclassed, or lack of luck – Danny was happy doing what he loved most. Then a young horse he was riding at a private track suddenly went crazy at the sight of a roly-poly burr, or tumbleweed, and fell over a ridge of dirt, tipping him out flat on his face. His nose split like a banana, revealing the bone, and had to be rebuilt. When he came out of anaesthetic, he said, 'Did they look at my ankle?' The answer was an embarrassed 'No'. Sure enough, it was broken and required a plate to repair it.

Then there was also the not-so-pleasant experience of being on a skittish horse in the barrier that managed to fall over, leaving Danny's leg caught, hooked up on the structure between the saddle and the starting gates, resulting in a bolt through his knee. Whenever he had to fill out an official Racing New South Wales form, he'd always give other jockeys a laugh by reading out the question: 'List any injuries requiring surgery, sustained while racing', then quipping, 'Jeez, I'm gonna run out of ink!' He attributes the surprising fact that he has no arthritis to the good food he has always eaten, especially since marrying Mireille. 'The saying "You are what you eat" is so true,' he says.

It was only natural that when women were allowed to become jockeys, he was concerned about them being hurt. 'But it was just a matter of time before females were given equality at the track, and horses go well for women – you can't argue with that. Pam O'Neill did a wonderful job paving the way for other girls to follow. My other opinion on the subject is that female jockeys should have separate changing rooms. If I had a daughter I wouldn't want her thrown in with the men and boys. Whether an apprentice is male or female, they must have dedication and be prepared to work hard, and not to make the same mistake twice. As for strategy – having good judgement where to position your horse and when to make your run – well, you've either got that or you haven't. During a race you have to make split-second decisions, and if you make the wrong decision you just have to get over that after that race, or you lose your confidence. It's also very important to be prepared to give up racing if you become frightened, because you will cause an accident. There are plenty of other jobs in the thoroughbred breeding and racing industry that a person can train for if they lose their nerve,' Danny says.

'Waiting in the barrier stalls can be nerve-racking when they are taking a long time to get all the horses in. Some horses naturally start playing up. We talk to each other while we're waiting and the public would probably get a laugh or two if those conversations were taped. You are on a big animal that's full of grain, fighting fit and raring to go, and it's shut in a confined space. That's where accidents can happen and it's often also the place where a race is lost due to a poor start. A horse might turn his head just at the crucial moment, or even worse, rear up due to nerves. One day some clever person might work out a way all the runners can be loaded in at the same time. That would make racing a much fairer sport.'

Danny is described by many people in the racing game as 'a champion bloke' and 'nature's gentleman of the old school'. He is a completely genuine person, and modest about the tremendous success he has experienced. When he received an award at a gala presentation ceremony in 2010 from Racing New South Wales for 'services to country racing', he told people afterwards, in typical self-effacing fashion, that he received it for 'just hanging around for so long'.

When he rode in what ended up being his last race at Armidale in

2010, his horse just suddenly dropped like a stone. It had a cracked pelvis. Danny was very lucky to survive that final fall. As usual, Mireille was watching with her heart in her mouth. For twenty-five years she had watched him ride in races with a mixture of dread and pride. This fall looked very bad. She rushed to him, fearing the worst. When she rode in the ambulance with him to the hospital, he did not recognise her. She is so grateful that her husband somehow survived, recovered, and is now back in good health. They love being together and although Danny will never ride another winner, he has won the game of life: adored and cared for by a beautiful person, and still able to enjoy his other great love: riding and training thoroughbred horses.

6.

Terry Gordon, OAM

COUNTRY MUSIC ENTERTAINER AND COMEDIAN

Terry Gordon is a naturally funny feller. A conversation with him is full of laughter. His audiences get double their value for money: a great singer with a distinctive, booming voice, delivering the best of country music, plus lots of laughs at his gags and hilarious, sometimes bawdy ditties. One minute they are spellbound by his fabulous rendition of a smooth Jim Reeves or George Jones hit, the next, roaring with laughter at the tale of Windy, his blow-up girl who accompanies him on tour.

The story of Windy is full of hot air, of course. Terry jokes that she's never been out of her wrapping. Like many entertainers, this larrikin has had more women than brekkies. Having toured Australia constantly for the past half a century, he's been in more motel rooms than the Gideon Bible, and his gigs would number literally thousands. He's had his own television show, toured with the greats, received a Medal of the Order of Australia (OAM) and is on the revered Roll of Renown at the country music capital, Tamworth. Terry is a happy man who's proud of his life. He's been a 'bit naughty' a few times, but he's only a man. He has many friends, including all his ex-wives, and he would not have an enemy in the world – a true-blue loveable larrikin.

Born to sing, as a young'un Terry entertained kids on the school bus that took them from their farms, surrounding Taralga, near Goulburn, New South Wales, to St Joseph's primary and high school, copying the singers he heard on his parents' wireless: Hank Williams, Buck Owens, Buddy Williams and Tex Morton in the 1940s, then Marty Robbins, Johnny Horton, Wilf Carter and Johnny Cash in the '50s. Because he was the first child to be picked up, at Bannaby Station, and the last to get home, his school friends and the bus driver were treated to plenty of songs from the willing performer. The bus driver would enjoy a cuppa both ends of the trip with Terry's mum and his dad, who was the station's overseer. His mother owned a small sheep property nearby, left to her by her father, shearer George Conner. That extra income gave them a comfortable living, back when needs and expectations of young married couples were much simpler than today.

A 'bloody wag' since babyhood, Terry's pranks landed him in trouble now and then, like the time he took revenge on the kids on his bus for pinching his stash of lollies while he was yarning with the driver. He went to Kitty Moonie's chemist shop at lunchtime, bought a heap of Laxettes (laxatives that look like chocolates) put them into a paper bag, and generously handed the lot around on the bus home.

Apart from the wireless, which he tuned onto 2WL's *Sunset Trail* hillbilly show every weekend, entertainment for Taralga people consisted of tennis matches plus the regular dances all over the district, where his grandad played the fiddle and his mother the piano. Men would sneak outside the hall regularly to charge themselves up on grog they'd have planted outside the hall. Young Terry found a bottle of muscat in a tree near the dunnies, had quite a few swigs and paid for it next day. So did one of his mates. Green around the gills,

Terry was singing in the church choir and suddenly chundered on his cobber in front of him. He was forgiven.

He loved to watch his grandfather shearing. He admired his smooth, clean, athletic style. He also loved helping his father check the stock and muster on Bannaby, a substantial sheep and cattle station that had been left to the Anglican Church by a devout follower. Life on Bannaby was stable and comfortable. Like his dad, Terry was a keen rider, winning ribbons at local shows. He was what they called in those days, an 'afterthought' – his brother and sister were much older than him, so his friends at home were the stockmen. At shearing time, he learnt from a very young age to be a handy rouseabout, and loved yarning with the big team in the ten-stand shed. He would have naturally picked up that dry humour of the bush – the love of a good, funny yarn delivered well – from these men. During their breaks, he'd happily sing their requests.

At the annual amateur concert in Taralga, Terry would be the star performer, the boy with the huge voice who the locals knew would go on to be a professional singer, like his idols. The highlight of his year was seeing Tex Morton and Buddy Williams' shows when they visited his little town. He couldn't wait to get up on stage every day and make records like they did. He saved for a guitar by rabbiting, using his pony to ride 'round, setting and checking traps. On school holidays he'd trap rabbits fulltime with his uncle Les Whipp, and eventually made enough pounds, shillings and pence to buy his first guitar from Les's brother Ron, a country music singer. He rode home on his pony with it across his back, proud as punch. He learnt to strum from chord sheets, thinking he'd be playing like his heroes Buddy and Tex in no time.

With his sights set on eventually becoming a professional enter-tainer, he left school at Intermediate and got a job as a postie. After just six weeks pedalling around town, he couldn't see himself achieving his ambition from Taralga, so left for the bright lights of Wollongong, where he lived at his married sister's house. His first job, at the Port Kembla steelworks, was as a 'watcher' – a job that carried a lot of responsibility for a young bloke. He had to ride on the little train, taking the slag from the furnaces to the dump, and watch the railway line for any traffic, warning them by pulling the whistle. One day the shunter had lent him a *Man* magazine – red-hot back then – to read. Terry was looking at the pictures of topless birds and not thinking about pulling his whistle. The train hit the rear end of a Blitz truck that was crossing the line and wiped it out! Fortunately the driver wasn't hurt, but Terry took off like a scalded cat and never returned.

He scored a good, cruisy job on a bread cart, which left him plenty of time to learn to play the guitar well. By the time he turned seventeen in 1959, he got his licence and was able to drive a bread van himself. He was also forming a band with four mates. Styled on The Shadows, they called themselves The Wanderers and soon had regular weekend gigs at all the surf club dances on the South Coast of New South Wales. They sang all the hits of the day, which included many country songs. Terry had honed his flirting skills with the housewives on his bread run, but there was little need, he found, to work hard on winning hearts once he was up on stage as lead singer in a band. There were plenty of pretty girls chas-ing him, even though his 'car' that he took them 'pashing' in, was a decidedly unsexy bread van!

Fun nearly always comes at a price. In those pre-pill days, if a bloke 'got a girl into strife', he did the decent thing and married

her. At eighteen, Terry was tied down with a wife and baby and living with the father-in-law from hell. His band was playing regularly
on a television show, they had a big following at the dances, and it
proved impossible for him to remain faithful. He could not resist
talking to a very pretty girl who'd been staring up at him on stage,
fluttering her eyelashes. Her name was Narelle and she said he could
take her out but he had to meet her mother first, as she insisted on
meeting every young bloke who wanted to take her daughter out.
(Good onyer, Mum!) Smitten, he rocked up in his multi-purpose
bread van a few days later, with anything but bread or singing on his
mind, and there was Mum on the doorstep, with a poker face and
folded arms. 'Are you Terry Gordon?' she asked without a smile.
When he replied yes, she said, 'Are you in that band that's on TV?'
Again he replied yes, and she said, 'Where do you live?'

Thinking fast, he replied, 'Um, with my sister at Corrimal.'

Mum had done some research. 'Oh really?' she said. 'Don't you
live with your wife any more?'

Gulp! That was the first of many awkward encounters to come
throughout Terry's fifty-year dual career performing both on stage
with his microphone and with women behind closed doors (of both
motels and bread vans). Before he left the 'Gong, he did manage
to have his wicked way with young Narelle, the groupie with the
formidable mum, and once again, the bread van was rockin' and
rollin'! 'When we got out, we had enough crumbs all over us to coat
five dozen lamb cutlets, fair dinkum!' he recalls with a grin.

As the old bush saying goes, Terry was always 'riding one and
leading one'. What used to go through his mind over the years as he
sang those heartfelt country songs about cheating men and 'wrong
done by' women? Remorse?

'[I felt] a bit of a twinge when I'd first been sprung,' he says.

'But that's how it was back then, especially in this business where females throw themselves at you. I will say, that I'm now mates with my previous three lovely wives – Helen, Margaret and Wendy – and I've been generous to them. I've given each one a baby boy, Terry, Ricky and Scott. We are all one big happy family now, and the boys came to my last wedding – which is, my *last* wedding. I've been lucky enough, at three score years and ten, to find a girl who I'll happily – in the words of Johnny Cash – "walk the line" for.'

Wife No. 4, Nan, quite honestly looks like she could be Terry's very pretty daughter, but she clearly adores him. Terry – in the words of one of his humorous songs, 'It's Better To Be Lucky Than Good Looking' – is indeed a lucky bugger, women-wise.

But he was not lucky enough to have had *the* Number 1 hit that would have made him a household name and wealthy. Despite his talent – an outstanding voice and rapport with his audiences – he was never able to write or find his 'Pub with No Beer' that would have put him on top of the charts. That said, Terry has had a tremendously successful career, consistently in work all over Australia, and is happy with what he's achieved and the life he's led since branching out solo from The Wanderers in the early '60s. He's toured with The Seekers, Tom T Hall, Slim Dusty, Normie Rowe, Jade Hurley and many other great performers. He was named Queensland Entertainer of the Year in 1995, the year he appeared at the star-studded Hodag Country Music Festival in Wisconsin, USA, performing with great artists such as Willie Nelson, Charlie Pride, George Jones and LeAnne Rimes. He was invited back there in 1998 and again in 2002.

His fifty-year career as a solo performer began, strangely enough, back in the shearing sheds. When it became obvious he needed to get out of the 'Gong, he saw an ad in a newspaper for a rouseabout on a shearing run around Roma and felt a yearning to be back in the bush. He knew he could do the job, and a plan formed in his mind – clear as crystal – what he had to do to break into the country music scene . . . his first love. He spent the next five months totally focused on achieving that. He slaved at his job, singing as he picked up and flung the fleeces, saved his money, didn't drink, smoke, or go 'out on the rantan' in town (despite appeals and rubbishing from the shearers), and memorised all the songs from word sheets he'd purchased and taken with him to the west. He put to memory countless popular country songs. At night and early morning, he also polished his guitar playing. This all-new, disciplined Terry Gordon treated it as a five-month rehearsal to present himself to an agent as a professional country singer. His baby boy, Little Terry, back in Wollongong with his mother and grandparents, was then twelve months old and Terry wanted to be able to provide for him. Little Terry was his inspiration to 'walk the line'.

At the end of the shearing run – the summer of '62 – he went to Brisbane, bought a new suit, and presented himself to the top booking agent, Bill South. Would-be country singers were prevalent in that era, but Terry's smooth and studied presentation, preparation and determination won the day. After Bill heard him sing through the repertoire he had rehearsed to the nth degree, he immediately booked him into one of the most difficult venues on the pub circuit, no doubt to really test his ability to win over an audience. Naturally, Terry will never forget his first, potentially difficult audience at the Palais Royal Hotel, Ipswich (a no-nonsense, former coal-mining town), billed as 'Tonight! Singing Sensation Terry Gordon!' The tough, sceptical audience loved him and he was away. All the top venues of that era, including the Lands Office, the Crown and de Brazil Nightclub, wanted him.

Bill South booked him over the border at Glen Innes' most popular venue, the Boomerang Hotel (now the New Tattersalls), as the regular entertainer and compere. The manager of the local radio station, 2AD Armidale, was in the audience. He invited Terry to run the new studio they were setting up in Glen Innes. He received a week's training by two great professionals, Barry Pierce and Kel Richards, and ran two country-music shows a week, *Country Requests* and *Terry Gordon Country Style*, sponsored by stock and station agent Col Say. He also booked acts for the Boomerang, including top names Col Joye and the Joyboys, Graeme Bell and his Allstars, and The Maori Troubadours, and got to know many entertainers – contacts that would be invaluable to him later. People drove for many miles from districts all around to the shows at the Boomerang.

At his desk at 2AD Glen Innes, he loved playing all his faves, as announcers were once allowed to do, before computerised 'play sheets' were enforced. One memorable event was Mackenzie's Department Store's outside broadcast during the Rose Festival. Terry was playing up at the Boomerang that day and asked a mate who had a ute to help him transport all the sound gear, plus his desk, with its two turntables, from the studio to the store. His mate was pretty shickery and took off flat out, gunned his ute to do a screaming U-ey in the main street, sending all the gear flying off the back. Terry saw the expensive studio desk, with bolts, screws and panels flying, skidding across the road, falling to pieces and sending the turntables heading towards the Club Hotel. *Shit, I'm gonna get the sack!* he thought. *That desk is f**ked!* He didn't get the bullet, but he had to do the outside broadcast, restricted to just announcing ads, while an announcer in Armidale played records. This humiliating situation continued until a new desk with turntables could be obtained for his Glen Innes studio.

The owner of the Boomerang, who had given him accommodation, bought a house in town for the staff to share, to free up motel rooms. The chef, who was a cranky old bitch, asked Terry to put her budgie out in the sun every morning, while she cooked breakfast at the pub. Terry had a bit of a whinge about this to one of the resident barmen, 'Knuckles' Parker, who could fight like a thrashing machine. Waiting to go on-air one day, the crabby chef burst into the studio and attacked him – gave him a hell of a time. He couldn't work out what she was raving about, but eventually discovered, after she'd stormed out, that Knuckles – who liked a joke as much as a punch-up, had let the budgie out, then locked the cat in the cage. No wonder she was furious! Of course, Terry had to cop it as a bit of fun, not wanting to take Knuckles on.

One of the regular entertainers Terry admired was Athol McCoy, leader of the Real McCoys Band. Although he was on a bloody good wicket, he couldn't resist Athol's invitation to join his travelling show, and toured right 'round Australia in '65 and '66. They went to every big and not-so-big town, every Aboriginal mission, every sizeable roadhouse in the middle of nowhere. Terry learnt a hell of a lot, but decided, after a year on the road with the show, that he 'never wanted to see another f**kin' caravan!' (He was featured in the *Post* magazine during the '80s as having stayed in an estimated 6250 motel rooms since that first tour. You can add at least 10 000 more since then.)

Athol taught Terry on-stage comedy – how to pause during gags for laughter and so forth. A lot of the sketches were strictly vaudeville but they worked. Terry could keep a straight face somehow while saying to the audience, 'My grandad was shot at Gallipoli.

He wasn't a soldier, he was just camping there and went over to complain about the noise . . .' A perfect Anzac Day yarn. Athol dressed him up as Nosebag the Naughty Clown for a routine the audience loved. But the laughs weren't all for them alone. 'At Tambar Springs Hall, a big fat sheila was in the front row, her feet up on the stage,' Terry recounts. 'She let fly with a tremendous fart and Athol and I couldn't stop laughing all through the show. Laughter is contagious – most of the audience hadn't heard her but kept laughing with us when we just couldn't stop. That was a funny, standout night. I didn't make a lot of money with Athol but the experience I gained on how to handle every type of audience, and make them laugh, was invaluable. I have to update my gags now and then, for example, "I was at a dance the other night and half the kids there had rings through their noses and eyebrows. They looked like they'd been tagged by the Wildlife Society. My girlfriend got one of those studs through her eyebrow. Then she got carried away and put 'em everywhere – I dunno whether to kiss her or give her a grease and oil change." '

Terry enjoyed a blowout in Sydney following the gruelling tour with the McCoys and, at the Chevron one night, yarning with the owner of the new (almost finished) Kings Cross Travelodge, was offered the important job of concierge. All the big-name stars of the era, like Shirley Bassey, Tony Hancock, The Seekers, etc., stayed there and Terry looked after them like an all-knowing friend, getting them, or arranging for them, whatever they wanted. He was also performing at gigs all over Sydney. Life was a hoot. Many GI's, their $800 R & R allowance burning a hole in their pockets, stayed at the Travelodge. One of them went off his rocker – a 'flashback to dealing with the Vietcong' was his excuse – and murdered a girl in his room. He shot through but was captured in Adelaide three days later. While the police were hunting him down, Terry decided to play a prank on the head porter, Norm. All the staff were on edge since one of them found the body. Terry hid in the wardrobe of a room near the murder scene when Norm was taking a guest's luggage there. He could hear Norm singing 'Everybody Loves Somebody Sometime', doing a fair imitation of Dean Martin's cruisy style, as he put the bags down, opened the curtains and so on. When Norm opened the cupboard to hang a coat up, Terry put on a scary face and yelled at him. Poor Norm needed fresh underwear and hated Terry ever afterward.

By then, Terry had met his second wife, Margaret, and they hooked up to run a Redfern guesthouse, which had been the Rose of Denmark hotel. When Terry relates a funny anecdote, like the Scaring Norm the Porter story, his facial expressions, with his huge eyes wide open, make it even funnier. Thus his recall of the Three Rats story should really be enjoyed in person. 'I always liked cooking, so used to cook brekkie for all the guests. One night I cooked up a big pan of savoury mince, leaving it to cool off while I got dressed to go out to a gig. When I returned to put it in the fridge, there were three rats in the pan having a great old feed. I smoothed the bite marks over, and the next day the blokes all said it was the best savoury mince they'd ever tasted.'

Terry once found one of the guests dead as a doornail in his room. The bloke hadn't been friendly and none of the other guests wanted to go to his funeral, so Terry went along, knowing that, to his knowledge, the man only had one son ('a prick who annoyed me with his attitude while going through his father's stuff') and no friends that he knew of. Because he was a returned man, the Mascot RSL were burying him. When Terry arrived at the Botany chapel, he was the only person there. He made a vow that when he died, he would arrange to have a front page ad in the *Sydney Herald* to make sure people would turn up. When another of the guests hanged himself in the laundry, Terry phoned a mate, Bugsy, who was a hard-bitten cop, and he brought along a brand-new rookie, straight out of the police academy. Bugsy asked Terry for a butcher's knife. When he cut the body down, it hit the ground and went 'Aarrghh!' Bugsy said, 'He's trying to yodel.' The young recruit had taken off like a jet, out into the street.

Another pal he had in the vice squad once offered to take Terry and a bushie mate on his rounds one night. Terry had organised a gig in Sydney for a famous country singer who was a fair-dinkum old bushie. The copper said it was bound to be an eye-opening experience for the bloke from the bush, which it certainly turned out to be! They were soon enjoying lots of free drinks at various brothels, and Dick, the vice-squad copper, was spinning a yarn to the madams and girls that Terry and his old cobber were Queensland plainclothes police in Sydney on a special mission.

After a while the old bushie was responding to the glad eye being given to him by a young and attractive pro, and Dick quietly arranged a '$20 special' for him, telling the pro to take him upstairs and give him a good time. The last he and Terry saw of him for quite a while was his moleskin riding trousers, tucked into his rodeo boots, disappearing up the steps. Two hours later – at about 4 a.m. – he appeared back at the bar downstairs, where Dick and Terry had been having a wonderful time with the free booze. He looked like a punter whose 100-to-1 shot has romped in. 'How did she go, old mate?' Dick asked. To which he replied with his slow drawl, 'Holy livin' Jaysus, Dick, that little sheila sure knocked a fart outta me!' (Young horses that are bucking or pigrooting often let out a big loud 'blurt'.)

It was an era when people could get away with many things that they wouldn't now. Terry was performing at the Courthouse Hotel in Surry Hills, owned by famous football coach Pat Gibson. He'd had a huge play-up that afternoon and was pretty much on autopilot, feeling a bit crook and wishing he was anywhere else. But the show must go on . . . On the stage, he'd set up his speakers between two large pot plants and was singing 'I'm Saving My Money to Buy You a Rainbow', when a couple who were very drunk got up to dance. When the bloke spun his partner around, her artificial leg flew off and hit Terry's stool. She crashed to the floor, her other leg flew up in the air and she had no knickers on. Terry, who has a very weak stomach, chundered voluminously into the pot plant next to his speaker, much to the absolute delight of the 'highly sophisticated' (not!) crowd. They laughed and laughed!

At a big city football club, he had secured a well-paid gig for himself and a successful female pop star whose records were on the radio hit parades of the time. Her live act featured wildly energetic dancing in sexy costumes, all over the stage, as she sang. When Terry finished his segment and went to see her during the drinks break, he found, to his horror, that she was stoned and blind drunk. This was really bad, as neither of them would be paid if she didn't deliver the goods everyone was expecting. He established that although she was incapable of dancing, she would still be able to sing. Thinking fast, he had the curtain drawn across the stage, then sat her on a barstool behind it, and gaffer-taped her legs to the stool so she wouldn't fall off. Her long skirt hid the tape. Then he introduced her in front of the curtain, saying that due to an accident that afternoon, she was unfortunately unable to perform her famous dances, but she was still going to sing all her hit songs. The audience clapped sympathetically as the curtain drew back to reveal her sitting, her head resting on her chest. The music struck up and away she went like a robot, singing all her hits. They got away with it, although Terry was worried the whole time that she would topple over, revealing their gigantic fraud.

When he'd had enough of city life he went back touring the country. Margaret was unhappy about being left behind all the time and took baby Ricky home to New Zealand. Terry was extremely popular at the new Tamworth Country Music festival and was asked by Channel Nine to host a new television show, *Must Be Country*. He moved there and presented twenty-eight weekly episodes, enjoying the adrenalin rush of performing on live television, introducing all the big names and giving young talent a go. By then he was visiting the Holy Grail, Nashville, to record his songs. But the beauty of Terry Gordon is, he didn't allow all this to go to his head. He has always been one of the most likeable blokes in the entertainment industry, who has helped countless youngsters with stars in their eyes to get their career started.

His *Must Be Country* television show was popular but didn't get a second run because it was so expensive to produce. However, the brand-new Blacktown Workers Club offered him a three-month contract to compere and perform, including at their gala opening night. It was a highly glamorous, no-expense-spared show, with an eight-piece orchestra and ballet girls, and before the big night, they all rehearsed for a week solid. On opening night, Terry strode out in the full-on, flash-as-chain-lightning atmosphere, in front of a packed house that included the directors and committee, to sing his first song, 'Heartaches by the Number'. He knew it backwards . . . normally. The over-rehearsing took its toll. His mind went completely blank. Disaster! The musicians were all looking at each other, the ballet girls bumping into one another. After dying a thousand deaths while la-la-ing, he managed to get his brain into gear for the last verse. The rest of the show went off perfectly and not a word was said about it. It had never happened to him before and hasn't since.

Every performer has experienced embarrassing moments onstage. At a Barham club one night, a lady handed him a beer coaster with something written on it. He assumed it was a request, so kept singing two more songs before looking down to see what she wanted him to sing. She'd written, 'Terry your fly's undone'.

There were a few more excruciating moments when he began managing the legendary Chad Morgan's tours after Terry had given Chad a star guest 'spot' on his TV show. Chad *was* conscious of his star status and could be a teensy bit difficult to handle sometimes. At one of their earliest shows together at a big New South Wales bowling club, a woman at a table in front of the stage kept annoying Chad by rudely yapping away with her female friends, while he was trying to deliver gags. It was very off-putting for him, knowing his punchlines were being drowned out. Eventually, Chad's years of professionalism allowed him to leave the woman in no doubt that she was disrupting his performance. He yelled, 'Hey, lady! Yes, you in the front with the blue hair! If you don't shut up, I'll come down there, set fire to your Tampax, and blow you through the f**king roof!' Unfortunately she was the club president's wife and he was barred from performing there ever again.

'There's hundreds more clubs and pubs, though, to get work in, and I toured with Chad for eleven years of ups and downs,' says Terry. 'Mostly ups, because everyone loves Chad. He's a tremendous drawcard. It's hard to imagine the Aussie country music scene without Chad and, as he's proved recently, you can't kill him with an axe. He's outlived all the old-timers and still loves entertaining. I'm proud to have been associated with such a mighty legend.'

Since that partnership, Terry has toured regularly with Col Elliott, Wally the Worker, and Sid Heylen (the comedian who played Cookie on *A Country Practice*), and even suffered (poor bugger!) touring around Australia with Electric Blue, the UK's most famous striptease troupe.

'That was a tough gig,' he says with a laugh. 'I warmed up for them with my really bawdy comic stuff, then they'd warm me up with their act . . . whew! They were gorgeous. Great girls too – we all had a lot of fun. That was a once-in-a-lifetime gig – and a sell-out everywhere. I took turns driving the bus with the soundman. We were driving along the Hume Highway once and, for a laugh, the girls all flashed their boobs at a semitrailer driver alongside us. He chased us all the way to Sydney!' One of Terry's warm-up skits for the Electric Blue show involved him dressing up in a hilariously camp outfit as Elton John (not a pretty sight), prancing out on stage in short shorts, with 'Cracker Night' sparklers sticking out of the heels of his high cowboy boots. One night, as he backed up near the drums, swaying his bum in time to his song, legs apart, the sparklers managed to set fire to a cardboard sign there. There was a flash as the drums caught fire. In the front row of the audience, a quick-thinking Noel McGregor, the president of the Showmen's Guild, tossed his jug of beer between Terry's legs and put the fire out. (Just another day at the office for showman Terry . . .)

Terry has a running gag he cracks whenever he walks into an RSL Club. He looks at the photo of the Queen, which is always hanging in their foyers, and wisecracks, 'Is she the next act after me? Think she'll pull a crowd?'

One of his favourite anecdotes is about the bowls club manager in western New South Wales, who either can't have been the sharpest tool in the shed, and/or never read the biography notes about the performers he booked. When Terry arrived there, he noticed that comedian Steady Eddie had been on the week before. Terry asked if his show went down well with the locals, and the manager replied, 'He really had 'em laughing, mate. They loved his gags. But jeez, he laid it on a bit thick. Even after he'd finished and was signing autographs, he still kept jerking and twitching and staggering around all the time!' Terry stared, speechless, waiting for the manager to burst into laughter, but that didn't happen. He obviously didn't realise that the whole point of Eddie's act was that he really is handicapped with cerebral palsy.

Buster Noble was a famous comedian during the '60s and '70s, whom Terry worked with on many tours, but apparently he wasn't quite as famous in North Queensland as he was down south. When they pulled up in a town that was apparently booked out, Terry went into the only motel they could find with a vacancy sign up. It was pretty daggy but they were buggered. The rough-as-guts manager said he only had one room left but it had twin beds. Terry said, 'That'll do, mate. There's only me and me mate, Buster.' The bloke looked a bit cranky and said, 'I won't allow dogs on the beds here.' Fortunately Buster was in the car, out of earshot of that remark, but he would have heard Terry laughing his head off after the initial surprise wore off!

More recently, Terry has, while still performing, taken on the role of entrepreneur, bringing top acts to Australia from the UK, including Isla Grant, Mary Duff and Charlie Landsborough. All three acts are hugely popular and the shows Terry organises for them are sell-outs. He takes a break between tours, at his Gold Coast home, which is full of memorabilia – photos and posters of him with all the stars from the 'old days' right through to the present, including Stan Coster, Gordon Parsons (who wrote many of

Slim Dusty's hits), Slim himself, Chad, Willie Nelson, Johnny Cash, the Everly Brothers and George Jones. They line walls of his fabulously restored railway carriage 'STAR BAR', set in his garden. Secure in the house are his many awards, the Olympic torch he carried in 2000, and the photos of his plaque at Tamworth's Roll of Renown and of the then Governor of Queensland, Quentin Bryce, awarding his OAM in 2005 for services to country music and charitable organisations. It takes quite a while to see everything that represents this terrific bloke's successful life, spent in the challenging but rewarding career of entertaining the public. Terry, you're a bloody champion who's loved by many people all over Australia!

Author's note: In Australia's bicentennial year, 1988, I toured over the southern half of Queensland (including isolated western communities) with Terry, performing country songs, bush poems and yarns, and skits, as 'A Pair of Scrubbers', for the Queensland Arts Council. I would have almost paid the Arts Council for the experience of travelling with one of the funniest and nicest people I've had the pleasure to work with. We laughed the entire time. The story of that tour alone warrants an entire book!

7.

Doris Wright

FROM THE COW YARD TO THE SEASIDE

At the truly grand age of ninety-eight, Doris Wright is as bright and chirpy as a willy-wagtail, loving life and making every day count. Living in one of Australia's loveliest spots, Tin Can Bay, in the warm climate of the blessed Sunshine State must help, as would the fact she still lives in her own home and is surrounded by young people.

She spent much of her first six decades milking cows, but since leaving behind life on the dairy farm, it's been fun and freedom – freedom from floods, droughts and the drudgery of being tied to the dairy twice a day, seven days a week, rain, hail or heat.

Born in August 1915, the eldest of five children, Doris helped both her mother and father with their chores from a very early age, on their farm at Kanigan, between Gympie and Maryborough in South-East Queensland. Her parents, from Pommy stock, never lost their distinctive accent and, as a child, Doris christened their farm 'Devonshire Valley'. When her parents took up their selection, their land was timbered, but between milking and other chores, her father swung an axe constantly to clear the land and give them more and more fertile acres. Once the trees were cleared, the virgin scrub soil grew first-rate pasture and crops. Doris vividly remembers picking crops of beautiful beans each year, packing them into sugar bags and sending them off to the southern cities. Naturally, the family grew all their own fruit and vegetables, and made their own butter from the separated cream. Cans of cream from the dairy were only picked up from the rail siding every second day but cream that had gone sour was still usable to make butter. Pigs were kept to drink the separated 'skim' milk, which no person would dream of drinking back then. It was 'pig's milk' and thought of as such until half a century later, when Australia's increasingly sedentary lifestyle led to the popularity of diets. In Doris's childhood, most people worked hard, and either walked or rode horses everywhere.

Children of dairy farmers are still expected to work before and after school, but their help was especially needed back before milking was done by machine. Although Doris rode a pony for 4 miles to her one-teacher school at Kanigan, she loved any excuse to ride it, be it helping bring in cows or doing other farm work. Her horse was kept during school hours in the 'pony paddock' beside the classroom. However, it was a bit of a rogue and sometimes got through weak spots in the fence to the 600-acre paddock next door, which meant Doris had to walk all the way home hoping she wouldn't run into any swaggies. On weekends, she'd ride several miles to piano lessons at a neighbour's farm, then further on to play tennis on another property on Saturdays, and then canter off again the next morning to Sunday school at the Theebine Hall. Her horse was very fit!

Her parents shared a big strong horse that was used for many purposes: ploughing, harvesting, scuffling weeds, pulling the wagon loaded with cans of cream to the siding, or pulling the buggy to the shop at Miva with Doris's mum driving. This horse was adaptable and willing – worth his weight in gold to a family that wasn't rich.

Dipping the cattle for ticks was another enormous task requiring the entire family to help 'encourage' the poor beasts to leap into a long, deep concrete trough full of arsenic-laden water, that would splash back over the helpers as the reluctant cows finally took a flying leap and plunged in. While driving the cows to the neighbour's dip, Doris would be waiting eagerly for rogues to dive off into the thick scrub either side of the track, hoping to escape their 'swim', as it was always an excuse for some fancy riding to bring them back to the mob.

Mothers on farms had to be nurses as well. If home remedies like soap and sugar poultices, Condy's Crystals, Friar's Emulsion and Epsom salts couldn't cure injuries and illnesses, it took a long ride in the buggy, then a train trip to Maryborough, to the doctor. A weekly dose of castor oil – foul-tasting stuff – was considered necessary to keep children healthy. Every child dreaded the appearance of the big blue bottle. As a little girl, Doris always rode to her neighbour's farm to line up with their children because she reckoned their mum didn't pour as much down her throat.

The Sunday school at Theebine catered for a mixture of Protestants. For some reason there were no Catholics in the district. There was a big divide in that era between Protestants and Roman Catholics. A rare outing for families was the once-a-year Sunday school picnic, with races and games in the paddock next to the Theebine Hall.

Doris vividly recalls the excitement leading up to, and during, a special visit to the neighbouring family who had bought the first wireless in the district. It was 1925 and she sat speechless – as her entire family were – listening in awe to a cricket broadcast from England coming out of a set that wasn't connected by wires to anything. Most people in the district didn't have electricity until Doris was well and truly grown up. When the dentist occasionally visited the tiny nearby settlement of Gunalda, he used his foot to pump a treadle that, in turn, drove the buzzing drill into the (usually) screaming patient's tooth. Although Doris's family would've loved a wireless set, her father chose to buy a piano instead. It was a tremendous procedure to get the heavy old piano up the high steps and into the house. She loved playing it and it was simply wonderful to have singsongs with the family, all looking to her to provide the music.

In her final year of primary school, Doris was top of the class. As well as that honour, she had really impressed the visiting school inspector by answering all his questions correctly – even the 'trick' questions. Her teacher, Mr Sheahan, uncharacteristically praised her on break-up day in front of all the children and parents, and to her absolute amazement, presented her with a gift, which her mother had helped him choose: a dressing table set with a brush, mirror and comb, which she was immensely proud of. (When I asked Doris if she was always good when she was young, she replied with a cheeky grin and a twinkle in her eye, 'Oh, my dear, you can't *always* be good!')

Then came the big grey cloud in her life. She was more disappointed than she'd ever been before when her father told her she wouldn't be going to high school – after all, he explained, she was a female and would end up being a housewife or farmer's wife, so what was the point of further education? That was the normal attitude, so she just had to swallow her disappointment and start looking for a job. The only work she could find was doing washing for some of the district women who could afford to pay her – a tremendously unappealing task to do back when it was all done the hard way.

She was only thirteen when she started that first job, which involved a full day of toil. Swirling the clothes 'round and 'round the copper full of steaming water and homemade soap, with a big strong stick, then lifting them out with the stick into galvanised tubs so they could be pushed through the mangle (two rollers that squeezed the water out), challenged her physical strength. Winding the handle of the mangle, or wringer, was difficult and potentially dangerous for tired hands pushing the heavy or awkward items such as sheets or overalls through. Sometimes squashed fingers – very painful – were the result of that extra bit of effort. Then the washing was rinsed by hand and put back through the mangle. One iron tub held starch for 'going to town' and 'Sunday best' clothes, pillowslips and doilies, another held water with a bag of Reckitt's Blue dissolved in it, to make whites blindingly white. The last items to go into the copper – which was kept hot with a small fire underneath it – were heavy work clothes. Doris would have to conserve an extra store of energy to enable her to manually scrub the dirtiest parts – usually saddle marks and manure stains. Hauling each basket to the line also tested her strength. For an extra shilling or two, she would also mop and scrub floors. She had learnt how to do that properly from her grandmother, having ridden to her place every weekend to clean her floors for pocket money.

It was exhausting drudgery for a young girl, and she had plenty of time to think about how much she would rather have been in high school in Gympie or Maryborough, learning new things and bettering herself. But she trained herself not to become bitter because hers was the fate of most girls.

Doris was in her teens before her father proudly brought his first car home – an Oakland. But she wasn't allowed to drive it. She learnt to drive after she was married, in a 'homemade' Chevrolet ute, back when farmers built their own utilities before they were available commercially.

Dances at the small hamlets in her childhood district relieved the monotony of working life, the band usually consisting of an accordion, a violin, and in some places, a piano. Doris was always danced off her little feet, but there was one particular young man – a nice-looking fellow – who had obviously set his cap at her. Doris had met her 'Mr Right' . . . who was, in fact, Victor Wright. In those early days in closely settled farming communities, young people knew all about each other and what sort of families they came from, long before they were officially 'stepping out' together. Although he attended the Theebine School, not her own, she had known Victor and his family all her life. While she'd been busy slaving over a hot copper for a few years, saving up for lovely things for her glory box – the carved chest girls filled with household linen, towels, and so on – he'd turned into quite a sort! Of course, he was a dairy farmer's son, and by allowing him to court her, she was consigning herself to that life, but he was quite irresistibly dashing on his noisy New Hudson motorbike!

Other girls were eyeing him off too, but Doris was smart. 'I didn't chase him. I made him chase me!' she recalls. 'I could hear him coming for miles on that noisy bike of his, and had plenty of time to brush my hair and kick my gumboots off before he arrived.'

Doris's old grandfather, a farmer all his life and still as English as the day he sailed to make a new life in Australia, was naturally a down-to-earth soul – a man of the soil. When he was told that Doris and Victor had set a date to marry, he drew thoughtfully on his pipe, leaned his cloth-capped, old grey head back and said in his Devonshire accent, 'Aye, I suppose they want to mate.'

Victor's parents were only too happy to retire from dairying, and move to the 30 acres they had bought at Redcliffe, closer to Brisbane, after handing over the running of their farm and their white-ant-ridden house to their son and his new bride. Doris's dad wasn't the retiring type. He kept dairying till he died. 'Some people simply cannot imagine life without milking cows every day,' Doris says wistfully.

The most heartbreaking experience of her life was the loss of a brother in World War II. She will never forget the day her parents received the dreaded telegram. They grieved for the rest of their days and she still thinks of him every day.

Doris and Victor's three children, Eunice, Maurice and Carolyn, were to grow up just as their parents did, helping with the milking and other chores, but with many more 'mod cons'. Milking machines had transformed the lives of dairying families. Victor, like most country blokes, was a great improviser. He used the same bank of batteries that drove the milking machines to operate lights in their house, long before they had electricity. A main form of entertainment was the weekly card games with neighbours. Sometimes the games would go on for so long that the lights would become dimmer and dimmer, until Victor would have to go out to the shed and crank up the generator to charge the batteries up again. It was a big improvement on the old carbide or kerosene lamps their parents had.

Their kerosene refrigerator, a Charles Hope Cold Flame, was a godsend. Doris's children, now all in their late sixties, proudly declare that between the fridge and their mother's cooking skills, they enjoyed 'the best ice-cream in the world' when growing up. Like most country women, she was a clever cook, making do without certain ingredients and substituting others, making nearly all the clothes they wore, plus the curtains and chair coverings. Everyone received a new 'best' outfit each year to go to the Gympie Show. One year when they were all getting ready for their big once-a-year day, Victor noticed a tail-light was broken on his farm utility that they all somehow squashed into for their rare outings. Not wanting to get into trouble with the police, he secured a piece of red rag over the busted light with a piece of tie wire. From a distance, in the daytime, it looked a bit like a tail-light! In those days, everything that was broken was fixed on the farm – nothing was sent away to be repaired. Victor was a very busy man and never stopped working. Doris often declared to anyone who'd listen, 'I'd get more attention if I was a Fordson tractor!'

Victor showed a lot of patience when teaching Doris how to drive the Chev ute, and his perseverance was rewarded the day she was able to save his life by driving him to town when he'd been bitten by a brown snake.

As simple as their farm life was, it often provided laughter. Doris always got a chuckle from seeing her children riding their bikes to the dunny!

Some of Maurice's most vivid memories from their happy rural childhood are of Sunday visits to Doris's parents, 7 miles away. They'd go to church on the way, then have a big Sunday roast meal, no matter how hot the weather. Above the table laden with delicious food and the 'best' crockery and cutlery, spun long streamers of sticky flypaper, covered in hundreds of victims hanging from the, fortunately, high ceilings. Maurice shakes his head at the memory of them and laughs, 'They were the most macabre dining-room "decorations" imaginable. Thank goodness some bright spark invented flyscreens.'

Maurice has many memories of just how different things were back then. 'An enterprising publican at Theebine put up lights on the tennis courts which were next to the pub. Tennis was very popular and of course the men would enjoy a few beers, the ladies shandies or lemonades. As we pulled up there one night, when I was about eight, I jumped out of the back of the ute and managed to break my arm between the shoulder and the elbow. In the darkness, Mum put my arm into what she thought was a comfortable position, then I was carried across to the stationmaster's house. He was known as a handy first-aid man. When we reached the light of his house, he saw my arm was twisted around and he unwound it a full revolution! Surprisingly, that did – eventually – make it feel a lot better. He then set my arm and it healed with no problems.'

Occasionally there would be an open-air theatre at Theebine, and the family's favourite movies were those of the Marx Brothers. The only time laughter was scarce in their peaceful rural life was when the Mary River, right below the house, flooded. The flood of 1955 was the biggest, when it literally rained feet, not just inches. Victor kept putting sticks in the ground to observe how fast the water was rising. Fortunately the cattle could all get to higher ground, but the house was in danger. They managed to put their furniture and household items up off the floor as best they could – even the piano was somehow lifted up onto drums! (Doris must have been very strong!) During the night, when the water was getting closer and it was still raining, they hurriedly packed a bag of clothes, woke their young children and, all wearing raincoats and hats, walked in the teeming rain to a farmhouse next door that was abandoned but high on a rise. At least they were dry and safe. By the time they had left their house, the river had reached the stumps.

What do dairy farmers do in a crisis such as that one? Keep milking the cows, of course. No matter what, the cows still had to be milked, so they returned next morning to do so and see whether their house had floated away or not. The water was running through it, but only 4 inches deep. However, when the water finally drained out, Doris was faced with an enormous task cleaning out mud and debris. Their neighbour appeared in a boat to see if they were all right and was pleased his old house had given them refuge. Several belongings in sheds, such as all the horses' harnesses, had floated away. Following that flood – the worst they had experienced – they shifted the house further up the hill. Floods had often ruined their winter feed, which was heartbreaking. If the feed did grow back in time, battalions of army grubs would then move in and decimate the new growth.

Victor could not see a bright financial future for their son on the farm, with profits soon swallowed up into machinery and other costs to operate it. Maurice became an electrician, gaining 100 per cent in all his subjects at Maryborough, then Mackay Technical College – an incredible achievement that saw him welcomed into a lucrative career in the coal mines of Central Queensland. The farm was sold to a neighbour in 1974, and Victor and Doris looked forward to a well-earned easier life at beautiful Tin Can Bay. No more milking – what a blessing! Victor was given what he considered a 'cushy' job working on a dredge for the local sandmining company that dredged sand to extract titanium. Until their house was built, they lived in their caravan by the ocean. Like many farmers, Victor had unfortunately left it a bit late to realistically achieve his dream of doing lots of fishing. Within a few short years, putting the boat in and out of the water was getting too hard, and it was sold.

They both became wholeheartedly involved in the tiny 'bush community by the sea', helping to develop the Country Club. Doris kept her CWA involvement going and encouraged the local group to cater for the Anzac Day march, as her Miva branch had done with great success. Until their morning teas, followed by two-up, became a 'must', many of the locals had marched in Gympie. She also was one of the main 'goers' who got the Ladies Bowls Club up and running.

Conservationists managed to get the titanium mine closed down, which put the men out of work. Doris convinced Victor to hitch up the van again, and set off to have a go at fruit picking, and see a bit of Australia at the same time. They loved it, working each year mainly near Shepparton in Victoria, for the season, then returning to their comfy ocean-side home. They were sad to sell it in 1999, due to difficulty for Victor – who died a year later – managing the high steps. They built a lowset brick house nearby, where Doris still lives, with Eunice in a separate unit keeping an eye on her. Maurice and Carolyn aren't far away either, so Doris is constantly in touch with, or being visited by, children, grandchildren and great grandchildren. Recently, at ninety-six, she stopped playing bowls and driving herself around, after breaking a leg, but her life is still full – her main mission now being to encourage more women to join the CWA. 'I've been a member for sixty years now, since joining the Miva branch, and I've *loved* it,' she says with feeling. 'When I joined, I dreaded getting up and speaking in public, as most people do. Being in the CWA has enabled me to overcome that, and I am always grateful. It saddens me that we struggle to get members because the young women would gain so much. They don't understand what they're missing out on. As the lady says on the radio: "We're not just about tea and scones."'

Doris Wright is certainly not just about tea and scones either. A young-at-heart, positive-thinking achiever, with a great sense of humour, it's a real pleasure to spend time in her company, having a lively conversation on just about any topic under the sun. It's impossible to get a grip on the fact she is almost a century old, that she was a baby when the Anzacs were attempting the impossible at Gallipoli. She loves reading books and newspapers and, amazingly, has never had to wear glasses. When I asked if she would change anything during her life, she replied without hesitation, 'I would love to have had more education. I think I would have made a good teacher.' That reply makes you reflect, that the 'good old days' were, quite often, not so good (especially for females).

Doris Wright may not have been allowed to achieve her dream of being a teacher, but she has contributed much to society both through her efforts for the CWA, which helps more worthy causes than most Australians realise, and by carrying out to perfection the most important job in the world, bar none: being a good mother. She produced three fine Australians, and with Victor's help, guided them towards having successful lives and contributing to their country. Doris, take a bow.

8.

Donald Cairncross Todd

THE PRACTICAL JOKER WHO 'MARRIED THE SEA'

Author note: In the interests of trans-Tasman friendship, and in the finest spirit of Anzac fellowship, I have included a story of a scallywag from the land of the long white cloud.

At age nineteen, Don Todd was bulletproof. Dying was something old people did.

It's quite normal for most teenagers to think they're going to have a wonderful adventure when, in fact, the outcome – whether they survive or go to an early grave – of what they're about to do depends entirely on what mood Lady Luck's in that day. At nineteen, I drove every vehicle as fast as it would possibly go, swam in rivers where there were crocs, climbed aboard horses that absolutely did not want me on their back, and worked with cattle that longed to turn me into a shish kebab, but I survived. Like the wild Far North ringers I worked with, I was mad as a cut snake . . . but I would never, *EVER!* have done what Don Todd did.

In 1950, he and his mate Des Rice set out in a badly made, little, leaky wooden boat that they'd built themselves, to cross one of the most dangerous stretches of water in the world. They'd constructed *Pipinui* by following a plan published in *Popular Mechanics* magazine and didn't have a clue about the finer points of boat building, like the desirability of having a proper keel and rudder, for example, and a thoroughly reliable engine – unlike the one they could afford and hoped would do the job.

Cook Strait, between the North and South Islands of New Zealand, is treacherous and unpredictable. It's claimed many vessels much larger and more professionally built than *Pipinui*, from large yachts and trawlers to cruise ships. It can be calm one minute and a maelstrom of raging winds and huge waves the next. Then there are the swirling, washing-machine currents that pose a challenge to the skills of the most experienced sailors and seamen. The large ferry *Wahine* encountered 120-knot winds during what ended up being its last crossing in 1968, and foundered with loss of life, while the other side of the strait was a millpond.

The two lads, knowing the strait's reputation and aware also of their extremely limited experience at sea, tried at first to get various boats to tow them across. Every skipper they asked took one look at little *Pipinui* and said, 'You're not crossing Cook Strait in that thing!'

Concerns about their safety led to them being 'dobbed in' to the Wellington harbourmaster, who told them with the sternest attitude, 'If you even attempt to go in that I will catch up to you and put an axe through it!' So they sneaked down the coast from Wellington to where they could leave without being seen by the authorities, and set out on their insane crossing. It was to become the adventure of their lives and would pass into Cook Strait folklore.

They were headed for the beautiful waters of Pelorus Sound, part of the magnificent Marlborough Sounds, at the top of the South

Island. Don was chasing his dream of spending his life 'mucking about on boats', a dream he'd had since he was able to say the word 'boat'.

Born in Wellington in 1931 in a hospital overlooking the harbour, Donald Cairncross Todd's first gulp of air was salt air, a smell he has adored ever since. As he loves to boast: 'My blood was impregnated with salt; my ancestry traces back to Captain Kidd.' Even as a toddler, he would point excitedly to boats, as obsessed with them as many young girls are with horses. Brought up by the sea, his grandparents would take him to the harbour, where he always wanted to go on board every boat he saw. At eight years of age, he finally received his first homemade tin boat and paddle. Until it rusted out a few years later, he spent every possible moment paddling around the harbour in it, his imagination running riot. As he grew up, he'd take himself to the wharves, mesmerised by the ships coming and going, loading and unloading. Eventually he had a store of knowledge in his young head about all the different ships that came and went into Wellington's busy harbour. His grandfather told him many stories of the sea and composed the following poem for young Don's entertainment:

Don would like to spend his time, in the Mercantile Marine
and learn to sing a proper rhyme, sea shanties all serene.
But when the sea gets very rough, and insides they are shaken,
he says 'I must be very tough!' then up he heaves his bacon.

A character full of fun and laughter from babyhood, a cheeky bugger who was to go on to become notorious throughout life for his practical jokes, Don inherited his sense of humour from his mum.

His father's name was Neville, and when anyone would ask Don's mother why she had so many children (six!), she'd reply with a laugh, 'Because whenever I saw Neville without his trousers on, I'd fall in love with him all over again!' His dad would tell people that the big family was his contribution to the war.

Don remembers women doing 'men's work' during the war, and frequently hearing his mum complaining about everything being rationed. It tested to the limits a mother's ingenuity with improvising while cooking. The two most frequently heard comments at meal-times were: 'Can I have some more please, Mum?' and 'Don't you know there's a war on?' By mistake – probably because there were so many children – his mother was posted an extra ration book. After a wrestle with her conscience, she put it in the cat's name, 'Willy'. During that time, little Don took a big risk to pinch a large tin of plum jam from the kitchen at the college he attended, to give to his favourite aunty as a gift. That would have been a welcome present then indeed, but he was caught and given the cane by the college principal.

He clearly remembers the fear of invasion by the Japanese and the citizens' gratitude to the Americans for going to New Zealand and helping them. 'The girls all loved them, of course,' recalls Don. 'They'd give them silk stockings with one hand and take them off with the other.' When the Yanks were in town, there were 'deflated balloons' in the parks and shop doorways in the mornings, and one day, Don took one home, to his mother's horror. 'Look, Mum, I found a balloon . . .'

Neville Todd had a successful engineering business and assumed his son would want to work for him then eventually take over, but Don grew up with other ideas. Always a larrikin, always in trouble, he was frequently caned at Rongotai College. On Sundays, Don and best mate Des travelled to church by tram and soon befriended the driver and conductor, who – foolishly, as it turned out – went along with the boys' requests to show them how to drive it. They'd stay on board chatting away with the driver till the tram went to the terminus to turn around. The men also showed them how to change the conducting rods over, eventually allowing them to perform that task while they went to the toilet at the terminus, before the return journey. It was too big a temptation for larrikin Don and one day he drove the tram a hundred yards up the street, giving himself and Des a real thrill, being 'in charge'. Then they enjoyed the biggest laugh watching the men walking back from the toilet, looking in horrified shock at the spot where their tram should have been. When they caught up, they were less than happy and gave them a good dressing-down, but Don felt it had been well worth it.

He was sent away to be straightened out at a strict boarding school, Nelson College, located at the top of the opposite island. He'd travel there across Cook Strait by the steamship *Matangi*, and soon got to be well known by the crewmen. Knowing he was starved for good tucker at school, they'd feed him in their galley, and were always astonished at how much he could eat, even during the roughest seas when every other passenger would be vomiting over the rails. Although he had always become carsick on trips, Don had 'sea legs', and did not live up to the poem his grandfather had written. Before his first trip back across the strait for the hols, he invested in a large bottle of Camroc ginger ale. Always thinking of ways to earn a few bob, he'd remembered the ad that used to appear on the trams in Wellington: 'Drink Camroc ginger ale – good for the stomach and seasickness.' When his friends started feeling sick and had taken to their cabins, Don visited them like Florence Nightingale, administering his ginger ale for threepence a dose. The result was almost instantaneous. Never has there been so much mess created by so few in such a short time. There was vomit up walls, on bunks, across floors – even on some ceilings! That was enough for young Don to create a deep, lifelong distrust of promises made in advertisements.

Because he was a favourite with the crew, Don was put in charge of organising the lunch on daytime trips back to Wellington, for himself and the other students. Usually he had the pick of everything he laid out on the table because everyone was sick, but on calm days he had to share anything considered special in those rationing days, such as jam. On one such trip, he worked out how he could have the jam to himself. He managed to catch a blowfly and stick it in the top of the jar, buzzing, before calling the others in to eat. They all passed on the jam, but Don dug some out around the fly, then took what was left home – minus the fly – and was therefore the hero of the household.

Vomiting chums aside, he loved these sea journeys and loved Nelson, a picturesque town located on the Marlborough Sounds – a beautiful stretch of water – with the warmest climate in what's known as 'the mainland'. He could never have imagined that six decades on, he'd be retiring there.

The South Island is not known for its balmy weather. At school he frequently received 'six of the best' across his freezing backside while touching his toes, the subsequent blood blisters and bright-red weals being a source of pride in the communal showers. The morning showers were supposed to be character-building, freezing-cold ones, but Don and his dorm mates enjoyed warm water after he broke into the workshop and ingeniously crafted a link from his dorm's plumbing to the hot pipes that led to the staff's bathrooms. Some yapping idiot let the cat out of the bag and it was six of the best again, plus back to cold showers.

Don joined the army cadets and soon found out that standing on the parade ground and sweating in the summer sun was for mugs. So, being as cunning as a shithouse rat, he worked his way into the medical corps. He'd seen the 'meds' enjoying the shade when they'd had to cart off the inevitable 'fainter'. On his first parade in this role, no one was fainting, so he turned around and punched a bloke behind him in the guts, hard as he could, and dropped him like a rock. That did the trick – off to the shade for young Don, carrying the comatose comrade. He was certainly a resourceful young fellow! He managed to fashion a boat from the float of an old Catalina flying boat, and loved to paddle it among the ships in Nelson Haven. These outings on the water, drinking in the atmosphere of the different vessels, managed to take the teenager's mind off females, for a while at least.

Describing himself as a 'testosterone bomb', Don ogled the chest development of the boarders from the local girls' college while in church, and lived to get closer to females during the college dance classes. Unfortunately for him and his fantasies, these stiff events were strictly chaperoned, with eagle eyes belonging to both the boys' and girls' college staff, searching for any couple dancing less than a foot apart, and male hands in places that were strictly out of bounds. One unforgettable day he managed to find himself in a paddock, 'getting to know' not just one member of the female species, but two. The girl he'd sneaked off to meet had brought a friend, and they were both, to his complete amazement, willing to discover some of the mysteries of life with him as a threesome.

'Well, I didn't even know how to handle one, let alone two, and I failed miserably as Romeo,' he says. 'It was a highly embarrassing experience and I slunk back to school, still a virgin, with nothing to skite to my mates about. After college when I returned to Wellington, my mate Des and I spent all of our time trying to find out either how females worked or how to build a boat. Both goals were just as difficult to achieve.'

When Don announced to his parents that he wanted to work on boats as a career rather than join in the family business, words could not describe his father's disappointment. His mother insisted he get a trade first, and arranged an appointment with an electrician who was seeking an apprentice. Like most apprentices, Don suffered all the usual leg-pulling, and his boss was a particularly hard taskmaster, but having that trade allowed him to follow his dream of working on boats. When he ended up in The Sounds seeking a skipper looking for crew, he found his talents with electricity in great demand. In fact, he was welcomed with open arms from one end of that magnificent stretch of water, lined with sheep properties, to the other, because there was no resident sparky and it was with huge difficulty one could be enticed there to wire up a house or business. Consequently, highly dodgy wiring, put up by sheep-station owners themselves, was a normal state of affairs.

But before Don arrived there like 'the 230-volt cavalry' in little *Pipinui*, he was to endure what would later be referred to as his 'Chatham Island experience'. Having finished his apprenticeship and become engaged to a girl he adored and was sure would adapt to the isolated life in The Sounds, he was suddenly lured to the Chatham Islands to fix the cold rooms operated by the blue-cod fishing company there. Now for most people, the isolated Chathams, about a hundred miles off the South Island coast, have about as much appeal as Siberia; their only redeeming feature being plenty of fish. Don was dubious, as any smart person should be, about going there, but it was a short, temporary job paying very good money – enough for him and his fiancée to set a wedding date.

In those days a fellow didn't marry unless he could afford to look after his wife. He was also assured the quarters were very warm and comfy, and the food excellent, so away he went.

The trip out there was a four-day nightmare in a rusty old boat chugging painfully through howling, freezing gales. When he finally arrived, the quarters were not just basic but in appalling condition, and the food matched. He insisted he wanted to go straight back on the same boat, but was told that he'd come out on what was the last one for six months. Trapped, he just had to make the best of it, but that was about as character-building an experience as you could get. He could only communicate with his fiancée by telegram – hardly a method of sending cootchie-coo, lovey-dovey messages about how much he missed her. He knew he was in trouble when the only woman who worked in the factory – the cleaner – whom he could hardly bear to look at when he first went there because she was so 'plain', gradually became more and more attractive, her body more and more alluring, to his famished eyes. Still, he remained faithful and the thought of returning to his girl, once this ordeal was over, kept him going. When he returned to Wellington, he found out she had abandoned him for someone else. It was time to chase his dream and head – finally – for The Sounds.

He and Des had built *Pipinui* using enthusiasm more than expertise, and with the wild optimism and immense naivety of youth, were going to sail her to Pelorus Sound, not realising how jerry-built their pride and joy actually was. When the harbourmaster forbade them to attempt to cross Cook Strait in her, they decided to sneak out in the middle of the night, at 1.30 a.m. They had barely enough petrol to make the crossing, no chart or radio, and little food. It was their first-ever journey in darkness and there was a considerable swell, but they forged on at a less-than-thrilling 4 knots, conserving fuel. When they hit the treacherous Karori Rip, where the sea was known to become 'confused', to put it mildly, their dodgy engine conked out. Fortunately it started again, and by daylight they could see the South Island in the far distance. Having no chart meant they could not find an entrance to calmer waters known as Tory Channel for a long time. A merciful God had steered the blithe duo away from the dangerous Wash Rocks, but as they weren't aware of them, they hadn't worried about hitting them. As they say across the Tasman: 'No worries!'

Heading south-west, they eventually were in calmer waters and headed for a house they could see at the water's edge in the distance. Tying the boat at the jetty, they asked the people who walked down from the house if they could buy some food. When they told them they'd just sailed over from Wellington, the boys sensed that they weren't believed. But they were loaded up with beautiful fresh milk and huge slabs of fruitcake. This was their first experience of the generous hospitality of the Sounds people. As they continued up the Kenepuru Sound towards their goal, their bilge pump suddenly went into reverse, filling the boat with water, and they had to frantically bail to stay afloat. A launch owned by a man they knew from past holidays, with a load of tourists on board, just happened to arrive alongside them to see if they needed help. When they said they were all right, as the bilge pump had gone back to normal, and proudly announced they'd just arrived from Wellington, the local man bellowed, 'You stupid young buggers! You bloody fools!' and proceeded to rip shreds off them. He was one of many from around there who had warned them not to attempt the crossing. They were shocked as they had never heard a man swear in front of women before.

Chastened, they chugged off towards Saint Omer, in Pelorus Sound. With 2 miles to go, there was a loud bang. Their propeller shaft had snapped in two. So they paddled to their destination. The *Pipinui* boys had arrived. Don kept it quiet that he was a trades- man – he wanted work that involved boats, but there wasn't any going at that time. Soon his financial situation was precarious, so he took the only job going: working with a professional scrub-cutter, who was desperate to get anyone to take on the hard toil involved. Don's poor hands really suffered for a long time. However, he liked the local people – tough, resourceful – all of them individual charac- ters who, in their isolation, helped each other out. By the time he'd become an expert scrub-cutter, he was offered an easier job milk- ing cows and being a handyman at Raetihi Guesthouse. (Des had returned to Wellington to work for Don's father.) Don had a won- derful time at the guesthouse, taking the carefree, holidaying young girls on moonlight cruises on *Pipinui*.

During one of the boat's frequent breakdowns, she was blown close to the shore by a strong wind. A big launch came over and Don was thrown a rope and towed to Saint Omer. When he was anchored safely, he asked the skipper what he owed him, and was treated to a curt reply. 'We do that for nothing around here.' This man, Wally Orchard, was to alter Don's life by teaching him sea- manship. He owned a barge carting stock and freight around The Sounds for a living, and was delighted when he discovered Don's trade. He'd been forced to wire his house up himself, as many people in that region had. No electrician had ever been interested in settling in that isolated region, so, after replacing Wally's highly dangerous network of wiring, he was soon flat out replacing the dodgiest wiring imaginable, on sheep stations and other places all over Pelorus Sound. In between, he was thoroughly enjoying his new job working for Wally, learning all about boating on the job. If he'd had a fraction of that knowledge a year earlier, he probably would never have set sail on *Pipinui,* so unaware he and Des were courting disaster.

Wally was a stickler for seamanship – doing everything right – and was renowned for never getting into trouble. His mantra he drummed into young Don was: 'You fix the problem before you start.' His main method of preventing problems was to always have a clean engine and clean fuel. Without radar, GPS or navigation lighthouses, Wally would always arrive at the right place even in dark or fog. For two years Don learnt from him, shifting sheep, cattle, timber, superphosphate, cars, bulldozers, wool and everything else, all over The Sounds to and from Nelson, Picton and Havelock. Balanced with exhaustion, chapped hands and other unpleasantries that went with the job were the beautiful sunrises and sunsets, starry night skies trying to outdo the phosphorescent wake, playful dolphins, and great mateship.

Don had a lot of fun for a while hooking up a Ford ignition coil to anything metal on the boat to catch unsuspecting victims, including a sheep buyer/passenger, who took a long time to recover from the shock. One cold winter's night, the prankster received his payback when he forgot to disengage it from the mast stay, and when he touched it, ended up overboard in the freezing water, watching the boat disappear. Until then, no one knew that Don couldn't swim. Fortunately, Wally had heard his yell when he'd received the shock, and rescued him as he floundered around in full wet-weather gear. The Ford coil was consigned to the deep, as Don had almost been, at just twenty years of age.

It was in 1951 that he really became busy converting homes, businesses and stations all over The Sounds to 230-volt power.

No more petrol-operated washing machines. No more 32-volt floor polishers and Mixmasters. Life became so much easier and better for many people there, thanks to the good old Lister Start-o-matic 2.75-kilowatt plants . . . and Don. To his great embarrassment, the locals began to refer to him as 'the man who brought the light to The Sounds'. He had a lot of trouble with his halo choking him! But it was wonderful not just being accepted, but actually welcomed.

He dreamed of having his own passenger boat, showing people the beauty of The Sounds, but that dream seemed very difficult to achieve. He needed to make more money and, in his youthful naivety, fell for the rosy picture of making good money if he invested his savings in, and helped run, a guesthouse. The couple who offered this opportunity had to sell their house in Wellington before they could move to The Sounds and contribute to its management. Don went to get it off and running with Des, who wanted to be the fourth partner. The isolated location was attractive but made things difficult logistically, and the buildings were very run-down – nonetheless they set to work and tidied it up for the first guests. Don collected them in *Pipinui*, oblivious to the need for licences, surveys and skipper's tickets when transporting the public.

Ironically, the guesthouse had no electricity. Lighting was provided by a carbide gaslight. The gas pressure was obtained by winding a heavy weight up to the top of a nearby gum tree every two or three hours, when the light dimmed. The wood stove took a bit of getting used to, and fortunately the first guests Don and Des looked after were very forgiving. Freshly caught fish seemed to make up for burnt veggies or lumpy mashed potatoes. Fish were plentiful then and Don was in his element, entertaining guests with his great humour and taking them out on the water. All that was needed to make his life complete was a big, comfortable, reliable launch to take more guests out at a time. At 5 metres long, little *Pipinui* was too small. However, the dream of a bigger boat was about to come true. He and Des were given the opportunity to lease a 12-metre launch, *Mahau*, which needed a new engine. They fitted her with a 1924, sleeve-valve Willys-Knight car engine that ran on petrol or kero. Its 26 horsepower pushed the launch along at a nice 8 knots.

But there's always a fly in the ointment. Don was too easy going and relationships became strained when the partners from Wellington disagreed on how to run the business and hadn't paid monies owed. Foolishly, Don had signed a personal guarantee for the rest of the finance on the venture, and he looked like being 'done', but he couldn't have cared less about the money – all he thought about was being in charge of a boat – a real boat – at last. He was slaving away doing far more than his share. He cut all the wood for the huge range, constantly washed up mountains of dishes, and was being paid barely enough to buy tobacco. After a nasty argument, he left and was able to secure ownership of *Mahau*, to operate her as a tourist boat out of Havelock. It was a small fishing village, but the principal town for those who lived around Pelorus Sound, and vis-ited by most tourists enjoying the magnificent South Island.

He was forced to leave little *Pipinui* behind, as he had fool-ishly included her in that hastily signed agreement as belonging to the guesthouse. It saddened him to later learn that she had been pounded to matchwood in a violent storm after being swept from her mooring. Now that he was seriously entering the charter boat business, he was finally cornered into applying for his skipper's ticket. Due to a bureaucratic cock-up, he was forced to sit the four-hour examination twice and has the dubious record of having two skipper's tickets.

Then he was required to bring the boat into survey, to legally 'ply

Bob Duncan has been a bulldozer artiste, truckie, fighter, buffalo hunter, croc wrestler, lifesaver and lotto winner. (*Photo by Kristin Williams*)

'Winki' Higgins…in the beginning!

Winki at Cryon Station in the 1950s.

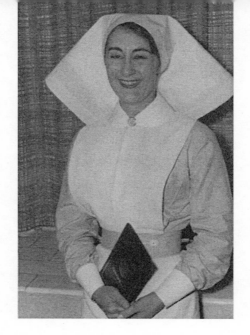

Winki at her graduation,
Royal Prince Alfred Hospital, Sydney.

Having a yarn with Winki is as good as a tonic.

William 'Dusty' Miller survived a remarkable thirty
air raids over Germany in WW II as a rear gunner.

Dusty and his wife, Lorna.

Roy Mawer in Vietnam.

Roy teaching his son, Wayne, how to be a waterski champion.

Danny Frahm as a young jockey.

Danny and his wife, Mireille.

Victor and Doris Wright
knew each other all their
lives before marrying.

At the truly grand age of 98, Doris is as
bright and chirpy as a willy-wagtail.

Don Todd and his wife, Joan.

Don (centre) speaking with then
Governor-General of New Zealand, Sir Paul Reeves.

Dot Davison with her husband, Jim.

At 97 years old, Dot is still bright as a button.

George Mansfield (right)
enjoying a drink with
an army mate.

Left to right: Corporals Jimmy Woods,
Sammy Farmer and George Mansfield
in Malaya, 1957.

To meet George is to encounter
an unforgettable personality.

Two good ol' boys of country music, Terry Gordon and Willie Nelson.

Chad Morgan and Terry had a lot of fun together on stage.

Bruce Blaikie (right) with friends in the 1970s.

Bruce might be in his eighties now,
but he's young in looks and attitude.

Spencer Spinaze in the air force during WW II.

These days Spencer keeps himself busy with farm
chores or relaxing on the verandah with a cuppa.

Beverley Rybarz making her debut in Adelaide.

Beverley's husband Stan with some Papuan friends.

Neville Greenwood (second from left) was always
quick with a joke during stock auctions.

Neville and his grandkids, Tom (left) and Josh.

Bill Ovenden loved to fish while on
Darnley Island in the Torres Strait.

Bill and his wife, Anne.

for hire'. *Mahau* was an old boat built in 1918 of kauri wood, but at thirty years old, some of her ribs were broken and she was 'nail sick'. The surveyor said, 'If you put a few new ribs and nails in her she may last a little longer, but take it easy in a big sea.' Don received his first Certificate of Survey in 1953, well aware that *Mahau* was not the most seaworthy of vessels. She leaked from the bottom and the top, having to be continually pumped out from the bilge. She was weak and twisted in the bigger seas, shaking all the repairs out. There was no GPS, chart plotter, radar, echo sounder or modern navigational aid, and for the first years Don owned the boat, no winch to haul up the anchor. But she was Don's and he loved her.

The toilet on a boat is called 'the heads'. On *Mahau* it should have been called 'the pinhead' as it was so cramped. One of his first legal charters happened to be a group of fortunately stalwart ladies with a collective sense of humour, from the Women's Division of Federated Farmers. They appreciated the fact Don provided a large shoehorn hanging above the seat, to enable the larger ladies to get themselves onto it. In their weekly column, published the following week in the *Marlborough Express*, a report of the excursion stated: 'The *Mahau* was an attractive vessel, but surely has the smallest toilet of any vessel ever built. It was necessary after opening the door, to back in, remove bloomers, then sit down with the aid of a large shoehorn provided, then close the door. This certainly added to our adventure in The Sounds, and was the subject of much hilarious discussion on the bus home.'

Don came to call Havelock home, a village surrounded by beautiful farms that is now the hub of an enormous mussel industry. In 1953, he had his eye on an attractive local farm girl, Joan Palmer.

He decided that as she was used to boats and to working hard, and was a good cook and housekeeper, that he should marry her. Apart from those qualities he believed were necessary in a wife, there was chemistry between them. This had puzzled him at first, because he had never been attracted to a blonde before. When he decided that Joan was definitely 'the one', he needed to wait for the perfect time to pop the question. He invited her to come on a trip on *Mahau*, with a group of tourists. Her parents accompanied her to the wharf at Rimu Bay, where he was to pick her up. Unfortunately the tourists all crowded up on the bow, obscuring his view of the wharf, where she was waiting. He crashed into the wharf, catapulting Joan into the water. He saw her swimming shoreward against the tide with one arm, pushing her lunchbox and knitting bag ahead of her. Her parents were glaring at him from the wharf and he decided it was not the time to ask for her hand in marriage.

Don then managed, in fine style, to blot his copybook with his intended future in-laws again, when he was hired to pick up people all over The Sounds and take them to a dance at a guesthouse. Naturally he had asked Joan to accompany him, and she brought her mother along. He was feeling unwell with what seemed to be an imminent flu, so the owner of the guesthouse took him aside to give him a sure-fire cure. He produced a bottle of Black Label Johnnie Walker whisky, and poured a huge nip. Away Don went, continuing to collect passengers, having a big nip of 'the cure' each time he arrived at the guesthouse with a batch of passengers. His mate was having one also, as 'preventative medicine'. By the time he had to start taking passengers home, Don was legless, almost incapable of starting the boat, so Joan took over. When she had delivered the last boatload home, he thanked her, apologising profusely for his condition, and gave her a big kiss, which was a bit off-centre, but he did his best, trying to emulate Clark Gable, despite his wobbly legs. That was all he remembered of that night, but the next day, Joan told him that she had driven his boat all the way to its mooring at Whatanihi, then walked home in the dark in the bush without a torch, and finally informed him that it wasn't her he had kissed so sloppily the night before, but her mother!

If there had been any doubts in his mind up till then about giving up his bachelor status, Joan's quiet, capable achievements – her ability to step in and handle a situation that could have been disastrous for his reputation, not to mention her forgiving him for getting blind drunk and pashing her mum – made him realise just how lucky he was. To his utter amazement and joy, her parents agreed to his request for her hand in marriage, and he knew he didn't want to dillydally any longer. However, just when he wanted to buy her a beautiful engagement ring, the boat needed a lot of repairs that couldn't be put off any longer. Priorities weighed heavily on his mind . . . hmm, new engine or expensive ring? Whew! Oh well, Joan was happy with what she received, knowing the sound of *Mahau*'s new Parson Pike motor made her husband-to-be very, very happy. Plus, he'd also lashed out on employing a plumber to put a septic toilet in his Havelock house. He did not expect his lovely bride to trudge to the 'long-drop'. How horrendous that would've been in the terrible winter weather!

He was able to save a lot of money by doing a deal to get the repairs to *Mahau*'s timber structure done by a local, self-taught shipwright in return for doing his mail run. It was actually a joy rather than a job, to be in charge of the 14-metre launch *Kowhai*, delivering the mail, bread, and so on to fishermen's homes, guesthouses and stations all over The Sounds.

Don hoped that his wedding night would be the longest night of the year, as he had much to learn. In those days, it was unthinkable to cohabit before you were married. By the couple's wedding day, to say young Don was as toey as a Roman sandal would be the understatement of the century. Their wedding, at St Peter's Havelock in 1954, was a wonderful occasion, with all the locals, who arrived by boat or tractor in the wet winter weather, overjoyed at their union. Don always wondered if that was because they had been desperate to attract a permanent electrician to their isolated neck of the woods and that 'their' Joan had managed it!

They flew off to what turned out to be a fairly disastrous honeymoon with many incidents combining to ensure both Don and Joan returned to the South Island still in their virginal state. It was as if the gods were against Don ever fulfilling his wildest dreams, and he felt by then he might be destined to die a virgin! Even worse (possibly) was the phone call he'd received while away, letting him know that, as the wedding guests partied on through the night, some had ended up on his boat, where one of the guests, casting off, had ended up in the drink in his suit, and while other inebriated guests tried to retrieve him from the water, *Mahau* had been holed and sunk. This news had not pleased him, but when they returned to Havelock, with him fearing she was beyond salvage, there she was, with all damage repaired perfectly and the boat resplendent with a new paint job. In fact, *Mahau* was in better shape than before. They had good friends.

When he had finally paid for *Mahau* and for her new motor, he did another deal to do the mail run for a while, in return for having her wheelhouse and cabin upgraded for charter work, which was increasingly available. The demand for his electrical expertise was also growing. Returning from a station on D'Urville Island, where he had installed a three-phase 16-kilowatt generator plant and wired three houses, a woolshed and several smaller sheds, he ran into gale-force winds, whipping up waves so high he couldn't turn back. Nearing the mouth of Pelorus Sound he was horrified to see a monstrous wave bearing down on him and his nail-sick boat. Before he could slow down, the wave poured through the wheel-house door, filling the cabin and swamping his new radiotelephone. As she headed downwards, it could have been curtains for man and boat, but survival mode suddenly kicked in and Wal's voice came back to him: 'Pull her out of gear and, if necessary, go astern.' This valuable advice certainly saved Don's life.

He had a few hairy trips in bad weather and fog, and was sometimes delayed getting home for other reasons, but Joan never worried. On that particular occasion, after surviving the deadly storm, he said to her, 'Weren't you worried?' As always, she merely shook her head and replied, 'No, I knew you would be all right.' Joan had every confidence in this man who had not only made her his wife, but was also 'married to the sea'.

Don not only loved Joan, his boat and the sea (hopefully in that order!), he also loved the warm feeling of being gradually regarded as a 'local' by the wonderful, generous people who inhabited that area. Everyone helped each other out and expected nothing in return. When he was stuck in a howling gale at the Trio Islands all night, with an oil problem, he was able to contact other boats by radio. The message came through loud and clear: 'Don't worry about the fishing trip you've got on tomorrow – we'll do that for you.' Fishing trips were his mainstay, bread-and-butter income and the locals who had responded wouldn't keep the money from that trip, insisting on giving the cash to Don.

In the late '50s he became a local hero by going out in his launch during a flood, to rescue two valuable cows. A farmer and his son had been swimming their herd to safety across the flooded Pelorus River, when two cows were swept away towards The Sounds. The men managed to catch Don's attention and he picked them up, then raced towards the terrified cattle. Somehow he managed to manoeuvre *Mahau* right alongside one, so the men could lasso her and tie her head to the bow rail, then they repeated the procedure with the other cow on the starboard side. When they pulled into the riverbank in calmer water to let the cows go, a reporter from the *Marlborough Express* was there with his camera to catch the action. Knowing a bit about cattle, and what their ungrateful reaction usually is when they have been rescued, Don called out to him, 'You'd better get through that fence. When we let them go, they might charge you.' The reporter laughed, saying, 'They're half-dead; they won't worry me!' and continued to snap shots. As soon as the cows were freed, he found himself running full pelt as they charged straight for him.

By 1963, Don was the father of three beautiful daughters (which meant there'd be three weddings to pay for in the future), and had to admit he was always going to make more money from his trade than from his boat. He formed DC Todd Ltd, operating an electrical business that would allow him to continue enjoying his charter and fishing trips – his first love. He started from a small shed near the Havelock cemetery, which he illuminated in the wintry darkness by hanging a fluoro light. When a state hydropower inspector called in, he almost had a fit when he observed that the cord attached to the light was strung through the trees to the cemetery office – highly illegal. Occupational health and safety did not occupy many of Don's thoughts. When his business grew big enough to take in a partner, Peter Slape (which allowed him more time in his boat), he had a wonderful time playing pranks, as usual. One involved pinching the bike that Peter rode to work and tying it to the top of a telegraph pole. Don was doubled up with laughter, watching from the office while Peter searched for it, mystified.

He also thought it was absolutely hilarious when he saw Peter, perched up on a ladder leaning against a power pole, foolishly cut all the wires on his side at once, causing the frozen pole to snap off at the base. As Peter, his ladder and the pole slowly descended to earth, he could hear Don's roar of laughter. Another day, Peter was making himself some toast for smoko at the shop as usual, and got a hell of a fright when the toaster exploded with an almighty bang! Don had put two big crackers in it, with their wicks on the elements. It was an old drop-side model and the two sides were blown off!

When Don was out and about on a job, he would tell any children he saw to 'go and get a tin of power from Peter for your mum'. They'd drive Peter mad, especially when Don had told them that they should take her a bottle of sparks too. They'd be dying to see the bottle of sparks and think that Peter was some fibbing grown-up who was hiding it from them. Don was asked to talk to the schoolchildren about the dangers of electricity, and to impress them, he held the silver paper from a cigarette packet to a couple of test leads. When he turned the power on, a giant blue flash shot out and one kid jumped up and yelled, 'Shit! I'm stayin' away from electricity!'

In the mid-1960s, Havelock's power finally came from the national grid. No more generators. It was an historic occasion in the little town and district's history, and a fitting amount of pomp and ceremony was planned for the act of turning on the lights for the first time at the town hall. It was packed with many dignitaries as well as townsfolk, and Don was tasked to switch off the old power, plunging the hall into darkness, then switch on the new supply. Standing up on the stage, he gravely carried out the first part of his duty, then, as the hall was darkened, and the anticipation of the audience was building up, he retrieved several jumping jacks from his pockets, lit the fuses, then gleefully chucked them out into the crowd. The scatter and screams were all he could have wished for.

A less-happy event in Don's life was the loss of *Mahau* by fire in 1967. He had owned her for fourteen wonderful years. She had provided him with much pleasure and pride and, due to her age, many challenges to do running repairs at sea. On one highly memorable trip, the steering rod snapped, then the radio broke down – two calamitous things. Fortunately it wasn't a charter trip – he was heading to an electrical job with his long-suffering (from Don's pranks) apprentice, Gordon Berry. Don rigged up some 'jury' (temporary, improvised) steering, steamed to Titirangi to do the electrical work, then headed home, incapacitated, with no radio, on a rising sea. Two more things then happened. The engine started overheating and the bilge pump went on strike. They made shelter at the Trio Islands and began radical surgery. Don did what he could with the engine while young Gordon repaired the bilge pump and connected it to the engine as a cooling pump. Don then disconnected the engine cooling-pump intake pipe from the seacock, to allow the bilge to flood at a rate that would allow the bilge pump to deliver the water to the engine. This enabled them to return to Havelock, slowly, to avoid overheating again, as the bilge pump had a lesser capacity than the engine pump. The trip took ten hours instead of four and a half, but boy, Gordon learnt a lot about improvisation at sea.

Mahau's replacement was the *Nancy Jean*. She was an 11-metre fishing boat from Port Ohope, built of tanalised Tanekaha timber and powered with a 140-horsepower Perkins. Don had her fitted with a Caterpillar 210-horsepower engine, which pushed the beautiful vessel along at 14 knots. His electrical business was going great guns; he'd built a large new shop in town, which sold everything electrical and also marine chandlery. His apprentice Gordon now had his own apprentice to order about. Don had asked the lad what his plans were for the future, and he replied, 'Become an electrician, get a house and a wife.' Don advised him, 'Get a wife first. She might already have a house.'

As the business grew, he had enough staff at the shop to enable him to keep taking on his charter and fishing trips, which were more like fun than work. He enjoyed playing practical jokes on the guests as soon as he sussed out whether they had a sense of humour. Joan was a tremendous help to him on these trips with her skills as both deckie and caterer. To be able to take people out longer than just a day, he eventually bought the *Ariki Tai*, a 15-metre Salthouse vessel that cruised at 12 knots, powered by a 230-horsepower Detroit Diesel engine. He lengthened her to 20 metres, and converted the fish hold to sleeping berths, which he called the Passion Pit. He'd tell prospective clients that it 'slept twelve people conventionally and twenty-four passionately'. From his humble beginning with little homemade *Pipinui*, he now owned the biggest boat in The Sounds. Over the years they looked after many celebrities and distinguished guests, including the then Governor-General Sir Paul Reeves, whose witty conversation and sense of humour ensured Don and Joan were completely at ease looking after the vice-regal party. They were very proud to be flying the Royal Standard on that trip, and treasure the lovely letter they received from Sir Paul and Lady Beverly Reeves.

One cold winter night while ferrying a local home across The Sounds, there was a tremendous 'CRASH!' as *Ariki Tai* hit a huge log. When Don saw the damage, he thought the boat would sink within minutes. He told the other chap to 'hold the wheel and *do not let go!*' When he closed the seacock, his hand was sucked into the pipe and he yelled *'Stop the engine!'* He was able to get his hand back out, and although the batteries were under water the boat miraculously started again. The log was jammed into the bow and – again, miraculously – stayed there like a plug. *Ariki Tai* weighed 25 tonnes. A smaller boat would have gone down. It took the two men to hold the wheel and not let it spin out of control, and steer the boat up onto a sloping mud bank with great difficulty. Don was able to identify the sawn log from its bark and to report that the plantation it had come from – where the logs were meant to be floated to a mill – had not secured it properly. It was important to make the owners aware of the accident he'd had, not just to get compensation for the damage, but to ensure it didn't happen again, as the results could have been fatal. Don still couldn't swim!

In 1993, during a magnificent holiday he and Joan were enjoying on the QE2, he became ill, which was most unusual, and discovered that he had developed diabetes. He closed up his shop and electrical contracting business, where he'd trained a total of eight young electricians, and moved to Nelson to semi-retire. He was sixty years old, and spent the next seven years commuting to Havelock to operate *Ariki Tai*, then reluctantly sold her. He had achieved what he set out to do in life and was content. During his so-called retirement, he has found himself busier than ever, delivering boats for people, maintaining navigation lights throughout the Marlborough Sounds, wiring houses, boats and businesses – everything, in fact, except a submarine – when he just couldn't say 'no'.

Over the busy years, Don had always found the time to be involved with and help his community as a member of the Lions Club, and could always be relied upon to liven up fundraisers and functions. He once jumped out of a big birthday cake dressed as a fairy, and at another function, attended by many dignitaries, waddled in dressed as a goose, his legs in purple stockings, occasionally squatting to drop boiled eggs from the rear of his costume. The Prime Minister at that time, Sir Bill Rowling, was in attendance and enjoyed 'Toddie's' entertainment immensely. He'd been out fishing with him earlier that day and had a wonderful time.

Always in great demand as an MC, Don's speeches were hugely entertaining and often rude, but never over the top. It was impossible for Havelock people to imagine that this extroverted larrikin had been shy and self-conscious as a small boy. Equally, it would have been difficult for his parents and sisters to foresee that he would one day become a mayor, but Havelock people knew he would run a tight ship and he was voted in overwhelmingly. In his speeches, both official and private, Don always gave full credit to Joan as 'my exceptional wife, who made me what I am'. After a busy but satisfying and happy life working together, they are enjoying their retirement at Nelson, including frequent visits from grandchildren, who just love their 'Grandon's' leg-pulling and jokes. Now in his active eighties, Don still refuses to grow up! Good on yer, mate!

9.

Brigadier 'Warry' George Mansford, AM

WARRIOR AND POET

George Mansford in his time has been a career soldier and a poet. That may sound like an unusual combination, but he is an unusual – that is, an extraordinary – man. He is an outstanding person who has contributed immensely in many ways to his country. To meet him is to encounter an unforgettable personality.

When you first see him, he is exactly what you expect a brigadier who's a veteran of three wars, and who has carried a formidable load of responsibility, to look like. Tall, well-built, handsome and totally confident in himself, George is a hell of an impressive person. His dignified presence commands respect, but he is not aloof – his expression is friendly, welcoming and open. Affectionately known to friends, particularly army mates, as 'Warry' (Warrior) George, he's a tremendously likeable bloke and a very popular man.

His soldiering included operations in several parts of the world and he learnt from his experiences. As well as writing beautiful poetry, he has also been a loving husband and father. There are several facets to this interesting boy from the bush. Born in August 1934 at Guildford, Western Australia, he was brought up near an isolated Aboriginal settlement close to Beechboro, where there were few white families and his black playmates still lived in gunyahs (roughly built shelters made from bush timber). With the Depression still on, his father was often away doing whatever work he could.

George clearly remembers being a small child and seeing his mother sobbing at the kitchen table, holding a newspaper with the huge, single-word headline: 'WAR!' His dad had volunteered for World War I and signed up again when World War II started. George recalls the inspiring sight of lines of soldiers marching through the centre of Perth off to the Middle East, bayonets fixed to their rifles, with thousands of people cheering them on. It was hard for a little boy to see his father go away and sense his mother's fear and sadness.

In 1940, when he turned six years old, he and his mother moved from Beechboro to the suburbs of Perth, where he began school. George remembers all the children helping the teachers dig trenches in case of attack and the sirens announcing air-raid practice, and windows being blacked out at night at home. During the Normandy landings, his teacher held a minute's silence and asked the children to pray for an end to the war. He recalls the tremendous shock and sorrow whenever one of the children's fathers was reported missing, taken prisoner or killed.

They had to move several times during the war years. George helped his mother as much as he could with chopping wood and other chores. He also sold newspapers to help with a few extra shillings. Even though they were poor, George's mum had high standards and brought him up in a caring, respectable environment, teaching him good manners, honesty, personal honour and respect for others, especially women. When they bought their first radio, they listened to a broadcast that London was being bombed with V2 rockets – 'buzz bombs'. The radio announcer claimed the Allies were no longer winning and that worried George.

Endless relief was felt when the war finally ended in 1945. After peace was declared, the young men from George's street who'd survived the war came home and life returned to normal. Ration cards from the war were still required to purchase certain items at the corner shop – times were very tight. Only rich people had cars. George vividly remembers the different vendors who delivered milk, bread, fish, rabbits and ice. Money was left on the steps for them and everyone's doors were open to allow them to take their goods inside if no one was home.

In 1947, when he started high school, he received his first pair of school shoes, and was always pleased to take them off as soon as he reached home. Like many other children, he had gone to primary school in bare feet. Swimming in the Swan River, diving off the old condemned convict bridge was the main pastime. At the occasional matinee, everyone stood for 'God Save the King', then before the movie began all joined in a singalong with the words to songs like 'Rule, Britannia!' or 'Don't Fence Me In' displayed on the screen. Every social occasion involved adults and children singing together.

George had grown up hardly seeing his father until after the war. He vividly remembers sitting around a fire with him one night, in a poignant and rare father-and-son moment. His dad uttered a quiet, profound comment that has stayed in George's mind ever since: 'Fire can be man's best friend or worst enemy.' George eventually worked out what he meant was that a fire can warm you and allow you to cook a meal, but it can also destroy property and kill people. Whenever he recalls that phrase, the memory floods back of sitting there with his dad, feeling so close to him. He died just two years later and it seemed to George that the family was once again on 'Struggle Street'.

In his early teens, he worked hard collecting and selling manure for the veggie gardens that were in everyone's backyards in those days. Aged fifteen, he left Midland Junction High School after Intermediate exams, and sat for the Post Master General's exam, finishing in the top three in the state. He trained to be a telegraphist, learning morse code and how to send telegrams, as well as delivering them and the mail. His mentors were excellent, teaching him how to do all tasks properly.

His mother was not happy when, on his seventeenth birthday, he joined the Regular Army with six mates to 'do his bit' for Australia in the Korean War, which had begun nine months earlier. He was sent to Puckapunyal training camp in Victoria, a very spartan and dilapidated army barracks that got so cold at night he had to pack the holes in the wall with newspaper and sleep in his overcoat, shivering. He excelled at the various exercises and tasks. One challenge, to throw a live grenade that had a four-second fuse and a 100-metre danger zone, had him thinking, *I can't even throw it that far!* His Corporal, a WW II veteran and tough nut named Wally Ogilvie, cut him no slack. When he overheard George being critical of the officers, he bellowed, 'An officer's job is to lead; yours is to follow. Now get off your arse and do just that!' He then put George through an extra hour of bayonet training every night, while his mates enjoyed a few beers. Criticising officers was a no-no. He learnt the hard way not to question or disrespect his superiors.

While he was there on basic training, he encountered older soldiers who had returned from fighting in the Korean War and were awaiting discharge. They were all big men, mostly WW II vets, wearing ill-fitting WW II jackets, some sporting the proud colour patch of the 27th Brigade. George observed that they had little respect for authority, said little and were content to play cards in the barracks, night and day, with large bottles of beer in hand. The biggest impression they made on him was their mateship. They were inseparable, yet they welcomed George for a yarn and accepted him. The advice they gave him on surviving and coping with barrack-room life was, 'Keep your mouth shut; stick by your mates; no bludging; watch out for orderly officers; thieves are fair game; and *never volunteer.*'

George was chuffed when he was made platoon mortar man, not realising how much his already heavy load of responsibility would be increased. The infantry platoon arsenal included a 2-inch mortar that could fire a variety of bombs, including high-explosive, illumination and smoke bombs. After two weeks of training, George was given the big test, in which his platoon were relying on him to dispatch a curtain of smoke, while a section was deployed around to outflank the 'enemy'. George was very excited as he sized up his target. While he was thus employed, his Number Two (offsider) was placing a smoke bomb down the barrel. George reported to the officer, 'Ready to fire!', confident he'd really impress him and everyone else. The officer barked an order George couldn't hear due to all the noise, so he turned his head to look for a signal, saw a very clear signal to fire, then heard the usual 'wumph!'

There was an unexpected recoil as two smoke bombs at once – an absolute no-no – slowly and lazily arched over and landed to their immediate front. His Number Two had placed two smoke bombs down the barrel. The only saving grace was that they weren't high-explosive bombs. So ended George's career as a mortar man, which probably saved his hearing!

Another lesson learnt the hard way was the importance of the rollcall being correct. The soldiers were given a leave pass once a month, as a privilege, if no one had stuffed up. George once got caught out on return, calling out 'Present' for a mate who he knew hadn't returned from leave. The Sergeant Major's sixth sense told him something was wrong, and commanded the Sergeant to do a headcount, after which he bellowed, 'One of you has covered up for a mate. If the guilty man doesn't step forward now, the entire platoon will march all night.' George stepped forward, and was none-too-politely informed that, 'The army has been calling roll-calls forever and a day and doesn't do them for your amusement. Not only do we do them after leave, we check after a withdrawal, we check after an assault, we check after an attack. We check and check to see who's *not* there. Now you, Mansford, turn up and want to change the whole system. Do you think you're Field Marshal Blamey? From now on you will be duty runner for a month and call the roll as well, and if you make one mistake I'll have your guts for garters.'

So George, the youngest in his platoon, became the duty runner. He managed to get into another spot of bother later on during training for trench-digging under fire. He had dug half a trench when suddenly machine guns and tanks were firing around him. George flung himself into the shallow trench, landing on top of the face-down platoon commander, which meant he was barely protected from fire. After a while in this embarrassing position, the platoon commander said, 'You have to move. I've got a cramp.' To which George, throwing all caution to the wind in the heat of the moment (for want of a better term!), yelled a most unmilitary response: 'You can go get f**ked!' – a response which, given the position they were in, could have been worded a bit more carefully.

When the names of those chosen to go to Korea were called, George had been left out. He was too young. Disappointed, he planned to be a stowaway. First on his list of what to do to accomplish this was to go to the pub and have a few beers (after packing his gear and shooting through from the base), then find a hiding place on the ship. Sprung by the provos (bugger!), he was placed under arrest and put in detention back at Puckapunyal. He and thirty other young blokes, who were in a 'holding pattern' until they'd be sent to Korea, were tasked to dismantle the huts at the old Watsonia migrant camp, which, before that, was an army barrack. Families were squatting there and had refused to move. When George started pulling the iron off the roof of a hut, he was, to his great surprise, looking down at a family sitting around the kitchen table. He suddenly slipped, fell through the hole he'd created, and crashed on his back onto their table. He apologised. Feeling sorry for the families being turfed out, he defiantly sought a confrontation with his superiors about what he believed was the unfair eviction of impoverished people. When he returned to barracks, he was ordered to front Captain Saunders.

Into his life marched Reg Saunders, who was to have a big influence on George's attitude and his future career in the army. Reg was the first full-blood Aboriginal commissioned officer in the Australian armed forces – a smart man who was equal to any professional psychologist at assessing men's character and frame of mind, and getting the best out of them. Summonsed into his office, George's anger was immediately neutralised by the Captain's first words, which left him in stunned surprise. 'Mansford, you are now a temporary lance corporal.'

'Why, sir?' George asked, flabbergasted.

'Because you're trying to run the army again.'

George let that sarcastic barb sink in and realised he'd over-stepped the mark.

'You are rations clerk [a lowly, despised position] until further notice,' came the dismissive order, and the seventeen-year-old 'rebel' who'd had the audacity to query the machinations of his nation's army left Captain Saunders' office in a fairly subdued manner.

George certainly didn't want to be a 'pogo' or 'blanket counter' forever, and after three weeks, he was again addressed by Captain Saunders: 'You've got a choice. Stay lance corporal and keep your pogo's job, or return to a rifle section as a private soldier.'

Later, when George became an officer, he looked back and realised that Reg Saunders' psychological tactics changed his thinking from that of a civilian to that of a soldier. By then, he was well acquainted with the legendary story of Reg, in the thick of a grim battle in the most terrible circumstances in Korea, on hearing a soldier say, 'This is no place for a white man!' yelling in reply, 'It's no place for a black bastard either!'

Another officer who young George discovered could anticipate what soldiers were thinking was Warrant Officer Joe O'Sullivan. When O'Sullivan looked outside the barracks the morning after George's platoon's last leave before going to Korea and saw a bra and panties flying from the flagpole, he just *knew* that George – who'd snuck in at 3 a.m. instead of midnight – was the culprit. As punishment, George had to guard the flagpole for the next four nights, marching around and around it, armed with a baseball bat, between 6 and 10 p.m. – the hours the wet mess was open.

(An entertaining book could be written on army punishments alone. When Joe O'Sullivan was in Malaya a couple of years later, a soldier who'd done something silly was ordered to water the hundreds of rubber trees around their camp every day. When the usual daily torrential downpour started, he came in and lay down on his bunk to read. He'd just got all comfy when Joe arrived and roared, 'Why aren't you watering the trees?' The soldier stuttered, 'But Sir, it's raining.' To which Joe bellowed, 'Then get a f**king raincoat!')

In Korea, George remembers the port where they disembarked, Pusan, was chock-a-block with cardboard shanty dwellings, holding literally millions of people. When they boarded a troop train to go north, it was freezing and he gave a thought to the original Aussie soldiers who were sent there without proper clothing for the winter – they would have suffered, quite probably to the point of getting frostbite.

In 1955, when George's unit was about to leave for Malaya, he decided he'd better marry a great girl he'd been taking out, named Maureen, as she was a bloody good sort and he didn't want to lose her while he was away. During his wedding speech, he mentioned that she was not only pretty, but also intelligent, and that the only time her intelligence left her temporarily was when she said 'yes' to marrying a soldier!

When they were honeymooning at Coolangatta, he went to buy bait on the beach from 'the old bait man', who noticed he had his Korean campaign jacket on. With the one-word query 'Korea?', the bait man struck up a conversation, and it transpired that this shy old fellow was a World War I veteran. He had fought at Fromelles alongside his two brothers, who were both reported missing in action during the time he was evacuated out with wounds. Pondering on the dreadful tragedy, George left to go fishing with his bride, never dreaming that the old man would enter his life again, fifteen years down the track . . .

On his second tour of Malaya, George, by then a corporal, was commanding troops who were ambushing jungle tracks along the Thai border. One day he felt something hurt his wrist and looked down to see two puncture marks on his skin and a snake slithering away. He was a three-day march from anywhere. Because they were deep in the jungle, there were no helicopters handy. There were only two radio schedules a day when they could contact the outside world, at 6 a.m. and 6 p.m. George was in deep shit. When he was able to radio the base he told the operator there had been a snakebite. The reply was that there was nothing that could be done to evacuate that day given the three-day walking distance and that bad weather made it impossible for a helicopter to be deployed. A doctor advised him to keep the patient calm and resting and matter-of-factly commented that if the snake was venomous, the patient would either be dead or alive next morning. Then he asked for the name of the victim. George bellowed, 'It's bloody well me!'

Apart from getting sleepy, George survived, and for five years or so, two little warts would appear now and then, where the fang marks had been.

It was a very different era in Malaya during that campaign. There were many Pommy soldiers posted to Malaya and relations between them and the 'colonials' were sometimes less than cordial. A British battalion occupied the area, including the city of Ipoh, and it was out of bounds to Aussies, due to animosity between both camps. One of George's soldiers had a fiancée located in the city and wished to visit her, so he and George took off to do just that. Soon after, George was drinking with two British types who were obviously from the enemy camp. In the subsequent conversation they were discussing what could be done to improve relations between both units. George suggested swapping some soldiers so they went on operations with each other. One of the Pommies immediately agreed and announced he was the Commanding Officer of the British battalion. Some weeks later, George and his sub-unit were relieved on operations by a fellow sub-unit. One of his mates in the relief group complained bitterly that they had been given three Pommy bastards for the duration of the operation and had been compelled to hand over his best scout and machine gunner to go and work with the Brits. The mob was cranky, and curious to know which bird brain of an officer had thought that one up. George, desperately holding back his laughter, shrugged his shoulders and agreed that officers were a strange bunch.

The greater military campaign was called the Malayan Emergency – instead of a war – and the reasons behind that are interesting. When the communist-backed uprising began in 1948, Britain was still in dire financial straits following WW II, and sent troops to Malaya because it needed the revenue from the tin mines and rubber plantations there. Any damage to them would not have been covered by insurers at Lloyd's of London had the uprising been declared a 'war'.

After George completed his second tour of Malaya, his Commanding Officer informed him that he was being sent to an officer's course at Canungra in Queensland. It was a very tough course, and George was one of just five out of twenty-five people to pass. He went back to his battalion as a lieutenant at twenty-nine years of age.

The 1950s and '60s were a tumultuous time in much of Asia. Indonesia confronted Malaya in a show of force; Korea was divided in an uneasy truce; and the French were kicked out of Indo-China. Vietnam had been divided into two countries, and when war broke out between the two, the north was supported by China and Russia and the south by the US and Australia. Conscription was stepped up back home and, once again, Aussie boys too young to drink in a pub were sent overseas to fight in what journalists were calling an 'unpopular war' – surely the most thoughtless phrase they could possibly have come up with.

In his speeches, George often states: 'Vietnam "nashos" were brilliant, dedicated. In a short time, you couldn't tell the difference between them and the regular soldiers. While more than 500 young Australian men lost their lives, the other tragedy is that because the method of conscription was very unfair, it in fact destroyed any future political intent to use national service as a tool to help develop future generations of youth.'

Many strange coincidences occur during wars, and one concerned George and the officer he was sent to Vietnam to replace. When he'd planned to stowaway to go to Korea after his initial army training, one of George's mates succeeded in stowing away and in subsequent years had been commissioned and gone on to fight in Vietnam, where he was killed. George took his place.

On another occasion when celebrating with students who had just graduated, he was approached by one of the graduates who was accompanied by his mother. The young man introduced himself as the son of George's mate who had been killed in Vietnam. The last time George had seen him and his mother was just after he had been born, some twenty-one years previously.

Members of the unit George served with in Vietnam, the Australian Army Training Team Vietnam (AATTV), won *four* Victoria Crosses.

In 1965, the seasoned veteran of three campaigns was chosen to take a platoon of soldiers aged eighteen and nineteen years old to an exercise in New Guinea, where they were to practise counter-revolutionary warfare against the Royal Pacific Island Regiment.

At the finishing stage, the AATTV reached the top of a mountain range, all buggered and starving. George told them they had two options: to take the easier track back down the mountain to the finishing point and surrender if ambushed (which was certain to happen as the Pacific Islanders played hardball), or take the hard way with him down an ankle-busting 'goat track' on a steep, rugged mountainside, in poor light, to avoid 'capture'. George was concerned that the unit, being so young and exhausted, might take the soft option, but was pleased and proud when they chose to follow him along the much tougher route, where they were more likely to evade capture. These young men all went on to serve with distinction in Vietnam. Many years down the track when senior officers were worried army training methods were softening, George would look back on this particular moment in his career and feel confident in his ability to inspire young, inexperienced recruits to find it within themselves to overcome pain, exhaustion, discomfort and hunger, to achieve a goal.

George learnt that a lack of understanding of the locals' culture and lingo could possibly lead to disaster. When he and his men had to cross a wide river, he asked a local man, 'Any puk puks [crocodiles] in dis pela place?' The man shook his head and shrugged his shoulders, which George took as a 'no' and then led the men into the water and across to the other side. The Papuans watched with great interest, and George was soon to discover that what their mate had actually meant with his reply was that he hadn't seen any crocs in that spot for a while! A leading news story on radio several days later reported that a tribesman on a raft was taken by a croc right where they'd been! The lesson learnt: ensure your questions are explicit, and don't believe everything you hear.

When George was best man at his mate Ken 'Rocky' Hudson's

wedding in '66, Ken thanked him with a new wallet, which became his good-luck charm. George was back in Vietnam when he was told, 'Rocky's copped it.' The proud new father of a baby son had gone missing while commanding an SAS patrol in Indonesia and was never found. George used the wallet till it literally fell to bits one day when he opened it in a shop. He is proud of the way he and other army personnel do what they can to assist the widows of their comrades who've fallen in action.

'These women were usually still very young – in their twenties, most with small children – and their lives changed forever,' he says. 'It's our moral duty to keep an eye on them.'

Back in Australia, where protests against Australia's involvement in the Vietnam War were escalating, unions had put a go-slow on mail and beer sent to the soldiers over there (bastards!). After quite a while suffering Yank beer, George vividly remembers his joy when finding a single can of 'Black Duck' (Swan) beer. He shared it with another old comrade to accompany their sumptuous Christmas dinner of tinned bully beef. Late that afternoon they bid each other farewell to return to their units and not long after, George's mate was killed in action. The memories linger and George wrote the following verse not so long ago for his fallen comrade.

How Could I Forget?

The killing stopped, well, just for a while,
it was a day of peace, or so they said.
So my mate and I met on a lonely hill,
shared a tin of meat, a brew and some bread,
talked of home and sweet love to fulfil.
Had other mates been wounded or killed?

We joked and laughed of better days,
then as shadows grew, we said hooray,
for I was going home and he had to stay.
I felt the power of that farewell embrace,
saw his final wave as I left him there,
heard his distant shout, 'You take care!'

Since then, so many years I have bid adieu,
now I have grandchildren, more than a few,
most of my dreams, but not his, came true.
I still think of him in many special ways,
more so of our meeting that Christmas Day.
I recall that familiar, welcome, cheeky grin,
a soft voice, ruffled hair, oh yes, it's him.
I feel the strength of that brotherly embrace,
pain of farewell etched on a sunburnt face,
see again his fond salute as I left him there,
hear faint echoes of a call, 'You take care.'
How could I forget? Who would even dare?

George came home from Vietnam and was posted to a training
position at Canungra's Battle Wing. He was suddenly a widower
with four young children when Maureen, tragically, died at a very
young age. In the aftermath, their son Peter was boarding at the
Southport School and it was impossible for George to have his three
daughters with him at Canungra, so they were living with their
grandparents in Brisbane. On top of this tremendous upheaval and
sorrow, he found his marriage allowance had been cut off because
his children weren't living with him. For two long, miserable

years he fought the bureaucracy of the army to redress this. Eventually he was forced to take the huge step of seeking help from the Governor-General, which was the last step in the appeal process. Shortly after, the Attorney-General, Lionel Murphy – at the Governor-General's request – rang George to apologise personally and tell him it would be rectified immediately, which it was. He was assured steps had been taken to ensure this would never happen again, but within a year, he was going in to bat for one of his men who'd lost his wife in an accident and had no choice but to place his three children with his parents, and was encountering exactly the same problem and wall of unyielding bureaucracy. At least this time it was an easier battle for George to right the wrong that had been done.

In 1970, he met his second wife, Helen, who, to everyone's – including Helen's – amusement, he always called by her surname, Wilson – a very military thing to do. As their first Anzac Day together approached, Helen told him that she always laid a wreath in memory of her three uncles, two of whom went missing in action at Fromelles. She said the third, who'd been evacuated wounded, just disappeared after World War I, no doubt mentally scarred by his horrible experiences in the nightmare scenario of Fromelles. George was astounded when he realised that Helen's missing uncle was 'the old bait man' he'd met during his first honeymoon at Coolangatta!

A sad footnote to this amazing anecdote is that in 2012, the remains of the two Wilson brothers were found where they had perished together in an enemy counterattack. They were found in an irrigation ditch, which would have given them inadequate shelter. Soon after they had been posted missing in WW I, their mother had died from a broken heart.

When George relates that story during his many presentations at both civilian and military events around Australia, he concludes it with the observation that 'the consequences of war impact long after the guns fall silent . . .'

After one of his presentations at Brisbane's Enoggera Barracks, the Regimental Sergeant Major, the most senior soldier in a unit, came up to speak to him. 'Sir, you may not remember me, but you spoke to us during our training at Battle School and told us that a good soldier always expects the unexpected. Just before our 10-kilometre run on the final day, we were all exhausted and very hungry from our constant training. I took the paper off my last barley sugar, and couldn't flick it off my finger, but eventually managed to, forgetting the golden rule, "No litter in a battle situation." You saw me but did nothing, so I thought, *You're getting old, mate – didn't you see me do that?* Back at the base, I could smell the barbecue cooking, was hogging for a beer and was daydreaming about lots of lovemaking when I got home, when you stepped in front of me, handing me a torch, and said, "You're going to need this before you get back from picking up that paper you dropped. I put a small rock on it so it wouldn't blow away. Away you go." So there was no cold beer or barbecue for me, and from having to do an extra 20 kilometres, I was too buggered for any lovemaking when I arrived home.'

In December 1971, Cyclone Althea struck Townsville, where George and Helen were living, and they lost everything they owned. George had been getting ready to go back to Vietnam and Helen was just two weeks off having their baby. George was part of the team organising the clean-up of the town. At what was left of a house that had been destroyed, he saw a little old lady searching through the rubble. 'I'm looking for my wallet,' she said. George gave her the $10 note he had in his pocket. She handed it back saying, 'Give it to children who need it.' After the clean-up, he had to board a helicopter to take off on his first leg of final training for Vietnam, knowing that Helen had been sent to hospital to have the baby – very tough on both of them. To give her spirits a lift, he organised for the three large Huey helicopters – taking him and a contingent of soldiers – to fly low over the hospital. This very noisy gesture cheered her up immensely but would not have impressed the hospital staff!

Two years and one month later, they again lost most of their belongings when the January 1974 floods ravaged Brisbane. George was based at Enoggera Barracks and had just returned from Singapore with his battalion. Once again he rolled up his sleeves as the army went to work to assist the community.

Later that same year, he was sent to Emerald, based at the Fairbairn Dam, to command Locust Force, a group of 200 soldiers in combat against a destructive invasion of locusts wiping out crops and pastures in Central Queensland. The plague was costing millions of dollars per day. George and his team researched the habits of the voracious creatures and found that they were most vulnerable in the mornings, before there was warmth to get their wings moving. An early-morning spraying campaign was set up, and when it proved to be winning the battle, George replied to a question from the group of journalists gathered at his base camp, that 'the body count is in millions.' The hierarchy of the army weren't exactly delighted with his choice of words.

The eventful year of 1974 concluded with yet another, even worse, destructive force of nature. Cyclone Tracy smashed into Darwin and George's battalion was tasked with hosting hundreds of refugees from the city. Soon after, he was sent to Darwin as second-in-command of the rescue and clean-up force. That would be a Christmas and New Year he would not forget. His bride and family were quite used to being without him. For his efforts as Operations Officer during cyclones Althea and Tracy, and the '74 Brisbane floods, and as Commander of Locust Force Central, George was awarded a Member of the Order of Australia (AM) for Civil Aid.

In 1979, when he was promoted to lieutenant colonel, the Chief of the Army summonsed him to his Canberra office. Putting his feet up on a chair and leaning back in a relaxed manner as though he was on his verandah at home yarning with a friend, the Chief said, 'George, the army's getting too soft. There's too much indoor train-ing. I want you to find a place to create a battle school, like we used to have.'

George soon found the perfect place. He wanted it to be a place where the climate meant that the troops would be often, if not always, in a state of discomfort, as you are in battle. North Queensland had extreme heat and humidity, which would result in exhaustion for soldiers marching or fighting, plus months of being extremely wet, which would be the icing on the cake! Flies, ticks, taipans and crocodiles were an added bonus.

The wettest place in Australia is Tully, south of Cairns, and there was already some old army infrastructure on a rugged property on Jarrah Creek, off the Tully River. To George, the conditions there, for his needs, were similar to what Hayman Island would be to hon-eymooners: perfect!

The battle school didn't take much setting up, as the troops would be living in pup tents. When they'd arrive, George would send them on a 15-kilometre march with full packs to assess their fitness. He taught them how to keep one uniform dry to sleep in at night, and to put their other one, soaked with sweat and rain, back on the next morning. He taught them everything he could from his vast experience of soldiering in a great variety of conditions – mostly extremely difficult and dangerous. He taught them that their level of fitness, their level of alertness and their professional attitude could all be factors that, alone or combined, might save their or their comrades' lives. Drummed into them over and over was the potentially life-saving mantra 'expect the unexpected'. Another difficult-to-achieve but vital attribute that George tried to instil was to 'stay calm under pressure'.

To give them the opportunity of honing these skills in the closest-to-real battle conditions, the objective of the school was 'to train instinctive reactions identical to the needs of combat, while the student is exposed to hunger, lack of sleep, physical exhaustion and discomfort. The ideal situation is a combination of progressively more demanding field exercises at platoon level, culminating with an unexpected night withdrawal, then being force-marched for 15 kilometres, interrupted with quick-decision exercises, finally engaging enemy targets from a standing position. Add adverse weather – e.g. monsoonal rain – and there is a significant challenge for the students.'

George was extremely proud of what he achieved at the battle school, at which he was Commanding Officer for three years. As it was a simulated war zone, he had no house there and no comforts. When each intake arrived, he would address them with these words: 'The oath you took to serve your country as a soldier did not include a contract for the normal luxuries and comfort enjoyed within our society. On the contrary, it implied hardship, loyalty and devotion to duty regardless of what rank you might achieve. We are here at Battle School to remind you of that oath.'

George also wrote a motto for the school: 'You can't teach soldiers to fight in a classroom.'

On the last day of one course, George saw an exhausted young soldier experience a stoppage in his rifle. He cleared it impatiently, then to his obvious fury, it failed again and he threw it on the ground, yelling that he'd had a gutful of being a soldier. George ordered the Regimental Sergeant Major to remove him and charge him. Soon after, George gave him a good dressing down. Thinking he'd had enough punishment and that he was remorseful for not 'staying calm under pressure', as he should have, George tore up the charge sheet, prepared to give him another chance. The silly bugger smirked, as if he'd had a win. When George saw this, he ordered him to remain behind when his mates left and start the course all over again with the new mob arriving the next day.

When George was welcoming the first US infantry company to be trained at the school, he received a message that their meals were meant to have been brought up from Townsville in hotboxes – a special arrangement for them – but wouldn't be arriving due to a highway accident. He asked the Americans to put their hands up if they'd had breakfast. They all did. Then he said, 'Good. Now you all should know that an infantryman only needs one meal a day, so you've had yours. Now let's get down to training.' Then on the last day of the course, it was discovered that the GI's had scoffed too much of their rations and had no food left. Their officer spokesman said to George, 'We have a problem. The men have eaten all their rations and we still have tomorrow.' George replied, 'No, *you* have a problem. There will be no resupply.' Apparently, on their return to base, they ate in a fashion reminiscent of newly released prisoners of war!

It's only natural to want to ask George – one of the toughest men in Australia – what he thinks about female soldiers. His reply: 'There are many tasks they are far better at than men, particularly those requiring patience and attention to detail, because a lot of blokes can be careless and untidy. Women, in my view, are unsuited to heavy, demanding physical tasks. So why reduce the efficiency of the army by taking them out of such jobs they do superbly, to do others they don't do as well? The biggest problem is that men will naturally, instinctively, take risks to protect and rescue a female. I saw a vehicle that had been hit by a mine. I was securing the area immediately after and saw a male soldier doing mouth-to-mouth, attempting to save a woman who was obviously dead, while a bloke beside her was dying from loss of blood. The other point against females being out at the very sharp end, such as long range patrol with young male soldiers, is the fact that after a couple of weeks, even the trees look attractive to blokes.'

Under that unmistakeable military bearing, George loves a joke and can be very funny. However, if you make an unwise remark it brings a transformation of his facial expression that reduces you to jelly. A thoughtless query, for example, about the burden that goes with a soldier's task of 'shooting people', and you will be thrown in the brig mentally, feeling much as a private would feel if they hadn't cleaned their rifle or boots correctly. Warry George will leave you in no doubt that soldiers don't shoot people by choice; rather, they are doing what they have to do to protect their country.

Many of this great Australian's observations on our country's history, and on Australians who've served, should be set in stone for future generations to read and respect. Perhaps with his father – who served in both world wars – in mind, and certainly the other WW II survivors he has met and worked with, he states: 'The World War II generation is perhaps the unluckiest, but the most magnificent generation of Australians. They saw the consequences of World War I, they were exposed to the Depression after leaving school, then in their youth, experienced World War II. They then made this country what it is.'

Another astute observation from him: 'Our armed forces are a mirror of society and given its softness and lack of discipline, it makes the military task of preparing youngsters for war even more difficult and hindered by political correctness and ever-increasing occupational health and safety requirements. We should never forget that success in war still requires a military which is tough, mentally and physically, and it cannot afford to lower its standards in developing such requirements.'

When hearing suggestions that our national flag should be changed, George has been known to talk of civil war!

In 1987, George was promoted to the rank of brigadier, a role he was born for. How proud his parents would have been! He retired in December 1990, but has since been associated with the army on a frequent basis, delivering motivational presentations to new recruits and speeches prior to officers graduating. From his secluded bush retreat overlooking the Coral Sea near Cairns, he's also been kept busy with wildlife and environment projects. George founded and is chairman of both the Australian Rainforest Foundation and the Cassowary Advisory Group, and is on the Wet Tropics Management Authority Heritage Board. He's a member and one-time chief of the local Rural Fire Brigade.

As well as speeches, he writes poems and books, which include *Tips for Training*, *Junior Leadership on the Battlefield*, and *The Mad Galahs*, a novel based on real life in the army. In 1993, George and Sir Sydney Williams organised the reunion for WW II veterans in Cairns. George has received a Paul Harris Award for service to youth and was made Citizen of the Year in Cairns in 1996 – the year he organised both the Peace Windows at St Monica's Cathedral and the Cairns Anzac Walk.

A man who enjoys life, good times with good friends, and the rewards from helping his community, he had looked forward to growing old with Helen by his side, but sadly, after a battle with cancer, she died in his arms a few years ago. How much sorrow can a man bear? In 2005, his son Peter suddenly went into a coma and died without warning. Today, George has four lovely daughters, who battle to make him look after his health.

On his living room wall, there's an eye-catching collage of photos of George, put together by the Cairns City Council. Between the photos are comments from prominent people about Warry George. 'To many of us, he epitomises The Digger,' said General Peter Cosgrove. Major General Ron Grey, AO, DSO, described him as 'an exceptional man of rare gifts, who by dedication and example has earned the devotion of soldiers'. The former Governor of Queensland Peter Arnison said, 'Perhaps his finest quality is his ability to bring disparate groups together to find a common ground in the interests of a successful outcome. He is truly a remarkable Australian.'

The accolades don't stop there. James Foley, Bishop of Cairns, called George a 'larger-than-life character who brings a unique blend of dignity, efficiency and friendliness to every task for which he is engaged'. Kevin Byrne, the former Mayor of Cairns, has praised his 'Australian spirit and ethos of mateship, fairness and equity'. While Dean McColl, of the Wet Tropics Management Authority, has noted that 'George plays a pivotal role in world heritage and conservation in his role as Chair of the Australian Rainforest Foundation.'

Australians owe a great debt to men like Brigadier George Mansford and those he served with. Without soldiers, we would not have freedom; without soldiers, there would be anarchy in many parts of the world. Australia's Baby Boomer generation – of which this writer is one – knows that without our soldiers, our country would have been taken over during World War II, and our mothers would have suffered a terrible fate. We probably would not have been born.

Lest we forget.

10.

Dot Davison

BULLOCKY'S OFFSIDER

When you meet Dot Davison, it's very hard to imagine that this dainty, feminine 97-year-old was once a bullocky's offsider – but she was. As a very young girl until she was fourteen, her job was to help yoke up a team of long-horned bullocks, and when they were hauling the logs out of the scrub at Buderim in Queensland, to use all her strength to apply the wagon's brake on the steep hills and gullies when needed. She also manned the big crosscut saw with her father, cutting the logs that the timber cutters wanted them to haul to the mill, into lengths to fit the wagon. From working hard since she could walk, Dot was strong, willing and disciplined.

She was also happy. She loved her father's bullocks and also loved being a great help to him. To her dad, Price Jones, timber carrier, her job was important – crucial, in fact – and she took great pride in never letting him down. She loved her beautiful mother – an English rose swept off her feet into the Queensland scrub by a big, handsome bushman – and her nine brothers and sisters. There was very little money in their household, but a lot of love and contentment. As is the way with people on the land, there was always plenty of good food, even in the toughest of times.

On 5 July 1917, floodwater had prevented her mother making it to the midwife in Buderim (near Noosa), so Dorothy Margaret Jones was born in Brisbane instead. She's proud of being the grand-daughter of Buderim pioneers Price and Isabella Jones, after whom Jones Road is named. They grew coffee and her clever grandfather invented a coffee grinder to process their beans.

Dot's mother, Ellen Tullett, arrived on the good ship *Limerick* in 1912, fell in love with Price Jones Jr, and was soon in the role of a country mum, learning how to cope with living out in the bush. Their isolation meant she had to learn the fine country art of improvisation, making do without all sorts of things not available where she lived, to keep her husband and the constant flow of babies – one every two years – fed and clothed. Being the second oldest, Dot played a big part in looking after the babies and children of a clan that eventually numbered four girls and six boys. She also helped to milk the cows, tend the veggie garden, feed the chooks and, as soon as she was big enough to climb up on the wagon, help her dad. He hauled logs for timber cutters Bill Short and Sons, to the Maroochydore sawmill, down a dirt road that was steep in places. He walked alongside the bullocks, talking to and encouraging them, while little Dot manned the brake. She was used to doing jobs that normally a teenage boy or a man would do. A crosscut saw required two people to take the handles either end and pull it back and forth through the timber. It must have been quite a sight to see: a big man and a young girl, working together in sweaty, puffing harmony, on what would be considered a 'man's job'. What a wonderful scene for an artist like Frederick McCubbin or Tom Roberts to paint!

After helping her father saw the logs and get them ready for loading, she watched the bullocks pull them up onto the wagon, her father guiding them. The bullocks all had their own personalities but worked as a team, understanding everything that was said to them. The two leaders somehow 'passed the word' down the line to let the others know what was required of them. How cattle actually communicate with each other is a mystery, but anyone who has observed bovine behaviour with interest can assure you that they do. Cows, for example, having given their babies their morning drink and allowed them to play for a while, then put their calves down for some 'quiet time', while they go off to graze further afield. How a cow actually *tells* her calf: 'Now, you stay there and have a rest and don't you dare move until I get back,' is a source of wonder, but they do, and the calf will lie down, and wait, and wait, for its mother to return. Even more astounding is the phenomenon of cows that are running in a herd appointing a babysitter to watch all the baby calves while the mums are away foraging. It has always amused this writer to imagine the 'cow-talk conversation' that must somehow take place: 'Now, Myrtle, it's your turn today to babysit. You keep a sharp eye out for dingoes, won't you?', then they mooch off, leaving all the 'littlies' happily playing under the watchful eye of 'Aunty' Myrtle.

Bullocks are castrated males that have grown past the size of steers, and are generally – unlike bulls – not aggressive toward each other. Team bullocks are selected for their strength and docility, and can be very intelligent. Watching the bullocks working, Dot could easily imagine them 'talking' to each other. She loved the way her father treated his animals so kindly. Unlike the bullockies in Australian folklore, he never swore at his bullocks or at anything else.

Both Dot's parents were kind, respectable people, who brought their children up in an environment of caring for each other. Dot cannot remember any cross or harsh words from anyone in her entire family when growing up. There were no toys to fight over for a start, so the siblings made their own fun when they weren't doing chores. One of their favourite games was creating 'bullock teams pulling loads' using stones and sticks.

There wasn't much time for Dot to play, as there were always plenty of jobs to do, but she accepted that as normal and did them cheerfully. When her big sister, Joyce, was old enough to go to school, Dot – who was only four years old – had to accompany her, as she was so upset about going on her own. They doubled on their pony for the 3-mile ride through the bush to the schoolhouse, leaving the pony to spend the day in a paddock beside the school. Dot went with Joyce for three months till she settled down and was happy to go to school on her own. Dot's help was badly needed at home to manage the chooks, tend to the veggies, bring in wood for the stove and so on, as well as to help care for the younger children. The only time she can remember her mother being annoyed was when she'd put a batch of soap at the back of the stovetop to soften it enough to cut into bars. Wanting to help, Dot put it in the oven and it all melted. Ninety years later, she can remember clearly how upset her mother was, and her relief at her mum's controlled reaction to the calamity. Despite her exasperation, she just said, 'Don't do that again, will you, dear?'

She enjoyed delivering billies of milk on her horse before school. She finished school at age twelve to begin working, which was washing for five local women (on five different days), being paid 2 shillings and sixpence by each of them for a hard morning's work, scrubbing garments by hand then lifting heavy, wet clothes out of the copper and pushing them through the mangle and so on. One unforgettable morning, she had her hands in water, rinsing clothes under an outdoor tin skillion that posed as a 'laundry', when lightning struck the house next door and she was thrown 10 feet. Ten feet's a long way for a girl to fly backwards! But, she lived to tell the tale to everybody (. . . and, eventually, to her twenty great-grandkids!).

In the afternoons, she earned a couple of shillings more on other people's farms, picking coffee beans, plus fruit and vegetables such as strawberries and beans. One week that stands out in her mind resulted in her earning the handsome sum of 30 shillings, but she'd had to work really hard every day for that. She happily gave all her money to her mother. 'I didn't want anything,' Dot recalls. 'Mum made all our clothes. I had a pair of shoes to wear to church. We had good food and Mum taught me how to cook. I loved making bread for the family – all twelve of us – and I won prizes at shows. Joyce went to Brisbane to work when she was fifteen, so I was then the oldest at home and took on more responsibility. I was always so busy, ever since I was little, and I've liked to be busy all my life.

'Mum ordered our groceries from Queensland Pastoral Supplies (QPS) and they'd arrive every Friday on the train, which had a steep climb to get to Buderim. One day QPS included a tin of condensed milk in our order by mistake. My mother decided she'd pay for it on our bill, instead of sending it back, because she felt we deserved a little treat. She gave us all a big spoonful each and we had never tasted anything so sweet and delicious. I will never forget that taste sensation. There must have been a new person packing the orders, because instead of sending us a big tin of arrowroot (for cooking), they sent us a packet of Arrowroot biscuits. One packet wouldn't go far between ten children!

'Back then, Buderim consisted of the station, school, post office, Middleton's general store and the blacksmith shop. I loved to pump the big leather bellows for the blacksmith to fire up his forge. I'm the oldest living pupil of Buderim School. Fancy that! I remember being sad when Dad sold his bullock team because he got a comparatively "cushy" job working on roads for the Shire Council. At thirteen and fourteen, I was sent on the train on Fridays to travel to Palmwoods to collect his pay.'

At age fourteen, Dot was helping her family pack up and move to a farm at Eumundi, where they were sharefarming. When it proved to be too small to support two families, they shifted to a bigger farm at Pomona, where she again helped with all jobs, including the milking. Their father ploughed and sowed crops using draft horses. One mare had a foal, and when Dot and her oldest brother rode her to a dance one night, all went well until they set off for home and she took off, bolting back to her foal. It's a looong way to fall off a galloping Clydesdale, but they somehow managed to stay on board and survive the exciting end to their night out. Even more exciting was the thrill of flying along in their homemade corrugated-iron canoe when the creek was in flood. Dot wasn't concerned that she couldn't swim . . . it was fun! 'It's strange that the rushing brown floodwater didn't frighten me, because I was too frightened to swim in the sea, having almost drowned during a Sunday school picnic at Mooloolaba when I was thirteen,' she says.

When the other children were getting big enough to help with the milking, Dot was able to accept work offered to her around the district, minding kids while their mothers were in hospital for various reasons. It was a tremendously big event in a girl's life back then to make your 'debut'. Dot made hers aged seventeen, at the Eumundi Hall, and remembers feeling like a princess in the gorgeous white gown her mother had painstakingly created. At age eighteen, she was invited to a house-warming party on a farm at North Arm, and that's where she met her husband-to-be, Jim Davison, whose father owned the farm and the new house. When the owners of the place her father was sharefarming wanted to return and take over again, they moved to a bigger farm with a very big house, at Coles Creek. Dot used to drive the horse and wagon to take their cream to the Pomona butter factory, three days a week. When Jim would come a-courting Dot, he was smart enough to bring a bottle of beer for her dad. He took Dot to all the district dances on his Norton motorbike. Dot was still under the strict control of her parents, who were devout Christians. She had never heard a swearword until she was in her twenties and moved to North Arm. The village there then consisted of a butcher, baker, post office, general store and busy railway station.

Jim was aged twenty-nine and Dot was twenty-two when they married in 1939 at the Church of England, Nambour, and honeymooned at Grafton, where some of Jim's family lived. His father, George, had driven his cattle on a horse across country from there when he bought his land at North Arm in 1907. That was quite an achievement to make that trip successfully on his own. He did well at North Arm and donated land for the school. Jim worked for him and eventually took over. The farm was always known simply as 'the Davison Farm', and still is.

Jim liked to call her Dot rather than Dorothy and she remained Dot throughout her married life. They returned from their honeymoon to the romance of the milking shed, cutting cane for the pigs with cane knives and harvesting bananas on the hillsides. Jim would send bunches zooming down on the flying fox to Dot, so she could pack them to go on the train to the Brisbane markets. A couple of times she miscalculated and was knocked flying off her feet by the speeding bunches of nanas. Apart from those mishaps, she loved working with Jim and loved her life at North Arm.

One thing that was needed to help make their life complete was a refrigerator. How she longed for one. Finally they had the money for the latest thing: an Edward Hallstrom Cold Flame, powered by kerosene. Like many young farmers' wives, Dot had learnt that things for the farm were considered far more important than things for the house. So she'd been extremely patient, battling on using Jim's homemade Coolgardie safe: a square, boxlike construction made from a tea chest and gauze, with a hollow timber frame that was packed with coke. Water dripped onto the coke, creating a cool atmosphere. The operative word was 'cool', not 'cold'. Dot had been to houses where she'd drooled with envy at their refrigerator. Wonder of wonders, you could open the door and instantly see everything that was inside. Not only that, but it was all lovely and cold . . . a farm wife's dream. She imagined how much she and Jim would enjoy a cold drink of water when they came in from the paddocks, how the icing would set beautifully on her cakes, how the vegetables would keep fresh and crisp for days. There'd be no more trimming the smelly bits off the meat . . . It was going to be wonderful, having a refrigerator.

Farmers! When Jim mentioned their intended purchase to his father, the old bloke snorted in disgust and said, 'You need a new tractor more than you need that newfangled gadget!' Being a dutiful son, Jim spent the money on a Farmall tractor, and bought an icebox home for his beloved the same day. An icebox – almost like an esky – was a very poor substitute for the long-awaited fridge. Dot was so fuming mad she could barely speak. When Jim asked her where he should put it, she only just refrained from making a most unladylike reply! Instead she muttered tersely, 'Put it where you like.' With that uncanny male sensitivity farmers have towards their wives' needs, Jim then blithely asked her where he should drill the hole to let the water from the melting ice run out (onto the kitchen floor!), and again, Dot, with admirable restraint, repeated her previous answer. It was to be another year before she would get her treasured Cold Flame. A postscript to this favourite family yarn is that while the Cold Flame was taken to the tip many moons ago, the old Farmall is still earning its keep on the farm. Their son Cecil, although a modern farmer, still appreciates 'the old girl' and finds jobs for her to do, resplendent in her brand-new coat of bright-red paint – the same as she looked when Jim brought her home that fateful day, many decades ago . . . the day North Arm residents might have heard a 'volcanic eruption', but didn't, due to Dot's good nature.

It was hard to say whether dairying or farming bananas was harder, but having two separate incomes was at times a godsend. On the land, everything has cycles of being up or down. Dot and Jim worked very hard to grow the best bananas possible and their efforts were rewarded when they won prizes at shows, including the Brisbane Royal. Like all farmers, it was hard for Jim to get away from his paddocks to enjoy himself, but he patiently taught Dot to drive in his Essex ute and was happy for her to go to tennis and also indulge in her new sport of bowls. At the blacksmith's shop in North Arm, she enjoyed winding the forge for Jim as he made horseshoes, just as she had when a girl at Buderim.

Fishing in the many rivers in their district was a favourite pastime during their rare leisure breaks. Their three children, Pam, Carol and Cecil, had a wonderful childhood in an idyllic place. Apart from fishing, Jim's favourite sport was shooting. He didn't have to drive anywhere to enjoy a bit of competition or just test himself, for the Davison Rifle Range was right there on his property. His father had built it at the start of World War I, with shooters firing into a hill.

It was originally built for blokes from the North Arm area who were going away to war to hone their shooting skills before heading overseas. About the time Jim and Dot were married, it was again starting to be used by local fellers who'd signed up to fight in World War II. Because Jim's two older brothers, Fred and George, had signed up, Jim was required to stay and run the farm. Dot had to be careful to stay in the house when the soldiers were there to practise, as their house was right next to the range.

Jim loved competing, but shooting didn't appeal to Dot, who offered to be the marker at the fortnightly comps and the big open comps, so that she was being a part of her husband's sport. It was an unexpected bonus that she earned a bit of pocket money for this during competition days: 2 shillings. By the time she'd finished doing it quite recently, she'd earn $15 for a Saturday arvo and $30 for a full-day comp – bingo and 'spoiling grandkids' money! The marker inspects the targets and keeps a tally of all the shooters' marks. Their allowance is not supposed to be danger money! But one day during a big competition, a bullet ricocheted off the metal frame around a target and three fragments of the bullet went into the side of Dot's face, miraculously missing her eyes. The man who had fired the shot was so distraught he never competed nor came near the rifle range again.

Dot was taken to Nambour hospital and was told that they couldn't remove the fragments that were in deep until they'd worked back out closer to her skin. Having recovered from the shock, she decided she could put up with the pain, and immediately returned to her job as marker on the same day, because 'it was an important competition'! To top her day off nicely, she accidentally knocked a big old telephone in a wooden box off a table and onto her toes, breaking at least one.

Jim achieved the highest possible score on the range of 105 with his .303. He passed on his marksmanship to Carol, who became a champion, and was selected as part of the State Ladies Rifle Team in 1971 and '72. Carol loves her .308 and makes her own bullets. The North Arm Shooting Complex, as their range is known, has separate sections for pistols, shotguns, sporting shooters (lighter rifles), and big-bore shooters, which is Carol's group. The targets are up to 700 metres away. The new targets, which certainly don't have metal frames, are electronically operated and a computer beside the shooters does Dot's old job and gives them their scores. She marked every fortnight, plus comp days, for half a century.

Carol tells a funny story about her shooting 'prowess'. She lives on a farm further north at Longflat, near Amamoor Forest, and a neighbour asked if she'd fire a few shots to scare off the flocks of ducks that were flying in and decimating his crop. Carol obliged and was horrified to discover she'd fired into the irrigation system! Naturally she has never lived that down.

In 1979 Jim and Dot enjoyed a long-awaited trip to the Melbourne Cup. Dot has always loved to dress in smart and pretty outfits. Despite doing what used to be considered 'men's work' for many years, she has managed to retain her femininity.

In 1980, Jim died suddenly of a heart attack, aged seventy-one. Cecil gave up his job at the local garage to come home and help his mother run the farm, by then producing sugarcane as well as milk. One day when they were dipping the cattle for ticks, the bull, which Dot loved, was refusing to go in and Cecil started to get cranky. 'Oh, don't be too hard Cecil . . . don't you like him?' Dot asked, to which Cecil replied, in a manner that clearly showed he meant every word, 'Mum, I *hate the bloody lot*!'

Dot got the message that Cecil preferred farming crops to

'stretching greenhide' in the milking shed. When the cows were all sold, Cecil became one of the first in the area to grow ginger as a crop and has been tremendously successful. A big milestone in the life of his dynamo of a mum came in 1997 when she turned eighty. They celebrated at the rifle range, with 300 people having a wonderful time. Dot has also thoroughly enjoyed three cruises in her later years.

'After Jim died, a couple of chaps hinted they were attracted to me, but I have never been interested in getting married again,' she says. 'No one could take Jim's place.' At ninety, Dot was still going great guns, playing competition bowls and bingo and remaining involved with many community clubs and volunteer organisations, when a bout of ill health put the brakes on her a bit. Then she deteriorated alarmingly and underwent a major operation at Nambour Hospital. Her condition afterward was such that those closest to her had cause for great apprehension – would this much-loved 'iron lady' pull through okay? Had all those years of hard work caught up with her?

After days of scaring the hell out of everyone, Dot the Dynamo's lights suddenly brightened up again, and she was back, raring to get out of hospital and mow her lawn or cook up a big batch of scones. By then though, her three children had decided she shouldn't live on her own any longer, and plans were made to move her belongings from her house at North Arm, where she'd spent seventy years, to Carol and husband Dave's property close to Gympie. That was a big wrench, but six years on, she is still happy there, looking at the cows, miniature ponies and menagerie of other animals, and refers to this phase as 'her new life'. Although she has let her licence go since her stay in hospital, her busy schedule keeps her mind and body active. She's still involved in local activities, still cooks up a storm, crochets, knits, plays bingo and enjoys seeing her nine grand-children and twenty great-grandchildren when they visit. Plus, she's a life member and patron of the nearby Yandina Bowls Club. When Carol and Dave took her to the 'Back to Buderim' historical celebra-tions recently, they were surprised, to say the least, that Dot – the oldest living pupil of the school and granddaughter of a pioneer-ing family – wasn't included in the line-up of legends. On asking why, they were informed that she wasn't eligible because she didn't live within the boundaries of the Sunshine Coast (which are within cooee of their farm) any more. They all found that very strange deci-sion disappointing and puzzling.

When you meet Dot for the first time and get to know her, it's hard to imagine her without a smile on her face. The image you may have had in your mind of what someone who's almost a century old would look like is replaced by the sight of a bright-as-a-button, smi-ley, alert lady with a smart, modern haircut and clothes. She's ready to chat about anything and everything. And while you have a chin-wag, you struggle to comprehend that this person actually worked with a bullock team, back when T Model Fords were just starting to appear on the dirt roads of rural Australia, Prohibition was hap-pening in America and it was only a decade since Pommy drongos sent our men and boys into Gallipoli. Whew! Amazing! It is such a privilege to meet and spend time with this wonderful representative of rural Australian womanhood. Dot's a true lady and a true legend!

11.

Bruce Blaikie

A TRAVELLER'S STORY

Bruce Blaikie is a traveller. After a working life journeying to interesting places, carrying out challenging and sometimes dangerous projects, he has spent his retirement years travelling to and enjoying even more exotic locations. He has created a lifestyle that would be the envy of most people, spending several months a year exploring Europe on his boat, and returning to the Gold Coast during our summer to enjoy living on the beach for a few months. Poor old Bruce!

Not that Bruce is old – he might be in his eighties, but he is young in looks and attitude. Constant mental stimulation – looking forward to seeing what's around the next corner – must be a first-rate recipe to fight off the 'dodders'. He avoids the 'r' word. 'When I'm not getting around in my own boat, *Zizz*, around Europe, I go on ships to destinations that are out of her reach, like the South Pacific islands,' he says. 'I get a lot of enjoyment from replying to questions from the pushy people I encounter on cruises – you know the type – about what I "do", by answering, "I'm out of work. Unemployed." The looks on their faces give me a good internal chuckle.'

There's an element of truth in that deliberately frivolous answer, because he never consciously retired from working life. He believes the stringent political correctness of the United Nations kept him out of the last job he *should* have had, but that's jumping many decades forward from his lofty beginnings: on nightshift in a pineapple cannery, stacking trays of heavy tins. Not exactly a job to kill for, but thankfully it was up all the way from there.

Between that humble start to his working life, and his later years spent constantly discovering and enjoying fascinating places, came a lot of study to gain the important pieces of paper that were his key to the upper echelons of the business world. Bruce has quite an impressive display of certificates that proclaim his status as a highly qualified accountant. It's a pretty fair indication of his sense of humour that they are displayed not on the living room or office walls of his Gold Coast base, but in the toilet. He is absolutely *not* your everyday, obsessed-with-figures, paper-shuffling accountant.

Born in 1931 at a private hospital, Ellendene, in Brisbane's Fortitude Valley, Bruce Walter Blaikie, a fifth-generation Australian, was not to endure the usual privations of the Depression years. He missed out on rabbit stew and bread and dripping because he had the good fortune to be brought up in his grandparents' huge mansion in New Farm, then a genteel riverside suburb. The Paltridges were prominent graziers from the St George district. Their daughter, Bruce's mother, had gone to live with them after the breakdown of her marriage to a man who was not a country fellow. Bruce attended New Farm Primary, then the prestigious Church of England Grammar School – commonly known as Churchie – and spent holidays with his older brother, Robert, at their grandparents' station, Minimi, near Nindigully. They also owned the Commercial Hotel in St George. A motor-car garage at the back of the pub was operated by the Jackson brothers, Bill and John, the latter of whom became an RAAF wartime hero. The Jackson airfield in Papua New Guinea (PNG) was named in his honour.

Minimi had been a Cobb and Co changing station when Bruce's mother was a child there. Bruce has a vivid memory of a truckload of Baltic refugees arriving in 1946 to start work there ringbarking. They were from a variety of backgrounds and had to be taught how to use their axes by Bruce's uncle Frank, who was managing the station for his father. They all spoke little or no English but one of them was appointed spokesman to ask the main question occupying their thoughts about their new life in the Australian bush: 'Are there any lions and tigers out where we'll be working?' Something like that sticks in a young feller's mind.

Bruce also recalls travelling out to Minimi with his grandfather, first on the train to Dirranbandi, then in what was known as a 'service car', a sort of limo service. Long before Reg Ansett started Ansett Airlines, he started his business life with a service car operating out of Mount Gambier, coincidentally the town Bruce's great-grandfather had ridden from to western Queensland in the 1800s, searching for land and opportunity.

The war years were the biggest influence in Bruce's young life – he was eight years old when it started. There was a submarine base at New Farm, which inspired him to apply, aged twelve, for an entry to the Royal Navy Midshipman College, but they accepted only ten boys from all over Australia and he missed out. He used to see the famous General MacArthur from the US watching his son playing with his Filipina amah (nanny) in the park near his grandfather's house. MacArthur lived in Lennons Hotel in Queen Street at the time, and Bruce clearly recalls the shock when he looked out from his tram one day to see the well-known general sitting in a car right beside him. He couldn't help staring and missed his stop!

Although Bruce was always top of the class in primary school, and was so bright he was jumped straight from Grade Five to Grade Seven, he was not an outstanding student at Churchie, just scraping through his exams, and didn't have a clue what he'd do when he left. In hindsight, he feels that not having the influence of a father as a role model to advise him was probably the main reason he had no motivation towards any career. His grandfather was old and deaf, and Bruce wasn't interested in the land, so there wasn't a close rapport there.

Jobs were easy to get then. Like many young people, he was keen to start at the top, or at least to earn big money, straight away. He heard that nightshift at the Hargraves pineapple cannery near the city paid 20 pounds a week, which was a princely sum in 1948. He soon found out why, and at the same time, discovered he wasn't cut out for either nightshift or hard physical toil. The job involved lifting big trays loaded with full tins up onto a high conveyor belt . . . all night! Somehow he forced himself to stay a week, then gladly collected his 20 quid and left, never to return.

An advertisement for a clerk for the City Electric Light Company gave him visions of rising rapidly to executive level, but when he started there, the modern open-plan layout of the offices gave him a very different vision. He could see from his desk that he was surrounded by middle-aged and older, grey-headed men, all shuffling bits of paper like he was – a very depressing sight. He thought to himself, *I can't do this forever like they obviously have.*

The next stop in his search for a satisfying job was A Harold's, record and sheet music distributors for EMI, in Elizabeth Street, as a warehouse clerk, from where he thought he'd climb the ladder to success. As well as attending balls at the famous Cloudland ballroom, he was enjoying sailing on weekends with his ex-Churchie friends, who had all gone on to uni. Their grand ambitions for their futures once they graduated made Bruce think he should study part-time to get some sort of qualification. He enrolled at the State Commercial College in the city (now QUT) to study accountancy. Because the first year of the course was almost finished, the head of the college advised him, 'You probably won't get through.' Those uplifting words possibly haunted him when Bruce sailed through to become an accountant in just three years, attending the course and also squashing in time to study at night while working full-time during the day. Naturally this makes you wonder just what he could have achieved full-time at university!

During that period, he had scored a decent job in the accounting department of Queensland Tyre Service Company at Milton. He had extra money coming in on weekends from using his most unusual skill as a square-dance caller. Square dancing was the craze then and he received 5 pounds per night from Friday nights at the Ashgrove Golf Club and Saturday nights at the Albion Bowls Club. Very handy extra income indeed. In the US, where the craze had started and grown to be hugely popular, top callers could receive a thousand dollars a night. The downside for Bruce was his inability to take part in long yacht races with his friends on weekends.

When he qualified as an accountant, he resigned from his day job to start a sports store at Toowong with his savings – it didn't pan out well. The store went broke and he lost what he'd taken years to save. However, it was a good lesson in how hard it is to succeed in business . . . there are many factors that have to add up.

Bruce went back to working for someone else and began to save

for another nest egg. Not wanting to be one of the herd, he endeav-
oured to push himself to give himself every chance of having a
successful life. He knew that he wasn't going to be a garden-variety
accountant, and that for him the qualification was merely an entree
to an interesting career in business and the beginning of a pathway
to the top executive level. So he continued to study at night for more
accountancy certificates and ended up with many letters after his
name. His attitude was always that 'the most important certificate
is the next one'. (Although after decades of experience in company
management, his credo is, 'What really counts is experience, not certificates or formal qualifications.') After closing his store, he took a
position with HB Selby & Co, makers of scientific instruments, in
their accountancy department and was very soon bored stiff. Two
weeks into that job, the manager informed Bruce in a most embarrassed manner that he had hired him without approval from above
and had been told to dismiss him. Bruce was so delighted he could
have jumped in the air! Then at last came the major turning point
in his life: a *Courier-Mail* ad for an Assistant Accountant at the
Steamship Trading Company in Papua New Guinea, at a salary of
1200 pounds a year, 'all found'.

Papua New Guinea! A land of excitement, intrigue, and opportunity with a capital 'O'. As a single man, he was first sent to
Samarai Island, to the bachelors' quarters. When he felt he was
ready to settle down, he returned to the mainland on a holiday and
proposed to Kaye, an attractive, well-brought-up girl he had taken
out in Brisbane and whose company he enjoyed. They married in
Brisbane in 1958 and moved into married quarters on Paga Hill,
overlooking Port Moresby harbour, with the household staff that
was a 'perk' every executive in PNG expected. By then he was a
company accountant, and with his hard-won qualifications was

offered membership of Certified Practising Accountants. When he
told them he didn't want to pay their fees they gave him a life membership! A case of being rewarded for complete honesty!

Steamship Trading Company was a diverse organisation that
owned shops – including department stores – hotels, coastal ships,
sawmills, copra, coffee and rubber plantations throughout Papua
New Guinea, and Bruce constantly travelled around the country
visiting all the businesses, checking on their progress and discussing ways to improve things with the staff. He eventually obtained a
pilot's licence to get around faster and relished the challenges of flying in one of the most dangerous countries in the world for pilots.
Flying in the Independence Day Brisbane to Port Moresby air race
was a highlight of his time in PNG.

After independence was granted to the country by the Whitlam
government, all government employees such as his brother Robert,
who was working there as a patrol officer, were paid out and their
jobs advertised as two- or three-year contracts. 'You had to query
the commitment to the country the new contract people had, compared with people like my brother, who'd regarded his job as a
lifetime career, with dedication to PNG's progress paramount on his
agenda,' says Bruce. Because of the very different natures of their
careers, the brothers rarely saw each other except when helping out
during times of crisis, like volcanic eruptions and floods.

Bruce developed great relationships with the staff scattered all
over the country and after twenty-five years with Steamship Trading
Company knew absolutely everything about it. He'd 'grown out of
being an accountant' and was a director of the company, actively
overseeing and managing everything that went on. From early in
his time in the accounting department of the company, he'd regularly see the 'forty or so company accountants in charcoal grey suits'

who'd get off planes at Port Moresby airport from the mainland, and vow not to become like them. He dressed in practical white shorts and shirts and relished his amicable working relationships with everyone – Indigenous and white – who worked for the company and knew he had their respect.

Social life revolved around the New Guinea Club and the Port Moresby Bowls Club. 'I was there during the end of an era. If you were a white Protestant member of those clubs, you were on the "top of the heap", socially,' he says.

He enjoyed going to 'reverse trade missions', mainly to New Zealand, brokering deals for their goods for the PNG market. It was during the time of Chairman Mao that he made many interesting trips to China, buying products. He always went to China via Hong Kong, which was described in China in that era as 'heaven for the rich, hell for the poor'. During those trips he stayed at large hotels in Hong Kong – his favourite being The President on Nathan Road – and would see GI's on leave from the Vietnam War, straight from the battlefields, getting around spaced out. 'That was not a good experience, seeing them like that. They were so young.'

In China, he saw many demonstrations with yelling and chanting Chinese crowds waving their copies of Mao's 'Little Red Book'. Long before the world's media featured the photo of the defiant young man standing in front of a tank in Tiananmen Square, Bruce looked out of his hotel window one day and saw thousands of agitated people marching past, headed for the Square. He asked the English-speaking Chinese hotel manager what they were marching for, and was given an obscure reply that was typical of that era: 'It's a beautiful day and they are going for a walk to a park.'

In 1976 he was made Assistant Managing Director of Steamship Trading Company and knew he was destined for the top job eventually. His initiative and tenacity in brokering a massive, lucrative deal between his company, Brambles and Ok Tedi was his proudest achievement.

Bruce naturally assumed he would be made Managing Director when the incumbent retired. So it was a tremendous shock when he told Bruce that another man had been given the job. In anger, Bruce told him to 'get stuffed' and resigned on the spot at the board meeting. It was a totally unexpected stab in the back of Gillard–Rudd proportions.

'I was the only person in the entire company who knew all the staff well in every business we had. No one knew the company like I did. It was *my* company. I had rebuilt it twice after disasters. To say I was upset is the understatement of the century. They said later that it was because I was too close to company retirement age, but that was just an excuse. It was sheer bastardry. I served out my month's notice with difficulty, only to say goodbye to the staff scattered all over Papua New Guinea. They presented me with an album with pictures of all of them – over 800 people. There were many tears during that time of farewell. It was a traumatic time,' he says.

'I packed up all the belongings Kaye and I had acquired in all those years – including six children who'd attended boarding schools in Queensland – and went back to the mainland, setting up house in Newmarket, Brisbane. Although I was feeling slightly shattered, I was completely confident I would be snapped up by another big firm. I was in for yet another shock. I found that in Australia in the 1980s, employers and agencies were only interested in people aged under thirty-five with a recent university degree. My vast experience was overlooked. I wasn't the only highly qualified person over forty who encountered that during that era. It was going to be very hard to make a fresh start at my age.'

He soon worked out he needed to go to London to seek another offshore job. From there he researched overseas companies and began applying. After a few months he was employed by the Malaysian government to run a large trading company, and was based at Kota Kinabalu, the capital of Sabah. After two years of his five-year contract there was a dodgy election held that resulted in a change of government. The new regime threw out all non-Malaysians, so it was back to London and job searching.

With his great organisational and people skills, Bruce then went on to carve out a successful second career helping to restore war-torn countries back to productivity. As a senior executive with AusAID and the International Labour Organization in Burma and Cambodia, he was in charge of projects like rebuilding bombed-out roads, restoring and modernising the dairy industries, getting water supplies flowing again, and, even more importantly, providing employment and housing for repatriated refugees.

He loved his time in Burma, which was a period of great achievement and adventure in a new and very different land. Kaye was also very happy there. When they arrived there was a picturesque little bamboo house beside the larger, more modern manager's house. The Burmese officials found it puzzling that Bruce asked for the smaller house. He preferred it as the building had great character. There was a separate bamboo office that had a deck over a little pond. Bruce would hold many functions there and would deliberately not have chairs for anyone to sit down. This forced the local officials, who were very class-conscious, to mingle with staff they normally wouldn't mix with.

His headquarters were set in an enchanting scene. He looked out over rice paddies with farmers working bullocks – a timeless vista. A bicycle repairman set up his shop by the gate every day and men would pass by selling samosas from baskets. Over the road was a monastery. Every morning, the monks – from the biggest down to the smallest – lined the street holding out their begging bowls for rice. People who gave them rice were considered fortunate, blessed for they had been given an opportunity to do a good deed. The monks and other people bathed at the water pump in the street, all dressed in their robes. Despite this hindrance, they all – somehow – always looked very clean.

Bruce learnt that all Burmese boys do a stint as monks in a monastery and only a small percentage stay on to follow the life of poverty and chastity. There are female monks – who wear pink robes – but they do not receive the same respect. According to a pamphlet Bruce has on the Buddhist religion in Burma: 'The fate of being born female is evidence of having led a poor previous life.' So much for equality!

The biggest project Bruce took part in during the late '80s in Burma was a joint Australian and Burmese government-funded (mostly Australian-funded) organisation called Mandalay Milk that was given the task of restructuring the local dairying industry. The aims were to improve the shelf life of the very popular sweetened condensed milk and improve hygiene in handling both the canned product and the raw milk, plus improve the nutrition and health of cows, and modernise the transport of milk. To be blunt, the dairy industry was about as primitive as it could be. The average farmer owned only 1.5 cows, but employed a milker to milk them – by hand, of course. Milk drinkers would not want to view those hands at work. Hygiene standards were non-existent. The milker delivered the cans of milk to the condensed milk factory on a pushbike and the cans were contaminated with a variety of substances. These included dirt and vegetable matter – and occasionally fish! – from the waterholes from which the milker topped up the cans, because he was paid for the *amount* he delivered. Bruce's organisation brought in hygiene, centralised refrigerated collection points, artificial insemination to improve the cows' yield, and control of diseases and parasites. Progress was slow but Bruce persevered until real changes were made and understood. A new factory was acquired when he was able to get a prefabricated building from Vietnam, where it had lain idle since the war.

Forty local vets, half of them female, were employed in the project. They were issued with motorbikes to get around the farms. The females were so tiny they were unable to straddle the motorbikes with their feet on the ground, so Bruce managed to acquire Australian posties' bikes for them, which were far more suitable.

While visiting villages to inspect progress he often had to abandon his 4WD after monsoonal rains and travel by bullock cart. The drivers would walk alongside, ever-watchful of how deeply the wheels were sinking into the mud. It always amused Bruce to see how they achieved 'turbo' propulsion when necessary: the driver would grab the nearest bullock's tail and bite it!

Covering long distances all over the countryside from his Mandalay base, he was eventually given a permanent driver, Aung Kyi, with whom he established a great friendship during their many long, weary drives and adventures together. Aung Kyi was a character, and very curious about Western life. After asking many questions one day about the Pope, he declared, 'Ah, so the Pope is the Catholics' Buddha!' Aung Kyi embraced the slang or Western phrases he picked up during their conversations. On an early trip, with a carload of white female staff, he suddenly pulled up. 'Why are you stopping?' Bruce asked, to which Aung Kyi replied, 'I need a piss!' This unexpected reply brought sharp intakes of breath from the rear seat passengers, then gales of uncontrollable giggles.

He was often the unwitting cause of laughter. One day, after driving slowly and carefully for ages toward Rangoon over a very bad road where foreigners hadn't been for about twenty years, Aung Kyi suddenly looked across at Bruce and said, 'Whose bloody bright idea was this, 'ey?' From then on, Bruce would catch the train to Rangoon.

Their friendship and mutual respect deepened over time, and in 1991, Bruce was extremely upset when Aung Kyi's teenage son was killed. He had been riding on the roof of a train, which was normal in Burma to get away from hot, overcrowded carriages, and had been wiped out by a low bridge. He'd never ridden on a train before and wasn't aware of the danger.

Aung Kyi visited Bruce in his office the following day, beside himself with grief, saying, 'My son came back to my house last night. He stood in the doorway and said, "Father, Father, I want to come home. Father, there is no room in the tree – all the places are taken. I want to come home . . ." ' (This refers to the Buddhist belief in reincarnation and in this instance the reference was to birds in a tree. There is no peace until it is possible to settle.) This incident upset Bruce very much because he shared his friend's sorrow and Aung Kyi's tearful tale of this dream made that sorrow even more painful.

Aung Kyi was Bruce's driver for four years and they shared many experiences. The number nine is hugely lucky in Burmese culture, and if there were eight people in the vehicle he was driving, he would put a stone in the car to represent a ninth person. The currency – kyats – was all in multiples of nine.

After the elections that saw former political prisoner Aung San Suu Kyi run as leader of the opposition, the country was in turmoil and projects such as Mandalay Milk were closed down. It was a dangerous place to be and Americans associated with the project were immediately flown out, but Bruce wanted to complete the project. His top six advisers on vital parts of the scheme, such as artificial insemination and construction, were given two weeks' notice to leave the country. Bruce managed to get his staff out on an RAAF plane, but he wanted to stay on. He advised his staff to only pack personal items in the large cardboard boxes he'd obtained for that purpose. At the airport, military personnel belligerently asked him what was in the cartons. 'Only personal items,' he assured them firmly. He had spent thousands of dollars on American Express to enable his staff to take their personal effects with them. Consequently he was not thrilled when the soldiers opened one of the biggest boxes and out fell a motorbike!

After smoothing this tricky situation over, he began talking to another Aussie at the airport, a journalist from the *Financial Times* based in Singapore, who told Bruce he had got in on a false visa. 'I'll lose my job if I get sprung, but I'm going to get a great story here,' he said confidentially.

After two days of particularly heavy fighting, Bruce asked the Australian ambassador what he should do and the reply was, 'I think you should get out! It's not safe to remain here.' He escaped to Bangkok, which was not easy, as roads were closed and civilian flights were finished, as was civilian train travel. After six weeks there he felt compelled to return to finish the joint-venture project that was so close to completion. His Burmese counterpart, who was not part of the corruption that was taking place, told him that the military regime operated like communists, and complained, 'No one can make decisions. I have to ask several different people if I may buy a pencil.' Burma soon went from being the biggest rice producer of Asia to becoming an importer.

Burma had thrown up many challenges and Bruce's work there had given him immense satisfaction. He loved the country and its people and was sad to leave. He was well equipped with experience to tackle his next project: moving hundreds of thousands of Cambodian refugees back to their own country. Before that he spent three months in Phuket, where he bought a boat, enjoyed life for a while, then sailed it to the UK. He sold the boat in Holland and there the seed was sown for his 'retirement adventure plan'. He decided he would spend his twilight years boating all over Europe's canals and rivers.

But first he had commitments to meet. In 1994 he moved to Cambodia, working with the Cambodian Red Cross for a UN subsidiary organisation, CARE International. Using his expertise in logistics, he helped repatriate 314 000 refugees from Thailand back to their homelands, equipped with pre-packaged housing and agricultural kits. This had to be accomplished in an organised manner and could only be done using trucks between the places where the railroads had been bombed. The trains, full of refugees, had a flatbed open carriage out in front of the engine, onto which any 'locals' could jump and ride for free. The only catch to the free ride was that if they hit one of the mines that was still placed on the trainline, the flatbed carriage would blow up first, thus hopefully saving the rest of the train!

The repatriation project had an end date, and after his year was up, Bruce was invited by CARE to continue on with them, but he preferred the offer from the United Nations Transitional Authority Campaign (UNTAC) to assist with the upcoming elections. During this UN-sponsored election, trouble was expected from the Khmer Rouge who were still active. Bruce was one of many employees of the civil administration of UNTAC who was drafted as an International Polling Station Officer, as there were not enough volunteers. He was sent to Koh Thom District in Kandal province a few hours drive south of Phnom Penh, and allocated, along with a young Brisbane lawyer – a volunteer – to a long-forgotten village in the middle of the jungle. They were each issued with an inflatable children's mattress, a mossie net and a supply of MREs (meals ready to eat), which are freeze-dried packs of food issued by the US military. These were supposed to sustain them for their time 'in the field'. They were meant to resemble roast dinners but when opened tasted like 'bags of plastic flavoured with ketchup'!

Travelling across a river on an ancient punt, then over many rural roads in a car, they eventually arrived at a remote village, where they were billeted in a local school that had no electricity or running water. A detachment of Bulgarian soldiers were there to protect them and the ballot boxes. They visited other little villages by canoe during polling, always accompanied by their heavily armed bodyguards in full battle dress and flak jackets. It was difficult for an Aussie to comprehend that people were actually being killed during an election.

After that extremely dramatic interlude, Bruce's next project was for the United Nations-affiliated International Labour Organization, running employment projects in Cambodia. People would be put to work making roads by hand for $1 a day. That would mean approximately $2000 a week would be injected into their villages that they otherwise would not have had. Bruce felt a great sense of achievement improving people's lives and bettering the war-ravaged country. There were really smart people in charge whom he respected and enjoyed working with.

On leaving Cambodia, he was off to the UN's headquarters in Zagreb, during the Serbo–Croatian war, to discuss an intriguing invitation from two Australian ex-army officers. They wanted him to join forces with them to unearth the whereabouts of $200 million worth of equipment that had gone missing. The officers were both Queensland engineers who had spent a lot of time in Papua New Guinea and they knew Bruce was the man they wanted. However, the politically correct policies of the HR staff of the UN, all working out of ultra-PC-conscious New York, declared that the team was 'top-heavy with both males and Australians'. Hence the job went to a female from an African country.

By then, Bruce was a single man, his children had all left the nest, and he was free to do whatever he liked. Europe and boats beckoned. Since then, Bruce and *Zizz* have tootled over many rivers and lakes and he estimates he has been through locks – which intrigue him – at least 500 times. He was moored near a lock in France a couple of years ago, in an idyllic spot that had induced him to stay a few days instead of meandering on. He'd noticed an attractive woman jogging past every morning and they started saying 'hello' to each other. On the third day, he dared to ask if she'd like a cup of tea or coffee, and she called out, still running past his boat, that she would . . . on the way back. Thus began a lovely friendship, and Marie-Terese, who Bruce calls MT, an independent and attractive lady with an apartment in Paris, has since accompanied him on many journeys and adventures. Two 'adventures' they could have done without were being attacked by gun-happy pirates off the Seychelles, and being mugged in Durban. In the mugging incident, MT managed to fight and scare off both men while Bruce, who'd been hurled to the ground, was trying to recover his senses.

'She goes to the gym every day and was at them like a tiger,' he says.

'When we were attacked by pirates we were on a cruise ship heading from Port Victoria in Mahe [in the Seychelles], to Genoa. They were either from the Seychelles close by, or could have been Somalis who'd come from a mother ship. Our ship's radar didn't pick them up and they attempted to board. We were sent to our cabins and heard all the commotion happening above. The Israeli security staff on board sent them packing and the bullet holes on the deck could be seen the next day, plus gaping holes from the rocket launcher the pirates had fired at us. We steamed to rendezvous with a Spanish military vessel, which unfortunately travelled more slowly than our ship, so we had to zigzag to enable them to keep up with us, until they could hand us over to an Italian military ship to escort us into the Red Sea. The Spanish ship had a helicopter on board, which regularly took off to do a sweep. The Italian ship never appeared at our rendezvous – we heard it was called to an emergency – and we were left to sail on alone. We made it safely to our destination and lived to tell the tale.'

Bruce has many tales of his adventures, journeys, and some unforgettable characters he has met worldwide, written and saved on his computer. If he ever gets 'round to publishing them, they will provide not only entertainment for armchair travellers, but also an insight into the bloke who decided as a teenager that he wasn't going to be 'one of the herd'.

12.

Beverley Rybarz

ADELAIDE DEBUTANTE MARRIES THE WILDEST
MAN IN PAPUA NEW GUINEA

The big hut stank of pig fat. Having been in Papua New Guinea for nearly a year, the pretty young girl with her blonde hair tied back in a bow was used to the stench, but it still made her nauseous. She had come here with her second husband, Stan, a fearless man whom the native men respected. Moulded by his hardline experiences in World War II and his tough upbringing in Poland, he was an unbending and difficult husband.

Since leaving her comfortable Adelaide home and genteel family to travel to the wilds of Papua New Guinea in 1950, Beverley had coped with many terrible, frightening and plain ghastly things. But the Papuan staff's habit of constantly blowing their noses everywhere with one finger up against one nostril – even in the cookhouse – was something she could no longer tolerate. She had narrowly escaped a stream of flying snot one day while tending plants in her garden, and had reached her limit of tolerance. She said to Stan, 'I can't stand them doing that disgusting thing any longer! You have to stop them!' and he had replied arrogantly, 'You tell them.'

Taking a deep breath, she let the men know in no uncertain manner – using pidgin – that they were not to do it anywhere near her or her hut. At first they were puzzled, then unhappy at a woman telling them such a thing, but they nevertheless let her know that she had been understood.

Beverley stared down their fierce glares. She knew she had to win this battle. Stan stared with grudging admiration for the bravery she'd shown, then finally stepped up beside her to let them know he backed her up, and that they were dismissed. No more discussion. No more flying mucous missiles in the cookhouse or near the woman.

'What would Mother have thought of this?' she pondered, not for the first time since she'd 'gone bush' with her bridge-builder husband. Beverley's mother, a teacher and a lady of great character, would no doubt have approved of her daughter's courageous stand, even if she'd found the circumstances appalling. And had her own father been present at that potentially dangerous incident in his granddaughter's life, he'd have been in his element, for he'd come to Australia from England as a Salvation Army brigadier to 'save the Aborigines', as was the common approach back then. Beverley's mother grew up a member of the Salvation Army and married a self-made, successful businessman who had spent his childhood, from nine to thirteen years of age, droving cattle with Aboriginals in northern Australia to help his mother out. Beverley was from good stock.

Born in 1929, she enjoyed her quiet, middle-class upbringing in Adelaide, never dreaming that she would one day marry a 'wild man' who'd carry her off into the jungle to live in a hut. By comparison, the most exciting thing that happened in Glenelg was if the milko's horse broke into a canter! Life was carefree, stable, secure and sedate. Nothing was locked. Children were safe anywhere. Men respected women and raised their hats to them as they passed in the street. Decent women didn't go into hotels. Everyone went to church and Sunday school. There were rigid standards of discipline in both schools and hospitals. The word of teachers and matrons was law. Like most Australians then, Beverley grew up in an atmosphere of complete, unquestioning loyalty to England and the monarchy, suspicion of foreign places, culture and people, and a vague but sincere belief that all Aboriginal people were well cared for by the churches and missions.

An only child, she still had many friends to play with and didn't experience the hard times of the Depression years. She attended a private school run by Anglican nuns she says were 'not known for their worldly knowledge!' Next door were the St Barnabas boys training for the priesthood. While she was playing tennis one day, one of them stuck his 'willy' – the first she'd ever seen – through a hole in the dividing fence. Staring curiously and giggling after the initial shock, she only just resisted swatting it with her racket. When the story got around the school, the nuns counselled her and advised her to 'pray a lot!' What exactly for, she wasn't quite certain . . .

Most children back then left school at age fifteen to get jobs. University was only for the very bright and they paid for the privilege of going there. Beverley did a year's course at Miss Mann's Business College and, while there, also studied three extra Leaving standard subjects, which she passed with Honours, delighted to trounce Miss Mann's opinion of her as a 'bimbo' (no doubt because she was blonde and attractive). Her first job was a temporary relieving position at the GPO – something she was apprehensive about, as the public service then was the province of Roman Catholics of Irish descent. Sure enough, she turned out to be the only Protestant there.

There was a deep divide between members of the two churches, who did not intermarry. Due to the force of her friendly-but-no-nonsense personality, she survived the initial hostility. Her first wage was 17 shillings and threepence, out of which she paid her mother 8 shillings board.

It was the era of jitterbugging frenziedly to Glenn Miller's 'In The Mood' at dances, and slow waltzing to 'Blue Moon' with a boy you fancied. If flirting wound up in pregnancy, a girl would most probably be sent to a home in New Zealand, where she'd scrub floors for her keep until the birth of the baby she would not be allowed to see, before adoptive parents took it away. An illegitimate child was considered a disgrace and if one broke the rules, society was harshly critical. Most young Adelaide girls couldn't wait to get engaged and, eventually, with their fiancés, build a 4000-pound house on the 200-pound block of land they'd save for. But at just eighteen, Beverley didn't want that commitment for a long time yet – she wanted to have a *lot* of fun first – which meant heading for Sydney! Before she could leave on that particular mission, however, Cupid had other ideas . . . She met Roy at a party, fell head over heels, and in no time flat, had a ring on her finger and was selecting a block of land with him for their love nest.

They also bought a yacht, which overturned on a terrifying, pitch-black night. When they both struggled to shore without having made any attempt to save each other, they realised that perhaps they weren't meant for each other after all! The ring was tearfully handed back. With her fabulous-crazy friend Carlien, Beverley set off for Sydney where the two well-brought-up glamour girls proceeded to have the time of their lives with all sorts of interesting and fun people – many from the entertainment world. They had a marvellous flat with a harbour view. Beverley made excellent money helping a friend create beautiful wedding gowns for an upmarket bridal boutique. While Beverley sewed on lace and pearls, Carlien's tales of her torrid love-life kept her enthralled.

Beverley was swept off her feet by Timmy, a Qantas pilot who'd been an elite night-time fighter pilot in the RAF during WW II, flying Spitfires and Beauforts. Shot down in flames, he'd had his face rebuilt with newly developed techniques and was still a handsome man, but completely different looking to how he appeared before the crash. Because he was young and didn't drink or smoke, his recuperation had been completely satisfactory. The surgery that replaced his eyelids, ears and other bits that had been burnt off, could not, unfortunately, transplant pleasant dreams to replace his frequent tormenting nightmares, during which his screams would wake her. They were married in Beverley's family's home in Adelaide, as her father was ill and dying. One of his brokerage agents had visited him and passed on Egyptian influenza. His medicine, imported from the US, was costing her mother a fortune.

Tim took a job flying in New Guinea, and after Beverley's father's funeral, she packed cotton frocks suitable for the tropics and flew to Lae, dressed demurely in pale blue and pearls. In 1951, Lae had 662 white people, and it appeared that most, if not all of them turned out to meet Tim's new bride at the airstrip, with – typically – a very boozy welcoming party. Walking to their new home, she was sweating one minute and being completely drenched in a sudden tropical downpour the next. When she looked around the inside of the galvanised tin shed with partial Arc-mesh walls where she was expected to live, she was uncharacteristically speechless! Tim had attempted to make it a little more homey by liberally splashing around gallons of awful green paint that had been given to him by friends for that purpose. He'd also lined the ceiling with a collection of parachutes that seemed to sag in odd places. Beverley discovered later that the strange shapes and lumps were snakes of all sizes, luxuriating in the unexpected comfort. There was a blue loo perched in the middle of an annexe, and she never did get used to the lack of privacy, nor the green frogs that leapt on her bare bum. Another regular adrenalin rush was provided by the appearance of spiders as big as dinner plates, while the sight of the local women walking along with a baby on one breast and a piglet on the other never failed to amaze her. There were many hilarious moments while she was learning to speak pidgin with her houseboy, Lamberto. Every aspect of life up there was about as far removed from what she was used to as you could imagine.

She got a job as secretary to the chief engineer of Qantas and enjoyed it immensely. Flying was very dangerous at times up there with rough landing strips, sudden cloud cover and treacherous thermals. When Tim was flying, she was often worried whether he'd make it safely onto the ground and back to her. Lae had a 230-inch yearly rainfall average, much of which fell between May and December. Clouds could suddenly close in, making it extremely difficult for a pilot to find a gap. Radio navigation aids were elementary in the '50s, but the New Guinea mountains blocked out the signals. A DCA officer told Beverley that 'New Guinea was being developed courtesy of the Pratt and Whitney company' (the engines that powered the DC3s). When Tim finally scored a job back with Qantas, they were given a nice house up on The Hill, as it was called, a definite step up the local social ladder. They should have been happy but somehow had drifted apart. With great sadness, they agreed to divorce.

A few months later, she found herself being courted in a mystifying but elaborate manner, by a fabulously handsome, vibrant, unforgettable character who was possibly the wildest and toughest man in New Guinea. Stanislau, or Stan, Rybarz had been an underground fighter during WW II for the Resistance movement against Germany and Russia, in his native Poland. He trained volunteers in using weapons and fighting tactics, organised sabotage operations and underground intelligence networks, and infiltrated prison camps, including Auschwitz, to gather evidence of what was going on inside them. In 1945, after Russia had occupied Warsaw and Stan was working his way back to find what was left of his family, he couldn't remember when he'd last had a bath or slept in a bed, or had a proper meal. He'd eaten grass to stay alive at times, and dog was his favourite food. At twenty-two, he couldn't remember how many men he had killed in many different ways to stay alive himself, but he knew much of the horror would probably never leave him.

When eventually he made his way to New Guinea in search of a new life, he was a man ready to seize whatever opportunities came his way to make something of himself and try to make up for his lost youth. Able to turn his hand to anything, he worked in road engineering, where he learnt everything he could, with a view to becoming a contractor himself. He had certainly wasted no time there catching up on all the female 'company' he'd missed out on during the war, and developed quite a reputation. But when he spotted Beverley, he knew she was 'the one' and that he must capture her heart. With all the cunning of a hunter, he planned his strategy to the nth degree. Eventually, the well-brought-up, young Adelaide lady fell head over heels with Stan the Wild Man, sending the Lae gossips into a frenzy. Perhaps it was his promise, in his Polish accent during their first romantic dinner together, to give her a baby, that did it?

Stanislau (or Stasiu, as his family in Poland fondly called him),

Antoni Rybarz whirled her off to his jungle hut by a river, taught her how to shoot to protect herself, and how to cook both local food and Polish recipes, then disappeared with his native 'boys' to resume working on the project he'd won a tender for: reconstructing the old Wau–Bulolo–Lae road. This was followed by work on the Markham Valley Road, and both these contracts involved building several bridges over wild, racing rivers. There was no way Beverley could communicate with him and when he arrived back at his hut (which had no electricity) one night, he informed her she must prepare 'plenty good *kaikai*' to feed fifteen important people! To describe Stan as blunt and demanding would be like saying Hugh Hefner was 'a bit of a flirt'. Amazingly, she managed to present a magnificent meal to the men who turned out to be from an Australian engineering company, interested in forming a business relationship with Stan. The fact she dressed in a Thai silk evening gown with pink satin strappy sandals matching the bow in her hair, somehow cooking and serving the food while teetering in high heels along the uneven boards of the hut, also impressed all of them, including Stan! To top it all off, she had Bach, Beethoven and Sinatra playing on her battery-operated record-player. The deal was struck and Stan looked set to make millions. But first, he informed Beverley in his matter-of-fact way that she would not only have to go back to her job to support him for a while, but also lend her considerable bank account to help him buy the machinery he needed. So they became partners in business as well as a grand love-match.

While Beverley earned the 'tucker money' at Burns Philp, the famous old trading firm, back in Lae, Stan went on to build many roads and bridges, which enabled major developments to commence – such as coffee and tea plantations – with Lae as the trading port. Beverley loved joining him at his work camps whenever she could, which entailed arranging for a temp to do her job for a couple of weeks. She admired not just the beautiful scenery, but also the constructions he was building, nearly always under immensely difficult and isolated conditions. The Papuans, who were so excited at how much the bridges and roads would change their lives, worshipped him and tried their best for him. The journey to get to these camps was always an adventure in itself – sometimes beginning with a short but scary-as-hell flight to and from bumpy airstrips. The one in Wau, for example, was built into a hillside and sloped steeply downwards, meaning that take-offs there were a heart-stopping experience, the plane racing down the steep slope to a precipice and 'falling or flying'! Then she'd continue on in big logging trucks or jeeps up and down terrifyingly precipitous tracks. Or she'd find herself on canoe journeys along croc-infested rivers or rafting through deep chasms with her heart in her mouth over the churning rapids. Beverley simply had to overcome her fears or she would rarely have seen her gorgeous man.

Her favourite district in New Guinea was the Chimbu Province, the beauty of which astonished her. She was dubious about visiting him at Kainantu, between Lae and Goroka, as it was known to be a place where people contracted the dreadful Kuru disease – known to locals as 'laughing sickness' – because victims died with a huge grin on their faces. Eventually she knew it was safe to go there when it was discovered that the disease was contracted by the locals not from a virus, but from eating the brains of their dead clan members during funeral practices.

At Goroka, she was mesmerised by the traditional dancing of the bizarre-looking Mud Men, who presented her with a shooting arrow that she still treasures. Stan had built several bridges in the valley carved by the massive Markham River, in a region known for earthquakes due to a fault line. When he took Beverley there on a trip to proudly show his bridges to her, a quake had struck since he'd finished his work, changing the course of the river. Consequently his sturdy bridges were standing over nothing! Typically, he laughed and said, 'Looks like I start all over again here!'

When his work took him away from Lae to Port Moresby to improve its airstrip, Beverley resigned – sadly – from her job at Burns Philp. She then suddenly went down with an acute bout of malaria, combined dangerously with blackwater fever, from which she was lucky to survive. She was sorry to leave beautiful tropical Lae, where she had many wonderful friends and where Stan had contributed greatly to building the large and lovely golf club, a social hub of the area. Port Moresby was completely different – more like an arid small town in Australia, with spindly gum trees. But here she was to get the most satisfying and interesting job of her life, as confidential secretary to David Marsh, Commissioner of the Central District of Papua. He was an outstanding man of great intelligence and integrity, with decades of experience working closely with the Papuans. In the early '50s, the district commissioners' responsibilities were immense and nothing was simple or easy. The Papuans and New Guinea people were enemies, and all tribes distrusted or simply hated each other. Only a few had received rudimentary education from missionaries; Western hygiene was non-existent. The indigenous people were protected by the representatives of the Australian government. Beverley was proud of that fact, and vastly amused when Stan was rebuked by a public servant about swearing at his 'boys'. He had up to 300 working for him and treated them well, and they loved him, but his mixture of Polish and English cursing was legendary. When he was told to stop it or else potentially lose the privilege of employing them – which meant he would be out of business – Beverley was treated to the immensely entertaining scenario of hearing him yelling at them, 'You b— [he stopped himself just in time!] jolly donkeys!'

One of the workers owed his life to her when she noticed his legs jerking around under a vehicle in Stan's workshop one day. In horror, she realised he was being electrocuted by a live wire that had fallen across his chest and was cooking him as well as shocking him. She pushed it away with the wooden handle of a spade. Thankfully, the hospital staff were able to eventually mend him. He was eternally grateful, but Beverley noticed he seemed a bit 'fused' after that.

Like David's work, Beverley's job at the administration building was significant and demanding. Her duties included recording everything that was said in land-title court cases, in both pidgin and English, screening the security files of everyone who applied to enter the country, and assisting with media statements to the outside world. David sent her to visit isolated villages, to 'get a feel' for that area and what was needed there. He did everything in his power to improve the lives of the indigenous people. During these expeditions, Beverley had many highly unusual experiences. One was learning, and having to calmly accept, a native method of greeting strangers, which entailed her having to stand perfectly still while they felt all over her body.

She vividly recalls her dismay on hearing that Papua New Guineans might be given independence. 'David Marsh was particularly concerned, as all of us Australians there were, that the United Nations and left-wing politicians in Australia, including Leader of the Opposition Gough Whitlam, were pushing for the grandstand gesture of giving Papua New Guinea independence, long before they were ready, and capable of governing themselves. I heard former Governor-General Sir Paul Hasluck, who was then Minister for the Territories, comment to David, "These people won't be ready for independence for another hundred years." ' (Whitlam eventually got his way. Self-government began in late 1973, with full independence from Australia formalised on 16 September 1975.)

On a short holiday to the geographically exquisite Madang, known as 'the Island of Contented Men', where Stan was tendering for contracts, he declared it was time for Beverley to stop working, marry him and have a baby. Naturally, she wondered how her conservative family would take to him, but on a holiday to Australia, he put on his Charming Stan hat, and won them all, especially her religious, refined mother! Their wedding in Port Moresby in 1957 was a huge and happy event. In 1960, everyone was overjoyed when it was known that little Jane was on the way – a baby with such larger-than-life parents was bound to be very special. As the day Beverley was due to give birth approached, Beverley's mother flew up to be there, and was shocked at the 'hospital' – yet another long tin shed with partial Arc-mesh walls. Jane arrived safely.

That night in the darkened hospital 'ward', Beverley woke to feel hands pinning her down, then mud being forced into her mouth to prevent her screaming, as men began raping her. In excruciating pain, she could smell the pig fat as she struggled to free her arms and throw them off. It went on and on, until a nurse walking in carrying a tray of pills screamed in shock, dropping the tray, and ran to get help. The men fled.

Nothing could be more unspeakable or more shocking than what happened to Beverley, the night of her daughter's birth. She could not bring herself to talk about it with anyone, including her mother. It was simply too terrible to describe or discuss. Of course, she knows now that she should have been flown out of there and treated for shock, but that didn't happen; and although she *was* in shock, she didn't realise it and tried to carry on, not confiding in anyone. The only people who knew were the investigating police and the nurse who witnessed it and had alerted the police. Somehow – at Beverley's fervent request – it was kept from both her mother and Stan, who was out in a bush camp where communications with civilisation were almost non-existent. The police willingly complied with her request to keep a lid on it, because they'd have known that Stan would have absolutely gone berserk, dealing out his own brand of justice. At their home, police found a well-worn path from a point in the road, leading through the jungle to their house, and sixteen peepholes drilled into the roof and walls. This news made her skin crawl – she had been being perved on in *every* room of the house for God knows how long.

During her violation, she had sensed some of them could have been white men. There were white men who had worked for Stan from time to time. The horrible result of this was that she no longer could trust *anyone*. On his return from the bush to see if his baby had arrived at last, he sensed something was terribly wrong with Beverley, as did her mother, but it was put down by them to 'baby blues'. Being a religious person, her mother insisted the child be christened before she returned to Australia. Somehow Beverley went through the motions of organising it, and during the ceremony she found the strength to force herself to act normally. Watching Stan drive off to first take her mum to fly back to good old safe and quiet Adelaide, then head back to his bush work camp, she was finally able to let go a flood of tears. On her own again with the baby, she found it extremely hard to cope with her fear. Were some of the perpetrators living right there in their compound among the

once-trusted house staff? (The guilty men were never found – identi-
fication proved too difficult.)

Somehow she soldiered on for nine long, terrible months, during
which Jane was her only source of happiness. Her baby also gave
her a reason to keep going, to try and not allow what had happened
to overwhelm her and ruin her life – or, at least, to prevent her from
being a doting mother. But finally the fear she lived with every day
and night when Stan was away became totally unbearable, and she
told him she had to go to Adelaide for a break. The man who loved
her could see that she needed to go, and knew he could not help
her himself to get over what was wrong. He was very fond of his
mother-in-law and hoped some time spent with her in civilised sur-
roundings would bring Beverley back to her old self.

When she walked off the plane, her mother was shocked by her
appearance. Her always-glamorous, vivacious daughter came down
the stairs, looking 'out of it', dishevelled and wearing slippers. With
typical Anglo-Saxon restraint, she merely took her granddaughter
out of her daughter's arms and said, 'You need a rest, dear. A long
rest.' She took over looking after Jane in her Adelaide home, with
enormous amounts of grandma pleasure, for the next five months,
until Beverley felt the time was right to move into a flat and get back
into the mainstream of life. Stan sent money for their upkeep and
visited when he could. In 1961, their business was doing extremely
well and they were financially secure.

Beverley's inherent kindness, which knows no bounds, saw her
unable to refuse a truly bold request from her crazy-as childhood
friend Carlien, whom she hadn't seen since their party-party-party
Sydney days. Life had not been kind to Carlien. Her husband had
left her, she was broke and unwell, incapable of properly raising
her two badly behaved, rude sons. To say they were undisciplined

and extremely difficult was a kind description. However, Beverley couldn't find it in her Phar-Lap-sized heart to say 'no' when Carlien asked if the three of them could move in with her. Carlien's life was a disorganised mess, she contributed nothing to the household except chaos, and Stan, during his next visit, was *not* pleased. The two boys behaved abominably to Beverley, their overly generous benefactor, and to little Jane. Stan doted on his daughter and when he saw this bullying going on, he told Beverley to chuck her parasitic boarder out immediately. Carlien did leave, but not until Beverley had promised her she would look after her boys. Most people would have said a big, loud, sensible 'NO!' but Beverley decided she would persevere with trying to train them and give them a home. 'It gave me something else to think about,' she says, with a characteristic downplay of her generosity.

One day when she had dashed across the road to the shop, leaving the children playing, the boys, who were eight and ten years older than Jane, tried to force her to drink a concoction they had mixed up with their chemistry set. Always blessed with a sensible disposition and high intelligence, Jane refused, went to get her coat from the hall, put it on and toddled off, aged just three, to find her mother at the shop. Fortunately Beverley was leaving the shop, saw her trying to look for a break in the traffic to cross the road and yelled out, 'Stop! Stay there!' Being a good child, Jane obeyed. Beverley hurried home and gave the fiends a well-deserved thrashing, telling them if they didn't stop being such monsters, she would have to put them in a home. She was thinking, 'If I end up in jail from doing this, it's worth it!' They began behaving in a slightly more acceptable manner, but Stan put his foot down during his next visit and Beverley organised their entry as boarders into a very good Catholic school. One brother went on to have an excellent career as a teacher, the other a highly successful and lucrative career in computers.

Beverley simply could not bring herself to return to New Guinea, as much as she had loved the country and its people. Jane flew up there regularly to have holidays with her father. Stan gradually accepted the hard fact that their marriage as they'd known it – the passion, the companionship – was over; but they stayed together as friends, never divorcing. He bought her a nice big house in Adelaide that faced a national park. Needing a new challenge to continue mending her life, Beverley turned the bottom storey into a creche. She felt that after looking after Carlien's boys she could handle any-thing any child could dish out! It was a great success and Jane was very happy with all her new playmates. Beverley gave the little chil-dren the incentive to be well-behaved at all times, with the promise that if they were good all day, they could choose a lolly to enjoy before their mothers arrived to collect them. She felt like the Pied Piper leading them all down to the lolly shop. Although she loved running the creche, it was time to get back into what she excelled at – being a secretary – so she closed it after a year and threw herself into building a new house on land beside her old family home.

She wanted to brush up her secretarial skills, and took a job in the administration of the Elderly Citizens organisation – a boring job but it served its purpose. She battled to succeed in mastering the newfangled golf-ball typewriter. When she saw a job ad for secre-tary to the CEO of Rank Xerox, a large company that sold office machines, she secured an interview and dressed to the nines for the first time in quite a while. They hired her and she found herself working for a dynamic organisation, mixing with twenty high-fly-ing, sharp and witty salesmen in a stimulating, fun atmosphere. Her boss was great to work for – a fascinating Scotsman who had been a squadron leader during WW II and was a gentleman with a professional attitude. She loved dressing up and looking her best after so long in the doldrums, but was a little taken aback to discover eventually that the salesmen, who she thought were so charming, were actually having bets before the Friday night parties, as to who would be first to get her into 'the cot'. She forgave them for that because they were, after all, only men and that sort of thinking was only natural to them.

Society was starting to become more materialistic in the mid-'60s and these men pushed themselves hard and were pushed hard to make sales. Their commission was huge, and when a Rank Xerox machine worth at least $1000 was sold, a bell was rung, a big fuss was made over the successful man and yet another party started up. After a couple of years, Beverley tired of the frenetic pace, the pressure and the superficiality. She left to take up the position of secretary to the director of the Children's and Adolescent Family Health Service. It was not only an interesting job in a more relaxed atmosphere, but it was with a worthwhile organisation that was accomplishing worthy deeds. The director and her executives were all good, smart women who contributed hugely to the welfare of neglected children. They also started up the first phone-in service for mothers who had no idea how to look after their babies. Some of them couldn't even boil an egg. Beverley loved being part of a genuine, intelligent team of women helping these unfortunate girls and their children.

She became embroiled in the controversy when the nurses associated with the service wanted to run it entirely, without the doctors who were on call for it. Beverley sided with the doctors, who insisted that they didn't want to run the service, but that it could not run properly without them and their professional skills.

Beverley felt that the nurses were led by 'stroppy feminists resist-
ing the [to them] superior attitude of the male doctors', and that
consequently the nurses were making decisions they were not qualified to make. This scenario became quite dramatic and frustrating,
and eventually, tired of the politics and bitchiness going on, Beverley
reluctantly retired, aged sixty-seven. Full of energy, her intention
was to throw all her efforts into running an orchard she purchased
in the Adelaide Hills.

During her 'third life' back in Adelaide after New Guinea, she took
many holidays to the US, often staying with a cousin at Beverley
Hills. When Jane was in her early teens, it was fun showing her everything over there that, in those days, was a big eye-opener. Before
Australia 'caught up', America was far ahead in many ways: the
flash houses with swimming pools, the big cars and freeways, the
theme parks, and, of course, the glamour of the movie industry.
They mixed with many interesting people, including her cousin
June's sister-in-law and best friend, the beautiful actress Jean Peters
(who starred in *Three Coins in the Fountain*). Jean had been married to Howard Hughes for fifteen years, and during his declining
years was the only person allowed in by his minders to see him.
The former farm girl and churchgoer still had keys to everything
he owned. Jean told Beverley that the only accurate book written
about him is by Peter H Browne and Pat H Broeske, simply titled
Howard Hughes.

After working for years in offices, Beverley loved the country
life on her orchard with lots of pets and farm animals. The orchard
produced strawberries, various other fruits, flowers and lucerne. As
well as Jane's pony-club horses, there was enough good grass to take

other horses on agistment. She never did master backing a horse float very well and on pony-club days the cry went up: 'Look out, here's Beverley!' Always a sucker to give strays a home, she found herself taking in a much-neglected, ancient ex-racehorse, Eddie, a foul-tempered, biting beast that anyone else would have consigned to the Pal factory. Apart from biting as many humans as he possibly could, Eddie also became famous for occasionally stopping the Adelaide-to-Melbourne train. When he heard the train labouring up the hill to intrude on his peace and quiet, he would open his gate and walk onto the line, standing between the tracks and staring the train down till it halted. To the passengers' delight, he would be trying to nip the driver and his offsider while they tried to move the cranky old bugger off the line. He was almost a tourist attraction!

Stan adored his daughter and visited them frequently from New Guinea. When Jane graduated to riding in one-day events, the big, attractive thoroughbred mare he bought for her turned out to be, unfortunately, not sound, but this predicament was to introduce them to the fun of becoming racehorse owners. The mare, Tresillian, was sent to a stallion and each of the three foals she subsequently produced were winners. Beverley found there's nothing quite like the thrill of seeing a horse you own win a race! Jane went on to become a state-champion eventer before the burden of university studies forced her to quit competing.

Unexpectedly, they received the terrible news that Stan had had a stroke in New Guinea. A female doctor in the hospital there became attracted to him and they moved to a property on the New South Wales coast. She cared for him until he died from a second stroke, several years later. It was hard to believe that this larger-than-life man, a legend in the jungles of New Guinea, where he had accomplished so much, was gone. Beverley began writing the story of his achievements – *The Bridge Builder* – and it was published in 2005 by Wakefield Press. The cover photo is an eye-catching, dramatic image of a well-built, handsome white man, surrounded by black Papuans in vivid costumes. He is wearing a prestigious headdress presented to him by them, in honour of and in gratitude for his superhuman efforts that changed their lives. The book contains the dedication, 'To Jane. To quote Stan: "We did good here." '

By then, Jane, who'd changed from a career in dentistry to accountancy, at which she excelled, had established her own practice in Cairns, then sold it and became the financial manager for famous movie producer Baz Luhrmann. After several years in the frenetic pace of the movie industry, she decided it was time for a quieter life and before filming began on *The Great Gatsby*, took on a position in Sydney with new and very different challenges. With her mother's blessing, she began searching for a piece of paradise they could share 'within cooee' of the Gosford area, which they both loved. At almost eighty, Beverley was finding running her orchard becoming too hard, and the income hardly worth her efforts due to the government allowing imported fruit into Australia. Where hundreds of people had once prospered in her area for generations, growing first-rate fruit for their fellow Australians to buy and enjoy, there were farms going broke, families no longer being able to work together as a team running a family business, neglected land and properties in receivership . . . very sad.

Beverley had also taken on the gargantuan task of compiling her former boss David Marsh's memoirs after she encouraged him to chronicle them before it was too late. He was then in his mid-eighties, and dictated to her his four decades of amazing adventures and great achievements in New Guinea. She then had to sort them all into chronological order and type them ready for presentation to a publisher, a task she recently finished. Her next project is writing a novel based on fact, about the terrible struggle a close friend, a professional man, has endured due to racial hatred. A person from the same profession has continually attempted to smear his reputation and ruin his life, because of religious differences. Beverley believes it is a story that must be told.

Jane – the light of her mother's life – found a beautiful small acreage property at Narara, a few k's out of Gosford, that was perfect for their needs. After four years there, they are both as happy as the first day they moved in. Typically, Beverley brought with her from South Australia an old friend of many years, Brian, who needed a home. After a stroke led to the onset of early dementia, he needed constant care and was going to end up in an institution. Beverley couldn't bear the thought of that, and this once-bright gentleman (now completely unaware of how lucky he is) is part of a happy household, instead of staring in a void at four walls all day back in Adelaide. Brian is included in all outings, treated with respect and loving friendship by both Jane and her amazingly generous (and exceedingly patient!) mother with the heart of pure gold. But wait . . . there's more. She has also taken on giving a home to, and caring lavishly for, not one or two, but *three* previously neglected dogs, seized from their cruel owner by authorities, who never expected *anyone* to take them on. They'd been used as breeding machines and their reproductive days were over. Apart from being starved of both food and affection, the dogs were ageing, suffering from a variety of complaints and completely untrained as well. When Beverley heard about them and saw the 'three sad little faces', she could not allow them to be put down. All their health problems have been fixed now, and the lucky little pop-eyed buggers live the life of Riley with their fleecy beds and gourmet meals.

Then there's the chooks. Surely Beverley is the only person whose chooks enjoy 'pre-dinner nibblies' each afternoon? Whatever she's enjoying with her Dewar's out on the verandah, the 'girls' enjoy also. (This writer has not given up trying very hard to get her to adopt me.) One thing is for certain: when she sits back with her 'sundowner', waiting for Jane to get home from the city, this fascinating lady who's lived life and loved it certainly has miles of wonderful memories to look back on and enjoy. Of course, she's always planning her next project too . . . surely the word 'fabulous' was coined to describe one-off ladies like Beverley Rybarz!

13.

Spencer Spinaze, MBE

CATTLEMAN AND CREATOR OF NEW ITALY

An intriguing, little-known chunk of Australia's history has been preserved in the middle of the scrub in north-east New South Wales. Drivers travelling just south of Ballina will see a sign 'NEW ITALY – Tourists Welcome'. While most people are driving too fast to pull up, many are curious enough to go back and take a look. They are all astounded at what they see, and what they learn. A collection of old buildings have been restored to show Australians and overseas tourists how a large group of Italian migrants who settled there many years ago worked, lived and died. They had journeyed there from Sydney in the 1880s to pioneer a tract of land on the Richmond River. Like many Italian migrants after them, they started with nothing but their will and energy, and they all did well, transforming the scrub-covered land into farms. Their descendants, now spread all over Australia, can be proud of them – very proud.

None could be prouder than Spencer Spinaze (Spin-ah-zay), who decided thirty-three years ago that all Australians should know the story of these resourceful migrants. To read about their struggles in the available literature is amazing, but it's a far more enriching and enlightening experience to visit Spencer's New Italy tourist complex to see firsthand where they toiled and to admire the old buildings that now house the photos and relics of their enterprises.

This significant site is an eye-opener to Aussies like me who thought they were well-read in our history. Stories like the settlement of New Italy should have been part of our curriculum, and should be taught in schools now. Its relevance to the development of our nation should be understood by Australian children, and they would definitely not be bored by it. Just the initial story of how these particular migrants arrived here is a riveting, sometimes horrifying tale of treachery, fortitude and death. Set out on storyboards at the entrance, the terrible saga brings audible gasps and surprised comments from those reading it. It's a story worthy of a big-screen movie.

In 1878, the Marquis de Rays, a French nobleman seeking a way to rebuild his fortunes, hit on the idea of starting a new colony, La Nouvelle France, to the north-east of Australia, on the island of New Britain in present-day Papua New Guinea. He found many willing investors to put money into his scheme, but he then needed to find people who would leave their homelands, settle there and start producing wealth. He proposed to give each settler a four-roomed house on 20 acres at an immediate cost of 1800 francs, or they could pay it off over five years. For those who chose the latter option, there was an upfront fee to board the ship – 250 francs for a single male, or 1000 francs for a whole family.

To the struggling farmers of the Venetia region of northern Italy, whom de Rays targeted, the scheme promised a future for them and their children that didn't exist where they lived. Their recent history – which included heavy warfare to free themselves from Austrian rule, regular crop losses due to floods, and the crushing burden of heavy taxes – meant they were eager to try life in a new land. Among those leaving were the fifteen members of two Spinaze families – Spencer's ancestors – from the village of Campiglione. By early 1880, fifty families and a few single men were ready to live under sunnier skies. However, by then, the French government had forbidden emigration to de Rays' proposed destination he called Port Breton, due to it being a 'sterile environment incapable of sustaining agriculture'. The Italian government also did everything it could to stop its citizens getting involved with the highly dodgy venture. The Royal Investigation Bureau of Milan had instructed authorities that no passport was to be issued to any Italian wanting to go to de Rays' 'colony'. Warning bells should have rung about this fraudster then, but were ignored by the desperate, half-starved people. Even when they found out they were to be refused passports, they still persevered, sneaking to the port of Marseille. Had they been able to foresee a fraction of what they were about to endure, they would have gone anywhere but on de Rays' ship.

While they waited for the vessel, their accommodation arrangements were so squalid that the local health authorities tried to get the Italian government to send them back, but the Italian government felt that should be at de Rays' expense. Meanwhile, de Rays arrived and managed to mesmerise the unfortunate people. They demonstrated noisily in front of the Italian consulate, until finally the Italian government wiped its hands of them and allowed them to leave.

When they arrived at Port Breton, they were shocked to find there was nothing – not even fertile soil – to make the place suitable for a colony, except for plenty of water. The promised 'four-roomed houses on 20-acre farmlets' were nowhere to be seen – a myth, a terrible lie. At last they realised they were victims of a monstrous deceit, but set to work trying to build shelters, clear the land and plant the seeds they'd brought. Deaths from starvation and hard toil swiftly began to occur. It's harrowing to imagine the sorrow as they buried their babies, children and parents, almost on a daily basis. When the monsoons began, it wasn't just the very young and the elderly who were succumbing, but also able-bodied men and women. An SOS was sent by ship to Sir Henry Parkes, Colonial Secretary of Australia, who allowed them to sail to Sydney as 'shipwrecked mariners'. When they sailed through The Heads of Sydney Harbour in April 1881, only 217 people remained out of the 317 who had set sail, full of hope, just nine months earlier.

Sydney's Italian community, the press and the general public all rallied to help them. Parkes arranged for them to be housed at the Exhibition Hall in the Domain, given food and clothing and offered temporary employment by members of the by-then prosperous Sydney community, to allow them to get on their feet again. He was later made Commander of the Crown of Italy by a grateful Italian government. The people he helped were determined to regroup as soon as possible and form a farming settlement somewhere. It didn't take them long. The Northern Rivers districts had just recently been thrown open for expansion. Antonio Pezzutti and Rocco Caminotti were first there to take up selections (Crown-owned acreage parcels which were put up for ballot) south of the Richmond River, where its two arms meet, at Swan Bay near Coraki, already a busy timber port for the cedar industry. They were followed in 1882 by a group of seven of the Venetia families, and then nineteen more the following year. No doubt there were big celebrations when news reached them that de Rays had been extradited from Spain, where he'd been evading arrest, and sentenced to four years in prison for what he'd done to them.

The Italian settlers pooled all their resources and helped each other with everything. They built ingenious houses from bark, wattle, daub and pisé. They dug 12-foot-deep wells, plus cellars for their wine and salamis, and built clay-brick ovens to bake polenta. Within a year of the first families' arrival at what had become known as 'New Italy', a travelling journo for the *Sydney Tribune* reported they were growing all types of fruits and vegetables and farming pigs, poultry and cattle. They had called their settlement 'La Cella Venezia' (The Venetia Cell), as a symbol of their closeness after what they had been through together, not because they were closed to outsiders. On the contrary, the Italians were known for their friendliness as well as hard toil and teamwork, and had a reputation for being fine, honest people to deal with. The men did work such as cutting cane and hauling timber, while the women ploughed and harvested the fields, which allowed them to pay off their selections, which cost 1 pound per acre, buy their livestock and machinery, and establish a sawmill, blacksmith shop and so on. By the late 1880s, they were all well and truly on their feet.

Their resourcefulness knew no bounds. Angelo Roder, who ran sheep, designed his own spinning and knitting machines for their wool. If you give a thought to what that actually entailed – building a machine from scratch with few or no necessary 'bits 'n' pieces' available (no hardware shop!) – you realise how incredible it is. In 1891, when the settlement was chosen by the Parkes government to begin a silk industry (Venetia had been a hub of the silk industry in Italy), and given a grant to get started, they invented their own reeling machine – another ingenious achievement. Acres of mulberry trees were planted to feed the silkworms, which were housed in bushel bags stretched over rough timber frames. When they'd first started, the silkworms were kept and bred in everyone's houses. A disastrous fire in 1893 wiped their silk-producing business out and crippled the settlement for a while. From then on, only individuals carried on producing silk. Dairying then became New Italy's most prominent industry. Because of the poor quality of the soil there, the settlers had to work twice as hard as those on good land, both to improve it and to nurture their crops and pastures.

These assets of tremendous inventiveness, courage and fore-sight to try something new, and the desire and ability to improve on nature, were passed on through the generations to Spencer Spinaze. Apart from continually nurturing his land and his livestock, this quietly spoken gentleman was the first person in the region, and one of the first in Australia, to try running Brahman cattle. In the 1950s, that took a lot of courage. The strange-looking, lop-eared, hump-backed animals were despised by the majority of cattlemen, who were also accusing anyone importing them of being hell-bent on ruining the beef industry. There were nasty scenes at saleyards and showgrounds, among usually affable country blokes.

Far from the image of his hot-tempered, northern-Italian fore-bears, Spencer is the opposite of a fiery bugger, and smiled off all the insults he endured, confident in his judgement that these were the cattle of the future – the breed that, when bred with British cattle, would introduce tick resistance, and thus make producing beef in coastal, tick-prone regions far more lucrative.

Born in 1924, he grew up on a dairy farm at Gundurimba, near Lismore. As a kid, on winter mornings, he'd stand in fresh cowpats to warm up his bare feet. His parents and his grandparents, who also had a big influence on him, instilled in him the values of thrift, hard work and education. With his lunch of bread and dripping and half an orange, he walked 3 miles to school, which he did not enjoy attending. He was shy and the teacher seemed to dislike him, burdening him with insults. This mean man regularly told Spencer to 'Go to the abattoir and get yourself a set of brains' – an insult that crushed his spirit and stayed with him for a long time. No one likes to be told they are stupid. He was to prove that teacher very wrong, as he made his way through a successful life of achievement and acknowledgement. Leaving high school at Lismore at fifteen, as most boys did, he immediately got a job as delivery boy at Piercy and Nott – wholesale merchants who supplied groceries to smaller shops. Because he'd been brought up on a farm, he already knew how to work hard and do tasks properly, such as balancing wooden boxes of tinned goods on his pushbike – not easy! But the place where he really wanted to work was at the produce and seed-merchant firm E J Eggins, because he was very interested in crops and harvesting seeds. It was a large and prosperous firm that also sold farm machinery and many products for farmers, with two other thriving branches at Casino and Kyogle.

Spencer eventually scored a job with them, rising to an executive position, as manager of their seeds and produce division, and enjoyed working for them for forty-two years, with four years (in between) spent in the RAAF during WW II. He was originally based at Uranquinty, repairing planes that had been crashed by trainee pilots, but a sergeant told him about a job that no one wanted at Amberley base in South-East Queensland. It entailed keeping the boilers going for a week, then having two weeks off. This appealed to Spencer because on his time off he could return to his family's farm and help out. Initially he hitchhiked to get home, and later he rode his motorbike.

After the war he went back into his old job that had been kept for him, and finally plucked up the courage to ask a girl he'd had his eye on – a pretty secretary named Doris Clarke – if she'd like to go with him to see *Gone with the Wind*. She agreed and her family were shocked when he arrived to take her out on his noisy Indian motorbike. Spencer knew she was the girl for him, but had to jump over an obstacle to make his dream girl his bride. When she told him her parents would never consent to allow her to marry a Roman Catholic (especially one who rode a motorbike), he immediately said, 'I'll become a Presbyterian.' In those days, that was a gesture of immense significance. He even became a committee member of the East Lismore Presbyterian Church, and thus began his many years of community service, being roped into committees hell west and crooked, including the Church of England North Coast Children's Home, nearby Alstonville's House With No Steps disability service, the Guide Dogs Association, the Seed Merchants Association, and the Lismore Show (better known as the North Coast Show). He was to be President of the Seed Merchants Association for twenty-seven years and President of the Show for twenty-three years.

When his four children, Ken, Margaret, Merran and Jenny, were small, he bought a 624-acre property 10 miles out of Casino. It was in a beautiful and peaceful spot, where the family would enjoy their weekends from then on. They continued to live in Lismore, because Spencer needed the income from his job, which he enjoyed, and the children were settled in their school.

The property's quaint 1905 timber house, lined with rosewood, had been built fifty years earlier with timber drawn by bullocks from Dorrigo. There was a lot of work to keep everyone in the family occupied because the property needed a lot of improving. He was happy to buy a cheaper block of poor-quality land because he knew he had the expertise to transform it. Aptly nicknamed 'Poverty Valley' by all his Lismore friends who visited there when he first bought it, the previous owners had struggled to scratch a living there, but Spencer could see its potential. The fact its water-holes dried up regularly was its main problem, but he was sure that where there were patches of grass that 'looked different', there would be underground springs. The first thing he did was scoop out a hole with a dozer. The next morning, it was full of water, and the level has never altered.

Improving the pasture was his field of expertise, but first there was some hard yakka in store for him. The hardwood stumps everywhere, left by the early settlers and timber cutters, had to be removed before he could get in with a tractor to remove the swamp tussocks and blady grass. With little money to spend, he lashed out on the biggest steel mallet he could buy, a 14-pounder, and smashed the stumps to the ground using a young bloke's muscles (his).

He'd observed the newfangled Victa lawnmowers that had just come onto the market and – *brainwave!* – using the same principle but on a bigger scale, he virtually built a slasher from scratch, to tackle the tussocks and blady grass. Pulled behind his little old Fergie tractor, it gave a 2-metre-wide cut, down to 18 centimetres height above the soil. This cut off the rank top growth, leaving the sweeter, lower pasture.

To improve the paspalum and couch grasses that grew on his property on the poor-quality soil, he decided to apply phosphate. As he couldn't afford a tip truck, he shovelled it from a flat-top truck into a fertiliser spreader. Then he found it was killing the earthworms, and researched a solution to that problem. He discovered that Alrock fertiliser had a high phosphate content but didn't contain whatever killed good microbes. The problem was, the factory had closed down. More research revealed there was a factory in Gympie producing a similar product. His next step was to begin establishing carpet grass, which also thrives on poor soil, so he could harvest the seed to sell to the US – a second income apart from live beef. Revenue from the seeds has always paid for his annual phosphate dressing, but for the past five years he has achieved the same result by understocking even more than he had always done in previous years, as a management strategy. (For city readers, 'understocking' means running less cattle per acre than your property is rated – by experts – at being capable of supporting.)

Through financial necessity, he started his cattle herd with the only cows he could afford – neglected, culled dairy cows for 2 pounds each. The saleyard staff and stock agents referred to them as 'dires': in such poor condition they were close to death. Drenched and dehorned on arrival, they were about to be saved with science. As the old-time Devonshire farmers used to growl assertively, 'The answer lies in the soil.' Spencer had studied nutritional deficiencies in that area and mixed up a lick for them that was his own concoction of salt, copper, cobalt and selenium. It's one thing to research solutions or cures, but a wise investigator then studies the reactions and results, which is what this thinking man did. He found it fascinating that the cows would immediately go to the troughs and start licking at something that wasn't particularly tasty or in their diet or familiar to them – their bodies were telling them they simply needed to get that stuff down their necks. He observed how they'd lick at the troughs for three to four minutes, then go and graze for about twenty minutes, then have a drink, and repeat the cycle. Within three weeks, those weak, starving animals were transformed.

He continued to buy these pathetic animals that no one at the saleyards around the district wanted, brought them back to health, and joined them ('in holy matrimony') to beef bulls. A herd of cattle builds up surprisingly fast, and eventually he had enough crossbreds coming along that he could begin selling some of the dairy cows.

When he sold eighty-four head to a young bloke who was going to start a dairy farm at Woodenbong, he was asked 'Where did you get these?' by a farmer who'd bred some of them and sold them, and didn't recognise them as the same cows! The young farmer went on to have the highest-producing herd in the district the next year, with those once near-dead animals.

In all this time, Spencer and his family only had the weekends to do all the necessary work on the property, but they all pulled together with a common goal. He kept buying and selling cows until eventually his block was stocked with excellent cattle, all fat and shiny. Because they needed dipping every three weeks – a time-consuming chore – and because he was a natural innovator willing to experiment with anything new that might improve his herd and his life, he was interested in trying out the 'yaks' – as Brahmans, then new to Australia, were scathingly called – to test their tick-resistant qualities.

Success! There was definitely less dipping required for the offspring. After years of heavy culling to weed out any trace of flightiness, bad temperament and poor conformation, Spencer was one of the first cattlemen in Australia to have a herd of purebred, big-framed, beefy Brahmans that were docile. His calm mustering and handling methods ensured they were both quiet and friendly – dispelling the image neighbours and visitors had of crazed, snorting, charging, fence-jumping ratbags. He learnt there were twenty-two strains of the breed, and to avoid Brahmans with long, narrow faces, which were usually poor 'doers' – difficult to fatten – and temperamental.

At agricultural shows, Spencer's cattle were great ambassadors for the breed, and soon his house was full of championship ribbons and trophies. One highly unusually marked bull he named Christmas even caught the eye of Prince Charles. Having just opened Murwillumbah Show, the royal was being driven to his next engagement when he spotted Christmas being led by Spencer from the Grand Parade, and asked his driver to stop. Spencer enjoyed a great old chinwag with Charles. In fact, when his driver pointed at his watch to hurry him up, Charles told him to pull his head in, and continued yarning with Spencer about Christmas.

Christmas loved going to shows so much that he would often voluntarily climb up into the trailer parked beside a shed and wait for Spencer to take him. He'd look around at Spencer mournfully, as if to say, 'Please take me to a show, boss.'

In the 1950s and early '60s, Spencer had a weekly half-hour show on Radio 2LM called *While the Billy Boils*, during which he talked about every subject of interest to the Man on the Land. He was able to talk from firsthand experience about the benefits of infusing Bos Indicus blood into coastal herds, as well as other subjects, such as how to harvest seeds, horse-breaking methods, and controlling blady grass. He never prepared anything for the show – he just went on-air and talked as if he was yarning on the stockyard rail with mates. Every farmer within range tuned in to listen to Spencer.

In 1963, he organised a reunion of the descendants of the New Italy settlers, which was a tremendous success. Big families that had spread far and wide across Australia were reunited, to pay homage to what the Venetia farmers had endured to give their families a better life in a new land. The ceremony was held at the monument Spencer had organised to be built to their memory, beside the Pacific Highway, on the edge of the land where they once worked, loved and lived.

In the early '60s, Spencer was able to purchase the neighbouring property, Wingara, meaning 'Valley of Springs' – a beautiful, lush former dairy farm of 880 acres. Within a few months he was able to finally move from Lismore and live there as a full-time farmer. The girls caught the school bus to Casino. Spencer commuted to Lismore frequently to keep up his commitments with a number of community organisations. Like many people, he'd been very shy when first called upon to stand up and speak through a microphone; however, this changed when he became a founding member of Toastmasters. His newly developed speaking skills were soon to become extremely useful. He was approached to become President of the Show Society, which had fallen on hard times and was in financial trouble. He replied by pointing out that he wasn't even a committee member, but the people who had asked him had done so because they knew he was the man to lead the society out of the mess it was in. Spencer threw his heart and soul into not only saving the show, but turning it right 'round back to its former status as the biggest show in New South Wales after the Sydney Royal.

He struck a mutually beneficial deal with local stock-car enthusiasts to start a Saturday night speedway, similar to that held in the Royal Queensland Show's ring, which was hugely popular. First, a solid, safe fence between the track and the spectators had to be built. Mustering a team of volunteers, Spencer supervised, hands-on, the erection of an oval wall of local ironbark-timber planks, 8 inches wide by 2.5 inches thick, bolted to the posts with 8800 bolts, each 9 inches long. He and his committee and the volunteers often worked till midnight, selflessly spending all that time and energy to create something that would benefit the community.

All who had opposed the speedway for various reasons had to

eat humble pie later when it proved to be a tremendous success. For years to come it was the main financial income to maintain and improve the showground, and to put on the subsequent shows – including the cost of paying entertainers, advertising, etc.

Lismore is nearly always drenched at showtime, and Spencer's first year was no exception – in fact, it was even worse than usual. Naturally, he became more and more worried as the first day approached, with no let-up from the bursting clouds. The committee were nervously asking him if he would cancel. The 'showies' and horse event competitors were already arriving, slopping around in the mud. After a lot of thought, he asked his committee members if they would back his decision to spend 200 pounds – a lot of money then, especially to a cash-strapped Show Society – on advertising on Radio 2LM to urge the public to support their show, rain, hail or shine.

To give the ads more impact, he voiced them himself. 'Come in your gumboots, or bare feet if you have to!' he urged the people of Lismore – and they did. On show day, to his immense relief, several thousand gumboots marched through the turnstiles! This was the late '60s, before the concrete paths that now run everywhere were laid.

Another new idea of his that he had to persuade many people to accept was employing the boys from the North Coast Children's Home as cleaners on the grounds during and after the show. These were homeless, neglected youths from difficult, tragic or undesirable circumstances. Even the local police warned him he was taking a big risk giving them this responsibility and that some of them had been involved in vandalism and petty theft. Spencer assured them they would be all right and that it would be good for them. His method of channelling their thoughts into doing something constructive and being good citizens, was to address them thus: 'You fellows make sure you keep a sharp lookout for anyone not doing the right thing on this showgrounds. If you see anything happening or anything suspicious, you report it to the police. Now, I'm relying on you to do that.' Wide-eyed, they nodded at this 'decent old bloke' who was not just being kind to them, but trusting them.

They did an excellent job and when Spencer paid them, he praised them for their work. A little red-headed boy, about ten years old, burst into tears. When Spencer asked him what was wrong, he sobbed, 'It's the first time anyone has praised me for anything.'

Within four years, the Show Society was well and truly in the black once more and Spencer was your classic modest local hero. He relished the challenge of finding new ways to entice people to continue supporting their show. One gimmick he dreamt up was issuing a challenge on-air to a Radio 2LM personality, to race him barefoot around the showground pulling a showgirl entrant in a trotting gig. The crowd loved it.

A large part of any country show was the parading of livestock by members of Rural Youth. Each year, Spencer arranged for every high school student in the district – usually around 600 of them – to visit the field day held at Wollongbar Research Station, to receive instruction on showing and judging livestock, poultry and veggies. This exercise would result in many of them – even students who weren't from farms – joining Rural Youth and becoming involved in exhibiting at shows.

Spencer ran the show for twenty-three years, till he decided he'd 'done enough' – a major understatement – and he resigned hoping new blood would come in. The Royal Agricultural Society presented him with a great honour, the 'Freedom of the Shows' award, allowing him entry into, and VIP treatment at, every show in New South Wales. He was also awarded a Member of the Order of the British

Empire (MBE) the following year in 1982, for his years of service to his community.

The MBE was richly deserved. A prime example of his commendable efforts was during the 1974 floods in the region, when he took it upon himself to phone the police and tell them they should be evacuating people in low-lying areas. He'd received a phone call during the night from Eureka Customs on the Richmond River to tell him 12 inches of rain had fallen in the hours leading up to midnight and heavy rain was still falling, so a big flood was certain to hit Lismore next day. The person had phoned Spencer because he was sure he would act immediately on the warning. Spencer rang the weather bureau to get further information, then at 3 a.m. phoned Lismore's Police Inspector and told him that a massive flood would hit the town between 8 and 8.30 a.m., and that police cars with sirens going should be immediately despatched to tell people to get out and move to higher ground. The Inspector replied, 'I can't do that,' to which Spencer insisted, 'Get permission from Sydney, right now, and if they waste any time, just do it. You can blame me if you get into trouble.' A wall of floodwater hit the town at 8.15 a.m.

Spencer made many things happen in his town. In 1981, a hundred years after the de Rays settlers arrived in Australia, he spread the word all over the country for New Italy descendants to attend a second, bigger reunion. When the initial response made it clear there were going to be far too many people to hold it at New Italy, he arranged to use the showground. As the day approached, rain was bucketing down, day after day. He was driven mad by people urging him to cancel it, including the police, who were fielding hundreds of phone calls from every state of people unsure whether to leave. Spencer held out till the last day, hoping the rain would stop, because he knew that many people had already left to travel there.

Finally he had to postpone it till October, but 600 people still turned up and had to be catered for. Spencer planned the meal to reflect what the settlers ate, so the main ingredients were salami and sweet potato.

On the October date, he and everyone else involved in the organisation of the reunion were stunned to welcome not 1000, nor 2000, but *3000* attendees! That posed a few teensy problems logistically, especially when the volunteer cooks in the new pavilion blew out the power. All the food had to be taken to the hospital and cooked there, then transported back to the showground.

Spencer put his idea to the crowd of preserving the history of New Italy with a museum on the old settlement site, and asked for donations. The money raised bought 14 acres of land from a grandson of a settler. It was situated off the Pacific Highway, where the original settlement site was located. Spencer, whose father had been the youngest survivor of the de Rays expedition, found himself president of yet another organisation: the New Italy committee.

Working bees then began to erect the first of the museum buildings. After Spencer researched the best way to make mud bricks, the Apex Club of nearby Woodburn volunteered to make them as their new project. Spencer's interest in mud bricks stemmed from a story he'd read about them being successfully used as the floor of a hotel in Canada. The bricks for New Italy were treated with linseed oil for a lovely shine and they remained firmly in place.

The New Italy complex became Spencer's pride and joy. A lot of sceptics said it wouldn't attract many people, but they were wrong – and now that it's on the 'grey nomads' map, its future is assured. In 1982 the Italian Consulate in Sydney presented him, on behalf of the Italian government, with a knighthood. The beautiful medal sits beside his MBE. A man who gets things done, in his own quiet way, Spencer has many achievements to be proud of. Perhaps his life is summed up in a few sentences put to me by his nephew John Barnes, current President of New Italy, who I met there after my tour. 'Spencer is a self-made man whose success can be put down to his independence – his freedom of thought that has made him such an innovator,' he says. 'As far as his career on the land goes, he is more than a farmer – he is a scientific but practical agriculturalist with the ability to blend technology with sound practices in an economically viable manner. Spencer is always improving things, for example bloodlines and pastures. He's a thoughtful person, generous with his time and advice, a deep thinker, well liked within his large family and circle of friends, and throughout his community.'

Sadly, Doris passed away in 2012, after sixty-four years of love and support, always at her husband's side. She just loved being with Spencer at Wingara. Her grave is on a peaceful hillside there and is visited every morning without fail by her border-collie-cross dog Bob, who spends some time there, then goes back home to Spencer.

Jenny, Margaret and Ken often visit and help with the cattle work. Their sister, Merran, lives in Melbourne but visits when she can. Like all farmers, Spencer keeps himself busy with chores, and his favourite relaxation after a hard day is sitting on his verandah with his thoughts and a cuppa, admiring his first-class cattle. Unfortunately these days, the word 'gentleman' is used erroneously, particularly by the media, but Spencer Spinaze thoroughly deserves the description and is a role model whose ethics and character all young Australian lads should aspire to emulate.

14.

Neville Greenwood

STOCK AGENT AND AUCTIONEER

Having always stood in complete awe of extremely talented auctioneers, I looked forward to meeting one of the best, Neville Greenwood, of Quirindi in New South Wales.

A successful auctioneer is not only an expert in his field – be it livestock, real estate or antiques – but also a market expert, psychologist, diplomat and entertainer all rolled into one. During his long and illustrious career, Neville was all of those things, and has retained the latter skill during his retirement, entertaining people with his hilarious yarns about both his auctioneering days and 'the good old days'. Up there on the auctioneer 'catwalk' in front of a crowd, you need to be quick on your feet and as sharp as a tack. A naturally witty feller, Neville has a comical turn of phrase and a smiley face that endears him to all. He has the appearance of a gentleman and the twinkling eyes of a larrikin.

The first things he auctioned off as a boy were his sister's plaits. Another sister had snipped them off to stop her sucking her thumb, which she did while twirling them. No amount of bitter aloes put on her thumb would stop her, so when this drastic action was taken, Neville attempted to inject a bit of humour among the wailing and drama by auctioning off the plaits. Even back then, he showed natural talent as an auctioneer.

The year 1932 was a momentous period in Australia's history, during which the Sydney Harbour Bridge was opened, the ABC was born, and so was Neville Greenwood!

Raised on a family farm named Wailuku, near Quirindi in the North West Slopes region, he was always glad his parents didn't stop at ten children, for he was Number Eleven (and three more would follow!). He is eternally grateful to them for taking the enormous amount of time and trouble to take him, as a tiny tot, to Sydney Children's Hospital no fewer than eighteen times for foot surgery to enable him to walk. Born with Charcot-Marie-Tooth disease (named after the three neurologists who first described it), he eventually took his first steps, with the help of braces, aged three and a half. 'In those tough years, my parents would have deprived themselves to give me the gift of being able to walk,' Neville reflects. 'When I was thirteen, a bag of wheat fell off a stack onto the back of my leg and really hurt my foot. The doctor told me it was a regeneration of my problem and that I would be in a wheelchair by the time I was twenty. Naturally, I was a bit slower getting around, but every time I heard one of my siblings say they would do some job rather than "leave it to poor Neville", I became more determined to try harder at everything I did. Eventually an X-ray revealed I had two broken bones in my foot from that falling bag of wheat.'

Neville grew up in a hard-working home where every child had jobs, but they also had lots of fun. They chopped wood, milked cows, fed pigs, chooks and horses, and helped with harvesting crops and keeping the bunny population down. 'We'd walk for miles hunting rabbits. Some mates accused me of always lagging behind, but my reply was that I needed to keep an eye on them!' Another of

Neville's natural skills is a talent for coming up with a quick, witty comeback – a gift we'd all love to have.

'My [rabbiting] dogs comprised speedsters, sniffers, pick-up dogs and killers – all possibly the best dogs in the world, or so I thought, and it has never been proven otherwise,' Neville boasts. 'With my brothers and mates I spent hours digging out burrows, until someone hit on the brainwave of getting ferrets. These smelly creatures really did change our lives – from digging out burrows to digging out ferrets! If the ferrets caught and ate a rabbit down there, they'd promptly go to sleep!' Younger people now could not imagine the ground moving with rabbits. Every town had a rabbit-freezing works. The one at Quirindi received up to 20 000 pairs a week, as well as umpteen thousands of skins from people like the Greenwood children, who did not have the means to store the carcasses. The money they earned allowed them to go to the flicks. Neville once experimented with a baby rabbit by putting butter on it then placing it among the cat's litter of kittens. The mother cat licked the butter off the bunny then reared it as if it was part of her own brood.

His father took part in hare drives, using his trusty Greener 12-gauge, and once shot 109 hares with 108 shots. As well as dairying, he farmed 300 acres of corn, wheat and barley, with ten drafthorses, spelling two at a time. His first wheat crop of 10 acres, which sold for 1 and sixpence a bushel, was sown using a single-furrow plough and harvested with a reaping hook. He had certainly progressed from that by the time Neville came along, but compared with modern methods, everything still entailed countless hours of hard work. They milked by hand and cobs of corn were still picked, shelled and bagged by hand. Wells were dug with shovels, bags of wheat were carried on shoulders, wood was cut and scrub was cleared with axes – all hard manual labour – but every farmer and their families were in the same boat and didn't know of any other way to do things. Hard yakka made them strong and healthy.

The first tractor Neville's dad owned was a cross-engined Case with steel 'spud' wheels (so-called because they had steel ridges) and Neville vividly recalls the 'difficult relationship' he had with this beast. It once backfired while he was cranking it, and the crank handle broke his jaw. On another memorable and highly painful occasion, it caught fire and burnt his hair off, creating his premature baldness.

He also clearly remembers the gigantic steam traction engines lumbering across the paddocks and along the roads – an unforgettable sight – and the thrill when their steam-operated chaffcutter whistle blew. Herds of camels passing by were a common sight, as were working bullocks carting wool, Indian hawkers, drovers with mobs of sheep or cattle and, of course, many swaggies, who would always be given food by Neville's mother. In return for a meal and some tucker for 'the track', they were invariably prepared to do some sort of work – they were just men on hard times. The Greenwoods were known as generous people. There was plenty of food, love and happiness in their home. The children respected their parents' instructions, guidance and house rules, such as 'no pudding till you eat your pumpkin', or 'your turn to wash up', because they knew when they said something, they meant it. Their word was final.

Neville remembers an unusual family in the district, the Burdens. They were huge eaters and were huge people. On Christmas Day they'd divide an entire roast suckling pig into three and put it on their plates. There'd be chicken and other goodies on the table as well. Neville went there one day and Mrs Burden had a bucket of figs on the ground between her large feet and was tucking into them heartily. She only paused for a couple of seconds to say (rather unnecessarily), 'I love figs.' Well, she must have, because she scoffed the lot! For a small boy, that was an unforgettable incident! They made their own wine, which was most unusual back then, and sold it commercially. It won prizes at shows, even though it was often described as 'a passable vinegar'. McWilliam's Wines eventually bought all their equipment after Neville's father took over farming their land.

All the Greenwoods had fun walking to the little school at Quipolly together, having races and playing games on the way. One of the girls was a left-hander. If the teacher caught her writing with her left hand – which was ridiculously against 'the rules' in those days – she'd cop a whack with a ruler. Consequently she could write with both hands.

The monotony of the milking shed was livened up one afternoon when twelve-year-old Lucy's skirt became caught on a nut on the big cream separator. In a flash, it had separated Lucy from her skirt, to her enormous embarrassment, but all the boys thought it was a great joke.

Every kid does stupid things sometimes, but possibly the silliest thing Neville did when young was to take up this challenge from his brother Ron, when they were pitching hay: 'Betcha you can't drive that pitchfork through my feet, Neville.' While Ron hopped madly about to avoid the fork, he didn't have his feet moving quite fast enough, because Neville certainly did manage to spear one of them. That took the cheeky grin off Ron's face! Fortunately he fainted, and Neville was able to pull the pitchfork from his foot while he was out.

Although their parents would have thought times were hard when they were bringing up such a large family, Neville says he wasn't aware of it. Life was good. The children were never bored.

Apart from chores, there were many fun activities, like playing in the Quirindi Creek with boats made from sardine tins, playing cricket using a pick handle plus a kero tin for a wicket, using sheep knuckles as jacks, riding billy carts made from fruit boxes and old pram wheels, and using jam tins and bits of string as 'two-way radios'. Using their imagination, they made stockyards with matches, filled them with peach stones in the place of cows and pretended to be branding or dipping. Their few toys were homemade and cherished. Although they were just 6 miles from town, the Greenwoods only went in on Saturdays. An occasional luxury item from the shop was a packet of saveloys to be used for sandwiches – whacko! When one of Neville's sisters brought home some crumpets – which were new then, in the early '40s – he had never eaten anything so delicious. With a mischievous glint in his eyes today, he declares: 'I've been keen on a bit of crumpet ever since.'

They didn't have a refrigerator, but made their own ice-cream on cold days, from leftover custard, eggs, sugar and condensed milk, put out on a post to set and freeze. Their first fridge was a second-hand kero-operated Hallstrom. To the family, it was a miracle to sit at night and listen to the serials and music coming out of the wireless set. Their dad's first car was a Buick – a big American car that still struggled to fit fourteen children. They squashed in somehow. Sometimes the neighbours, who didn't have a car, would hitch a ride on the running boards. Like most horsemen of that era, their father was a terrible driver. Fortunately there were few other cars on the road in those days of petrol rationing. Like everyone else out in the bush, they somehow coped with floods and grasshopper and mice plagues, and hung wet sheets in doorways in the big dust storms. The grasshoppers would be so thick when a cloud of them rose up around the vehicle, it was impossible to see where you were going.

Despite hardships, the Greenwood children all agree they had a wonderful childhood and were rich in many ways. Sunday nights were an enormous family gathering. Eventually, as the children all married and had their own kids, it became impossible to fit over a hundred people in the old family home. However, they *did* manage to squeeze ninety in!

Conversations on every topic with visitors enriched their lives. When a visitor turned up – often unexpectedly because there was no phone – an extra place would automatically be set at the table. It was just taken for granted that they would be given a meal. On Sunday nights there would always be a lot of visitors, as well as family.

Their mother was amazingly capable. She once drove the horse and dray into town, carting the cans of cream, then went to the dentist, had six teeth pulled out, waited to collect her new dentures, then drove the horse and dray home to prepare the family meal.

Tragically, she died, quite suddenly, after their youngest sister was born. The stress of having a son taken as a prisoner of war after the Fall of Singapore – and the lack of information about his health – must have taken its toll on her heart. Neville was eleven at the time. 'Our poor father must have suffered terribly, losing her, and with Bob missing,' he says. 'Bob died on the Sandakan Death March, along with 2500 other fine young men – a tragic waste. My brother had been a strapping young feller and a great sportsman – he was so popular in our community when he sailed off to fight for Australia. I look at his picture every day and feel sorrow for our loss and the torture he endured.

'When Mum died, Dad then reared us single-handedly. He was a wonderful, loving father who never got angry with us or lifted a hand against us.'

All thirteen of the surviving Greenwood children have had

productive lives, but they have all been especially proud of Neville's success in business. His three older brothers were working on the farm when he finished school, so he found employment that was closely related to the land, working with a stock and station agent. 'He was a good honest man, but, unfortunately, an alcoholic,' he says. 'I learnt a lot from him, but learnt even more from watching what he did wrong. Clients would always want him to go to the pub with them for a beer while they were in town – that's a trap an agent has to learn to deal with wisely. You can always have a lemonade during working hours. I had learnt a valuable lesson when aged eighteen, I drank alcohol for the first time at a wedding and became horribly ill. I didn't have another drink until I was thirty-nine. By that age, you are – or should be – considerably more capable of controlling your intake and not allowing alcohol to control you.'

Neville always had the ambition to work for himself, and the day he turned twenty-one, he applied for his stock and station agent's licence. By then, he had five years' experience. He was able to buy his own business and premises from an elderly agent, D T King, who had dementia and was in his daughter's care. After Neville painted the dilapidated building and moved in, the poor old fellow turned up for work every day for a couple of months, which was sad. Neville bought his furniture and old typewriter for 40 pounds, and still has his old swivel chair. So there he was, twenty-one years old, with no clients, money or income. The old bloke's clients had all drifted away over the years and gone elsewhere. Naturally Neville was apprehensive, but he suddenly was overwhelmed by the support of several locals who thought they would give a young bloke a chance to get on his feet. These wonderful people remained his loyal clients for the next three decades.

Before his first auction sale, he practised like mad, auctioning off every corner post, gate and light pole he drove past, for weeks. He got through it and was again pleasantly surprised by the support given by tough old stock buyers, who could have chosen to give him a hard time. They have their ways of upsetting a sale while trying to get cheap stock, but they went easy and gave the 'young goer' a fair go.

Neville says he learnt two valuable lessons very quickly. 'One: don't give advice, because it soon becomes clear that the only advice that's ever remembered is when it turns out to be wrong! When it turns out to be right, it's always *their* idea. Two: when you are twenty-one years old, don't try to tell an eighty-year-old farmer what he should do.'

Other lessons passed on to him to help him succeed in business were: be reliable, be punctual, don't ever think that old people can't tell you anything, and if anyone offers you payment before it's due, just say, 'That's appreciated, thank you.' Don't ever say, 'No need for that. I'll send you an account.' It was all valuable advice from people with a lot of life experience on the land or in business. But what always stuck firmly in Neville's mind most was this saying, so full of wisdom: 'It takes several years to build up a reputation, which you can lose in just minutes with a bad decision.'

He worked bloody hard to establish a solid reputation and drove long distances to inspect livestock for clients, chain-smoking to stay awake. Eventually, through desperation, he developed another method to fend off sleep – he'd lift the bonnet and stick his finger on a spark plug. The shock would leave him wide-awake and keep him going for at least another hundred miles! (Don't try it with a modern car with electronic ignition.)

Due to his dedication to looking after his clients, he became so busy he wasn't able to spend enough time with his children. So he took on a partner, Geoff Keen, to share the workload. During the thirty years he was in business, Neville had three partners and never had a cross word with any of them. They were all fine men he held in the highest regard.

Quirindi is a solid town with good amenities. It was once a renowned sheep district, but now predominantly features cattle and other farming. Although it's a relatively safe area, even secure locations have droughts and hard times. Neville gets cranky when he hears city people say, 'Why don't the cockies sell their stock at the start of a drought instead of getting into debt feeding them?' His reply is that, 'No farmer can tell when a drought is starting, but it's quite amazing that city fellers know.'

Neville could fill a book with stories about the characters he's met and dealt with, but one who stands out in his memories was his mate and favourite client, Horrie Smith. 'Horrie could be hard, but he was a loveable larrikin with the biggest belly laugh – a laugh I'm sure he employed at times to get himself out of sticky situations with people, such as the Pasture Protection Board rangers, or traffic police, or victims of his practical jokes, such as the publican and clientele of the Max Hotel at Moree, who were livened up once by a big goanna that Horrie threw in amongst them.'

As well as a big laugh, Horrie possessed a big heart. In 1954, Neville was a very hard-working 22-year-old businessman who had not accumulated any money to speak of. In what was to him a very big deal, he sold a lot of stock for a total of thirty-one clients to a meat wholesaler and dealer who then had him biting his nails while he waited for his cheque. He needed it to be able to pay the suppliers of the stock. When it finally arrived, he wrote out cheques to pay them, then found out from his bank that the meat buyer's cheque for

22 000 pounds (a *lot* of money then) had bounced. Consequently twenty-seven of Neville's cheques to the vendors had also been bounced. He was pondering this terrible predicament when in walked Horrie Smith, who'd heard about the turn of events. He put a signed cheque in front of Neville and said, 'Fill that in for whatever you need to keep you going.' Neville's father also offered to help him out, but he rejected both offers. Many decades on, Neville still has no words to describe the gratitude and appreciation for the trust and faith they had in him, but at the time, he knew he had to work a way out of the situation himself. Legally, he wasn't really responsible for payment of stock 'sold in the paddock', but he felt morally responsible to ensure everyone was paid.

'My strategy was to go to the dealer's house in Maitland and get twenty-two cheques for 1000 pounds each, which I presented to the bank,' he explains. 'Eight were honoured, allowing me to start paying my clients who needed the money the most or were being the most demanding. I left the balance of the cheques at the offender's bank with instructions to credit them at every opportunity. Before he was eventually put into bankruptcy, I managed to pay all thirty-one of my clients, but I had to put in 3000 pounds of my money to make this possible. Everyone knew what had happened, so that episode helped my reputation rather than hindered it. But it was a stressful and distressing time, particularly as I was about to get married and, in those days, a prospective son-in-law was expected to be "solid", with the means of supporting a wife comfortably and providing her with a home.'

The year 1955 was a big one for Neville. He married Pat, the girl he'd had his eye on since high school, and he bought his first house, a one-bedroom home in Quirindi.

Down the track, when the couple's fourth child was on the way, he decided he needed to build three more bedrooms. He didn't worry about council approval; he just taught himself to build as he went along, and made a tidy profit on the house when they moved.

Neville is a bloke who doesn't blow his own trumpet and will tell a story against himself. For example, he grins when telling anyone that on his honeymoon at Surfers Paradise, he was offered an acre there, overlooking the ocean, for 7000 pounds on very easy terms, but because rural land was what he knew and understood, he decided to let it go. He thought, *The bubble there will burst and I'll be stuck with it!* (Oh well, nobody's perfect!)

He found his work auctioneering livestock fascinating. Standing on the rail, he could observe the collaborating, cartels, secretiveness and other methods used by buyers to try and cheapen a market. As an agent, he felt an obligation to the vendor to try to stop that and get as much money as he could for them. Conversely, he felt it was a matter of integrity to never run a buyer past the reserve price. The auctioneer he admired most was Malcolm Capp of Dalgety's Gunnedah, because 'he spoke with absolute authority. If you don't keep control of a crowd at an auction, you're a goner,' says Neville. In his opinion, a few unwritten requirements for a good auctioneer are:

1. Keep a sale moving – don't let it grind to a steady pace.
2. Don't let anyone make you lose your patience or temper, because getting wild appeals to no one. The first person to raise their voice will lose.
3. Know as much as you can about what you're selling. It's no good having the best stock auctioneer selling antiques.
4. If there's a dispute involving more than one bidder, resolve it quickly and move on.
5. Be absolutely alert and don't miss a bid, which might be the slightest movement of a little finger under a rail!

6. Be honest and fair. Don't ever think you're going to outsmart
   anyone.

With regard to Number 5, he was once attacked by a furious
meat buyer who, not wanting his mate to know he was bidding
against him, barely wiggled his finger under the rail. Neville had
missed it, and the meat buyer was so cranky he called him a 'bat-
eyed whore'. To add fuel to his fire, Neville found that absolutely
hilarious. When he was able to stop laughing, he said, 'If you could
waggle your finger half as well as you waggle your tongue, that
would be very helpful.'

Being such a humorous character, Neville always tried to make
clearing sales entertaining. If people are having a laugh they're loos-
ened up and more likely to bid. In the pre-political-correctness days,
a bloke could get away with a lot more. At his sister and brother-
in-law's clearing sale, after selling their motor garage, Neville sold
a couple of vices then moved down the row of tools to a hydrau-
lic carjack and simply could not resist telling the crowd that, 'Bob's
got rid of his vices but he's still got the jack.' A few older ladies pretended to be a bit shocked, but even the local constable who was
there enjoyed a good laugh. But the crowd really got going when
Neville picked up an old chamber-pot and said, 'Now this is a perfectly good po – the only reason Bob's selling it is because Carmen's
arse is too big for it now.' Fortunately, Carmen, his sister, joined in
the laughter.

One aspect of an agent's duties that Neville found quite unpleasant was being called out to value a property where obviously a
couple or family were fighting and it had to be sold. There are a lot
of sad stories out in the bush.

After many years of selling properties, Neville can verify that
the old adage 'Good quality land is never dear' always rings true.

He always found that you can easily sell good country, but it's hard to sell mediocre country.

An observation he's made recently is that as farm incomes lessen, with returns not keeping pace with the rises in running costs, older blokes are still working hard because sons won't work that hard for such a poor return. It saddens him to see eighty-year-olds still slaving.

In recent years, he's been disappointed to see people backing out of a deal saying, 'I may have said that, but I didn't sign anything.' Even the toughest old dealers he dealt with would never say such a thing. It used to be the norm to do deals for properties or mobs of livestock on a handshake. (Neville himself bought a property recently from a neighbour with his handshake sealing the deal.) During the first half of his career, he would ask both parties if they wanted a contract, but they were nearly always happy with a handshake. It took over ten years for him to use up his first contract book.

His favourite aspect of being an agent was meeting and dealing with the great characters of the bush. 'A client I'll call "Fred", who spent his life collecting money, was a good bloke – scrupulously honest and trustworthy. His only "fault" was the fact he would not spend a cent on anything that would provide him with comfort. His dilapidated old house was filled with scrap iron, old engines, papers, you name it. There was no running water. He allowed a quiet, little heifer to regularly wander through the house, until one day he informed me she was no longer welcome. On asking why, I was informed, "Because she allowed the bull to follow her in and he made a hell of a mess!"'

A friend of Neville's went to Fred's house once and remarked, 'Hey, Fred, there's a sick rat in that corner.' Fred peered at the rat and said, 'Yairs, he's been a bit off for a few days, that one.'

When one of his neighbours, Campbell Copeland, was away, Fred kindly kept an eye on Campbell's wife, Gail, checking to make sure she was all right and didn't need a hand with anything. He even took her a special gift – a bag of frozen testicles from a mob of bulls he'd marked. Gail thought they were for her to cook up and, although surprised to say the least, thanked him. When he saw her in town at the supermarket shortly afterward, he bellowed out across the aisles, 'How did your dog like those bulls' balls, Gail?'

He once hired a bloke with a crane to shift a windmill. He said he wanted it shifted upright and the driver said that was impossible and that it'd have to be slung horizontally. It turned out penny-conscious Fred was worried about losing the 2 litres of oil that would run out of it! Then again, he could be the most generous man when it came to donating to worthy causes. He just hated spending money on himself and on 'luxuries', like a hot shower! He was inter-viewed just before he died and attributed his long life to 'good food, good living, and no women!'

'Another local character was in my office one day, just after he'd bought a new pair of glasses,' Neville says. 'He explained they were newfangled things called bifocals and that they took a lot of getting used to. He said, "The first time I went to the dunny, I looked down and saw two dicks – a big one and a little one. Well I knew the big one wasn't mine, so I put it back 'n' blow me down . . . peed down me leg!" He was a wag with a stock of great stories, one of which was about one of his old female relatives who asked the local priest if he would take her to visit a very ill sister in the Werris Creek hos-pital. This was in the horse-and-sulky days and the priest was urging his fat, lazy pony back home from the hospital, at a smart trot as it was freezing. The pony kept slowing down and at one point he lost his temper with it and gave it an almighty thrashing with his buggy whip. The pony reacted by pigrooting and letting out a tremendous fart, much to their embarrassment. Later on, when nearly home, he said, "I'm very embarrassed about that incident back there. I admit I lost control. It was disgraceful and I apologise." She replied, "You shouldn't have said anything, Father, I thought it was the horse."

Neville's most unforgettable client, an old-timer called Dal, was a real one-off. No matter how funny the story he was telling or the remark he was making, he had a permanently, completely deadpan face, which of course made everything even funnier. He wasn't a rude or objectionable man but was a compulsive and habitual swearer. One night Neville was at a party and asked Dal where his wife was. He explained, 'She hounded a man to buy one of those f**kin' newfangled kero fridges, which I did, and I didn't know that a man had to light a f**kin' fire under it and leave it burning all f**kin' night. So I told her it's her responsibility to stay at home and look after he f**kin' bastard of a thing!'

Neville was yarning with him one day at his place and he was 'f' this and 'c' that, non-stop as usual, when Neville informed Dal that his ten-year-old daughter was standing behind him. Dal turned to her and said, 'What are you doing up here where us gentlemen are talking?' He turned back to Neville and said, 'We could've been talking about things not suitable for young people's ears.' He then looked back at her and said, 'Get back to your f**kin' mother!'

When Dal was giving up dairying to run sheep, Neville arranged for him to inspect a small flock. Not knowing anything about sheep, Dal took himself to the sheep sale in Tamworth, then to one in Gunnedah, to observe prices, etc. He then felt those experiences had given him full knowledge of the sheep industry and the market. When he inspected the sheep belonging to Neville's other clients – a father and son who were good churchgoers, he addressed them thus: 'Gentlemen, I know the time and f**kin' sweat and toil you have put into the breeding of these bastards and I congratulate you on that. But let me tell you that I went to the f**kin' Tamworth sale on Monday and I could've bought the same hairy-arsed little sluts for half the f**kin' money!'

Neville was at his place when a bureaucrat came to check on whether he had a wireless licence, which were then compulsory. With his usual deadpan expression, Dal said he didn't have a wireless. The inspector didn't believe him and said, 'Don't expect me to believe that – everyone has a wireless these days. Have you got it hidden somewhere?' He received this very definite reply: 'I don't have a f**kin' wireless, and have never had a f**kin' wireless, and what would I want one for anyway – to listen to f**kin' music?'

During 1974, a catastrophic year for beef producers, the top price achieved one day at the Quirindi saleyards, with 1500 mainly prime cattle, was just *12 cents* per kilo. Neville had some Jersey cows in the yard, their vealer calves drafted off them for weighing next day, and the mothers were sold for *50 cents* each. Desperate, Neville told the buyers that those cows had at least $2 worth of milk in their udders, to no avail. For him, that was a shocking and depressing experience. He felt so sad for the vendors. That day, a local taking his calves back home because he hadn't received a bid, stopped at the Wingen pub to cheer himself up. When he went back to his truck, it contained *twice* as many calves. Someone else apparently didn't get a bid!

Neville loved the times spent travelling long distances with clients, hearing their life experiences, especially the old-timers whose memories went back to the 1870s. 'How I wish I had kept a diary back then,' he says. 'Some of them were reared, or reared their own

families, on 40-acre dairies with no irrigation. One man told me he
made a living on a 20-acre orchard, supplemented with income from
bees and catching rabbits. Rabbits also gave poor people the protein
needed to perform all the backbreaking tasks they tackled each day
to survive on the land. In 1929 they brought 4 pence to 5 pence a
pair and the export value of the meat and skins was worth 52 mil-
lion pounds to Australia. In my childhood, some children earned an
adult wage after school and on weekends, with a .22. Those who
didn't have a rifle and used traps would catch around eighty pairs
a night back then. After myxomatosis was introduced, most people
wouldn't eat bunnies.

'It's a very different world now,' he continues. 'I have done
well and given my wife and children a comfortable and secure life.
Now I enjoy helping others through Rotary and am so proud that
Rotary, amongst innumerable humanitarian deeds, have stamped
out ninety-seven per cent of the world's polio.'

Neville was also immensely chuffed this year when he was
awarded the Community Service Award by his club, which he's
belonged to for forty-one years. The Quirindi club also donate survival boxes to people who have been left homeless and devastated
after a disaster. The boxes contain a ten-person tent, medical supplies, cooking facilities, bedding, a water purifier, and more. Neville
never misses a chance to urge people of all ages to join Rotary or any
service club. He's often asked to be the auctioneer at charity fundraisers and with his cheeky and funny remarks, can usually manage
to get double or triple what the items are worth.

That wit of his is now part of local folklore. When a city-based
dentist was visiting Neville's daughter, Neville just happened to have
a toothache and the dentist was happy to take a look. She said to
him later, 'It amazes me how you farmers can tell the age of your

horses or stock by looking at their teeth.' To which he replied with that characteristic cheeky twinkle in his eyes, 'It amazes me that just by looking in my mouth, you can tell I need root therapy.' Wife Pat just rolls her eyes when he's being 'naughty'.

That sense of fun has always ensured his office was a happy workplace. 'I am fortunate to have had wonderful, capable, reliable and pleasant people working for me,' he says. Jill Hoswell, who worked for him for ten years and has known him all her life, describes Neville as 'a great man, a great boss, a great friend. Neville is a unique person, very caring, always helping people out with their problems.'

At age fifty, Neville decided to retire. He sold up and walked out the door for the last time. He had always run cattle on land at Wallabadah and a contract harvesting business 'on the side', but he wanted to farm fulltime. Fate had taken him off his family's land into the world of business and, at last, while still young and strong, he was able to purchase a large, quality property called Maloka. It was a beautiful place with a lake on it, stocked with fish, and yabbies were plentiful. Beautiful crops of wheat, sunflowers and sorghum flourished. His cattle fattened easily and were a source of great pride. But even on a beautiful property, there's plenty of work to be done and times of strife. Like the time a bull sent Neville under an electric fence and, because his clothes were all hooked up, he was zapped nine times until it shorted out!

One time Pat and Neville's then five-year-old grandson, Josh, came to visit, then went home and told his mother he knew what 'f**k' meant. Absolutely shocked, but deciding to sort this problem out calmly, she said, 'Well, what does it mean?' Came the innocent reply, 'It means the electric fence is on.'

Maloka contained 2000 acres of the 22 000-acre Goran Lake.

Neville wanted to farm the golden carp and yabbies commercially but was refused permission by the relevant bureaucracy. Consequently, when the lake dried up in a drought, thousands of fish flapped in the mud till they died – a wicked waste. It turned out that they aren't even a native fish! The yabbies, of course, dig themselves into the mud and survive somehow until it rains again. A mystery of nature. Yabbies have been found up to 20 feet below the ground, continually following moisture. Neville worked out a plan to circumvent the ridiculous rules put into place. He allowed a large, licenced commercial enterprise, which supplied the Sydney market, to keep yabbies in tanks on his property until they grew big enough to transport and sell, and charged them $4 a kilo agistment! The yabbies are transported packed in ice and bark. They can survive being frozen for quite a while. They are amazing little creatures . . . and delicious as well.

Neville and Pat have recently sold Maloka and their big two-storey home in Quirindi, and scaled down to a townhouse. They commute frequently to their retreat on the glorious Clarence River at Iluka, where Neville built the large block of holiday units with a partner, thirty years ago. He is a man content with his life, who's worked hard for what he now enjoys and has many friends who look to him for advice and a lively, humorous conversation. 'I'm privileged to have lived in Australia in the earlier times and to have shared my life with Pat, my children and all our extended family and friends. If my theory is right that "true wealth is measured by family and friends", then I am a rich man. Without them, you have nothing.'

15.

Bill Ovenden

THE MAN WHO CONQUERED THE DUCHESS

When Bill Ovenden first laid eyes on her, it was absolutely, definitely not love at first sight.

She was at her most unattractive in the blast-furnace temperature of a North-West Queensland summer. Not even the shimmering waves of heat could soften her hard, unwelcoming face. The Duchess was even more unappealing in reality than Bill had visualised in his mind.

He wrestled with a burning desire to climb back onto the train. Then he called upon all his courage to help him endure what lay ahead.

As the Inlander chugged away up towards Mount Isa, leaving him stranded in an ocean of red dirt and hot gibbers, he stared around him in dismay. Half a dozen corrugated iron buildings baked beside the railway line. Crows lazily mocked him – 'har, har, haaarr' – and for the tenth time that day, he cursed the bastards in the Education Department who'd sent him to this godforsaken place.

This would not be the last time in his long career that Bill would harbour those thoughts. A man with his passion for improving children's lives, and his outstanding ability to inspire them to want to learn, would inevitably fall foul of the crusty old dinosaurs and legion of brown-nosers in the department during that era. It was fortunate, for the sake of educational standards of the isolated children he was to teach and guide, that Bill Ovenden was not a quitter, for what he had to offer would have been lost. Being sent to Duchess, a remote settlement that was the least desirable posting in the state, to live under deplorable, primitive conditions in terrible isolation, failed to crush this young man's zeal. So . . . this feller who managed to conquer 'the Duchess', what was he made of? What moulded his special character that would leave such an impression on so many lives?

Bill was born on 20 June 1936 in Cairns, to Emily and Albert William Ovenden, who ran Palings Music Store at Innisfail. They were both musicians and Bill fondly remembers them practising at home with their band, which included his Uncle Ted on saxophone. His father could play every instrument and was an especially talented French horn player. He toured the world for four years with the Australian Commonwealth Band. Bill had an older sister, Patricia, and a younger sister, Pamela. By 1942 the family had moved to Brisbane, where he was enrolled, aged six, at St Ambrose's Convent, Kelvin Grove. The threat of Japanese invasion saw the family evacuated to Tenterfield in 1943 for a year. Bill's father wasn't well and died in 1944 of lung cancer. For some reason, their mother didn't tell her children that he'd died until after the funeral. Consequently they found it hard to understand and accept his death. They had seen him, laughed and chatted with him in hospital, only three nights earlier. How could he be dead? It just wasn't possible!

This affected Bill, who was only eight then, for a long time. He searched for his father's face in every crowd for many years. His mother would not, or could not, communicate with them about their loss. A hairdresser, she worked from home to pay the bills. During the last year of the war she accepted a position as manager of Meredith's Salon in Toowoomba, and put the children into boarding schools. Bill went to Marist Brothers, which at the time was in Eagle Heights, Tamborine Mountain, and his sisters went to Star of the Sea Convent in Wynnum. When the bus pulled out to take him away to the unknown, he saw his mother standing on her own, waving and crying, and finally his well of emotion spilled out.

As an eight-year-old boy pining for his father, he was lonely for a long time at the new school, where bullying was common. He suffered being belted up many times – almost every day – behind the toilets. The kind and caring principal, Brother Harold, who was a Spencer Tracy lookalike, took Bill under his wing, coaching him in self-defence. Bill took to boxing like a duck to water, thinking of all the scores he had to settle, which he did, well before the year was out. He gave the bullies who'd tormented him a 'bloody good hammering', one by one, in the ring, with Brother Harold refereeing. By the end of the year he was acquitting himself well in championship matches. His mother saw him taking part in one and was completely surprised by his aggression in the ring. Brother Harold was a mentor to Bill – a man who was equally handy with his fists, a shovel, an axe, or when hurling a lump of chalk. All the brothers were kind and decent and Bill enjoyed helping them in the big veggie garden.

At the end of 1945 his mother moved back to Brisbane and the family were reunited, living back at Red Hill, then later in a big home in Norman Park with views of the city. Bill went to Marist Brothers, which had moved to Ashgrove, as a day pupil until 1951, when he commenced secondary schooling as a boarder.

In 1954, Bill's senior year, his dream – the dream of every senior boy, to be in the First Fifteen rugby team – came true. He proudly states that the team of that year, during which he played hooker, is reputed to have been the 'best ever'. Dual International star Des Connor, who was declared 'best Australian halfback of the century' by the press, was in Bill's team. The following year he enrolled at Kelvin Grove Teachers College, and hooked for their First Fifteen, then for the Teachers' Team in '56 and '57. The rough and tumble of the rugby field and the boxing ring prepared him for the difficult challenges ahead in his life. Although everyone has sympathy for what many teachers encounter these days with undisciplined, disrespectful children, Bill's mettle was tested to the limits early in his career by different situations brought about by his superiors.

During 1956 and '57, Bill was an assistant teacher at Redland Bay State School, where many of the pupils were from the fruit and vegetable farms that surrounded it. At the end of each season, the pupils and teachers would pick crops ready for harvest, and the money earned was spent on library books for the school. Bill introduced rugby to the school and organised an inter-school competition. So the girls weren't left out, he also taught ballroom dancing and held dance nights for the older pupils. He was popular with the children and really enjoyed educating them about the world beyond their little farms. The fly in the ointment was the head teacher, who was as antiquated as the school. He had ultra-rigid, old-fashioned views on education, considering perfection in copybooks more important than educating the children in the literal and broader sense of the word. He and Bill did not see eye to eye. This is possibly why Bill ended up at Duchess. When, at the end of 1957, he reached the status of teacher, he wrote on the application form for a preferred school that he was 'prepared to go anywhere in Queensland'. Possibly egged on by his nemesis from Redland Bay, one or more of the powers-that-be in the Education Department must have thought, *Let's teach this young smart-alec whippersnapper, with his modern ideas, a good lesson*, and sent him off to hell.

While Bill was at Redland Bay, he served three months of national service training during 1956, reaching the rank of corporal of his platoon. He was involved in a very nasty, unforgettable episode called by the press at that time as the 'King George Square Incident'. He was in charge of the men in his hut at Wacol Army Camp, a number of whom were older fellows who'd deferred 'doing their time' as long as possible. They were several years older than Bill. Consequently, at age nineteen, he had to be assertive and stay in control of them. On Easter Saturday they had enjoyed a night out at the Police Boys Club in the city, in uniform. Bill had instructed them to all be at King George Square next to City Hall to share cabs back and be in camp for the 23:59 (one-minute-to-midnight) curfew. There was animosity towards the 'nashos' (national servicemen) from the so-called 'bodgies' – generally not-too-bright young blokes who wore clothes and haircuts that they thought made them look tough. The bodgies would sneer at the nashos with their immaculate uniforms, tidy hair and glossy boots, and bravely pick fights when they outnumbered them. Strangely there was also animosity towards the nashos from Regular Army soldiers.

The streets were crowded that night at that hour, especially outside the Tivoli Theatre opposite City Hall. Waiting for his entire platoon to catch up with him at the cab rank, Bill could hear a disturbance and saw one of his blokes forcing his way through the crowd towards him. When he asked what was up, the reply came, 'Army blokes are picking on us.' Suddenly a car pulled up, then a bloke in a suit got out and immediately swung violent punches at one of Bill's lads, called Sweeney, until he fell flat on his face. The other men in the car, who turned out to be plain-clothes policemen, ran into the crowd chasing the nashos who'd been being picked on by the Regular Army blokes, through King George Square opposite the Tivoli. Women were screaming. As the belligerent cop was hand-cuffing the hapless, completely innocent Sweeney, a woman said to Bill, 'What are we going to do about that?' When Bill called out the cop car's number plate to her to write down, he swung around yell-ing, 'Who called that number out?' Suddenly Bill was being arrested and dragged to the police car by the angry cop (who'd decked Sweeney), who stank of rum.

Sweeney was hurled in the back seat as well, and they were con-stantly threatened with the big fist of the angry cop smelling of rum, every time they tried to protest their innocence on the way to the police station. Sweeney was charged first with being 'drunk and dis-orderly', and chucked in a cell, then they said the same words to Bill, who protested, 'I've never had a drink in my life!' All the drunks in the cells then started mocking him, repeating the words – which were completely true – over and over. Bill was thrown into another cell full of blokes who started chanting, 'There's a soldier in here.' In contrast to their threatening, frightening tone, he could hear the rest of his platoon chanting outside: 'Illegal arrest! Illegal arrest!'

When Bill was able to return to Wacol, charges of assault were pressed against the bad cop. Some months later in the Supreme Court, Bill was called as a witness for the prosecution, and had to identify him from a line-up. Still only nineteen years old, he had to look the big furious cop in the eye.

The witnesses for the prosecution had to stay outside, only being allowed in one-by-one to give evidence. Bill, who actually saw the cop punching Sweeney right in front of him, felt disappointed as he listened to the discrepancies from the witnesses about the number of punches that were rained upon Sweeney. They were guessing, and that weakened their case. They should have said they weren't exactly sure, which was the truth. On the bad cop's side was the formidable team of the best two barristers in Queensland, named Casey and Brennan, paid for by the Police Union, and they led the witnesses up the garden path then cut them down in flames. The defendant was not only exonerated but promoted as well, after a trial that went for a year. Yet another case of 'whoever has the best barrister wins'.

Meanwhile, Bill continued to enjoy his teaching at Redland Bay, despite the head teacher, and enjoy his strenuous testing activities with the national service. He relished the 5-mile race in army boots, with full kit and pack, won it handsomely, then was made captain of the long-distance running team. Bill had his eight runners up ready to go, fully kitted up, every morning at five o'clock, for their gruelling training, to ensure they were unbeatable. It gave him a good feeling to see blokes who'd come in as dropkicks changed into useful men thanks to national service. They were then a part of the Reserve Army and went on three compulsory camps a year. Bill's number did not come up in the 'lottery' to go to Vietnam, to his mother's great relief. She had remarried that year to George Adams, who owned the Metropolitan Hotel at Bundaberg. Bill had a very good relationship with his stepfather. At eighteen, he had visited his father's grave in the military section of the Lutwyche Cemetery and finally, after ten years of mental torment, found closure and stopped searching for his dad's face in crowds.

Then came his great twenty-first birthday present: a year in Duchess. It took him a while to confirm his suspicions that this was a punitive move engineered by the Redland Bay headmaster and other archaic types associated with the Education Department. After battling his urge upon arrival to run after the departing train, he stood there, holding his suitcases containing all his possessions, the only human being visible for many miles. Had he been sent to a ghost town for a joke? No, he had received a letter from the school's Parents and Citizens (P & C) secretary, the policeman's wife, suggesting he should stay at the pub when he first arrived. Squinting, he could make out a large building a hundred yards away and began walking towards it, across the hot dirt, struggling with his heavy bags. Gradually he could make out the words 'DUCHESS HOTEL'. The two-storey timber pub still served the cattle station people and railway fettlers who remained in the otherwise abandoned mining town and was the only building not constructed of corrugated iron.

He was made welcome by Charlie and Maria Kelly, and taken upstairs to his ultra-basic room, which led onto a verandah facing the ancient Selwyn Range. He realised there was no electricity when he saw a wet hessian bag thrown over the keg at the bar to 'cool' the beer. Ah, that's why there were no fans! Tossing and sweating in his little bed that night, he thought about what he'd left behind: a lovely girlfriend who promised she'd write every day and all his rugby mates. He was thousands of miles from anyone he knew, didn't have a vehicle and the train only went through twice a week. There was no telephone. He promised himself in the soporific darkness that he'd rise to the challenge of running this school, which had the lowest classification in Queensland, but . . . it would be his school to run the way he wanted to run it.

The next day the policeman's wife, Netta, picked him up to show him the school. After driving along the dirt track through the spinifex for a while, he asked if it was in the next town. She replied it was over a mile and a half from town – a leftover from when the main town had been closer to the now-abandoned mine. When she pulled up in front of two little galvanised-iron huts surrounded by orange-red bare dirt, Bill's jaw dropped. The teacher's hut was 'furnished' with an ancient bed, a decrepit wood stove, and an old hurricane lamp. Everything was dusty and dirty, including the table, which had no chairs. Spiders were everywhere! At the rear was a tiny attached shower room and laundry tub. The loo was a 20-metre hike and definitely not the sort of place you'd linger with a book. Bill was relieved he could stay at the pub until he could fix this dismal little place up a bit.

The powers-that-be had succeeded in driving him to drink. He had previously promised himself he would continue to abstain from alcohol, but the urge to try a cold beer and join in the locals' fun and laughter at the bar proved too strong to resist that afternoon. They made him welcome and introduced him to the local ritual of 'Once Around the Bar' – trying a nip of all the spirits, port wine, etc., on display. The night became a blur of hilarity and fiery liquids. The resulting hangover left him comatose for twenty-four hours.

Upon recovery, he forced himself to tidy up the little school, set up his teaching tools, and begin planning ahead. Teaching twenty-two children from Grade One to Scholarship would prove a challenge, so he intended to be completely organised with goals set for each class. His 'school' was a corrugated-iron box set on low stumps, with iron walls about waist high, then flywire to the ceiling. No windows!

After walking the distance back to town, he found himself being hijacked as he passed the bar. It was a case of 'You're either with 'em or agin' 'em!' The locals were good company but he was very careful from then on about his alcohol intake. By the time the first day of the school year arrived he was well organised. The pupils mostly came from the railway workers' houses and a cattle station. Completely confident and friendly with the children, Bill found them a good bunch, likeable and responsive. They lived in such isolation that they were short on many life experiences. Two had never seen the sea.

The walking track to the school was quite dangerous as it passed close to the derelict open-cut copper mine, abandoned at the start of WW I. The mine flooded and was full of toxic green water and the open shafts had become the graves of unfortunate wandering stock. Jack's Creek cut across the track and was dry for ninety per cent of the time, but it filled twice during Bill's time there and he was totally fascinated to see small crabs crawling around in the shallow water. Where were they when it was dry? he wondered. All around Duchess were blue-green stones, rich in copper, and just outside the town was a dolomite mine, with its beautiful, multicoloured crystal. Bill heard many rumours of gold waiting to be found in the Selwyn Range.

Throughout Bill's long career, Duchess proved to be the only school where he had to devise willy-willy drills. Spiralling winds frequently blew across the desert, gathering up dust and roly-polies of spinifex, then, due to the unique 'architecture' of the school, blew straight through the classroom, playing havoc with books and eyes. Bill would yell a warning, 'Willy-willy!', and the children would slump facedown on their books on their desks, clasping their hands over the backs of their heads until it passed through. A thick cloud of dust then hung in the room, and as it subsided, the cleaning up would begin, all joining in. Some willy-willies were like mini-tornadoes. One actually took the school's water tank away.

After a couple of months he decided not to move into the daggy little quarters. The publicans treated him very well, and he looked forward to the company and laughter they and the few patrons provided. Adult conversation on a variety of topics was welcome after what were often trying days at school. One night a group of fettlers in the bar overheard Bill suggesting to the P & C, during their meeting at the pub, that he teach boxing at the school. They took the hat around and collected enough money for two pairs of boxing gloves. The children were delighted. The 'ring' was a square cut into the hard gravel in front of the school. No one was hurt because Bill focused on teaching defence as well as punching.

If Duchess was a furnace in summer, in winter it was the opposite. One freezing morning just before school started, he heard the children yelling outside that the pub was on fire. Flames were leaping from the windows and by the time Bill sprinted the distance to town, most of the hotel was engulfed and he lost virtually everything he owned. All he salvaged, after climbing up the fire escape, were two left shoes. Bugger!

For the Kellys and the rest of the residents, it was a tragedy. That evening, the railway workers 'borrowed' ice from the Inlander train to chill a keg that had been salvaged. Everyone from near and far sat beside the smoking embers of the pub and drank to 'the beer with no pub'. It was 1958, the year Slim Dusty had recorded his hit song 'The Pub with No Beer'. Bill had to catch the train to Mount Isa to buy new clothes and other essentials. None of his belongings were covered by insurance.

The fire forced him to evict the spiders from the tin hut, turn the grubby mattress over, set up his 'chair' – a fruit case – in a really comfy position, and begin life in his fabulous bachelor pad. For quite a while he lived on tins of Tom Piper sausages and veggies. With the shops so far away and his limited cooking 'facilities', it was like it or lump it. He found it very lonely but was able to visit the Kellys, who continued to sell lukewarm beer from the galvanised-iron laundry – the only section not burnt. To the ringers from the vast outlying stations, it was still 'an outing'.

Eventually the Works Department answered Bill's pleas for some furniture, but considered a refrigerator a luxury item, so he bought a second-hand, kero-operated bitch of a thing. It never worked properly so he lost a lot of food from time to time. He was living in real hardship. The Department sent an itinerant painter to paint the 'quarters' while Bill was on holidays, and when he returned all his clothes had been stolen. The local policeman tracked the painter down in Normanton and the clothes were returned.

During the cooler months, he enjoyed joining in the tennis matches on the bitumen court, his team playing competitively against Mount Isa, and he also took part in the three-way cricket competition with Dajarra and Boulia. At the end of these sporting days, they (and 5000 flies) would all enjoy a keg of beer and steaks brought along and barbecued by a cook from one of the local cattle stations. After six months, he realised he had to make the effort to go to Mount Isa every second weekend to keep himself sane and keep in touch with other teachers. For company he bought Fritz, a dachshund, who was a great little character but became infested with cattle ticks and had to be sent to Bill's mother and stepfather at Bundaberg. Bill was on his lonesome again, but a sympathetic local gave him a kitten and a cockatiel, which became good friends. He had by then become a virtual hermit, quiet, withdrawn and heartbroken. It had been a bitter blow to find out that his girlfriend had fallen for another bloke during his absence. On top of that, he realised all his friends from college and football days had disappeared from his life. Each day he took his frustrations out on the punching bag he'd hooked up. To give himself something to focus on apart from his loneliness, he enrolled in an external course towards his teaching degree, studying by hurricane lamp. He won a radio in a contest run by 4LG Longreach for an essay about their service, and that radio became his best friend.

The Department of Education hierarchy would've been astounded when he signed up for another year in Duchess, but he did so because he wanted to see 'his' Grade Sevens through to their Scholarship exam. He was overjoyed at the end of 1959 while on holiday at Bundaberg to receive telegrams from his five Grade Eights to tell him they were successful in their exam. Bill was regarded as a hero for pushing his Grade Eights over the line, and the next year there was once again a cause for celebration when he'd 'done it again!' Back then, the Scholarship exam was considered very important. One has to wonder whether these children ever realised how fortunate they were to have such a dedicated and noble man helping them get over the first step towards their secondary education. The Department of Education completely neglected young male teachers in remote areas and many resigned, having been forced to live in appalling conditions. Some became heavy drinkers and some suffered nervous breakdowns in their early twenties. To complain was to be classed as weak and carried the risk of being sentenced to an extension of time in 'the salt mines'. A common joke among Department staff at that time was: 'Well, you wanted sun, sand and sea, and two out of three ain't bad!'

One young teacher in a tiny school north-east of Duchess had to depend on a local station owner for accommodation. When he wrote to the Department saying he was going to get married during the Christmas vacation and wanted a transfer to a school with suitable accommodation, he was ignored. The couple lived for some time in a small enclosure they rigged up on the school verandah, but he eventually resigned and found work in a bank . . . lost to the teaching profession. Remote teachers were also poorly resourced, receiving little, if any, support from the Department, and were usually the poorest-paid person in their location. However, they were expected to set high standards of behaviour, work with multi-grades and perform miracles with the Scholarship exams. The District Inspector, located at Longreach with a gigantic area to cover, only visited Duchess once during Bill's two years.

Towards the end of his time, he began to doubt his sanity, as he was finding himself getting quite attached to its rugged landscape, brilliant red sunsets and wide star-filled night sky. Still, when the brown envelope arrived containing his transfer to the Bundaberg area, he had to admit he had had enough of the hardships and solitude. The Duchess had forced him to endure a tough apprenticeship, but the character-building experiences and the challenges he had risen to and conquered with the students stood him in great stead for the rest of his career.

Now, having read Bill's story so far, you would think that he would be rewarded with a good appointment, but instead he was sent to another of Queensland's lowest-grade and most poorly resourced one-teacher bush schools. Blessed with the prestigious-sounding name of Mullet Creek, his second school was in a very depressed, lower-socio-economic area, with no electricity, phone or reticulated water, accessible only by rough gravel road. He had no choice but to stay in a dilapidated, grotty farmhouse opposite the school, and fled it gratefully on weekends to his mother and stepfather's hotel in Bundaberg. He encountered the notoriously cranky School

Inspector, 'R C', who made his and the children's day (of his visit) utterly miserable. A ray of light during this depressing two years was meeting Anne, a nurse at the Mater Hospital. When Anne had to move with her family to Dalby, where she would complete her training and become a Sister, they became engaged. In 1962, Bill was given the post of district relieving teacher, based at Bundaberg West School, and lived in his parents' beach house at picturesque Elliott Heads. At last things were looking up!

The following year Bill and Anne were off to their Great Adventure. Part One: getting married; Part Two: flying to the Torres Strait to Bill's new appointment as head teacher of Darnley Island School, just 30 miles off New Guinea. When he had casually mentioned to his brand-new mother-in-law that the locals were still quite primitive and were reputed to have been cannibals before the London Missionary Society arrived there in 1871, her reaction was a horrified, 'No daughter of mine is going up there!' Anne, aged twenty, was very excited and managed to calm her mother down. She was to be in charge of the nursing station, the Medical Aid Post, near the school. They were expecting challenges and they got them! Darnley was beautiful and the islanders were friendly, but Bill and Anne frequently went through the white-ant-ridden floorboards of their house, which like everything on the island then took months to get fixed. There was no power – which meant no cooling, lights or refrigeration – no phone, and sometimes no water when the islanders would cut it off for a while. A boat arrived once a month with mail, papers and tucker. After a week they were sick of eating fish, fish, fish, and asked what else there was to eat. One of the locals, Bill's school janitor, promptly presented them with three huge lobsters!

It's possible to also get sick of eating lobster, so the janitor then presented them with a pig. Bill couldn't bear to kill it, so two island girls carried out the deed, then proceeded to clean the animal with paw-paw before cutting it up for them. This was a little different to what Anne was used to, but she took it all in her stride, and was kept busy treating patients for hookworm and malaria, and a variety of injuries. The janitor, who'd been given rum by some fool on a fishing boat, literally bit the bottom lip off his mate in the resulting drunken rage. Anne had to patch the victim up as best she could, which wasn't made easy by the fact the janitor had spat the lip out into the ocean. The janitor was extremely contrite. He liked to take Bill fishing and became very jealous if he went with anyone else.

In October, their first son, Mark, was born at Dalby. He was a month old before Bill saw him. As the only white child on Darnley, the islanders treated him as very special, and presented him with an ongoing wardrobe of lava-lavas – the native costume.

The school had close to 100 pupils enrolled and they were happy, lovely children who responded to Bill's encouragement. He asked the elders – men and women – if they would come to the school and teach the old crafts, including erecting thatched huts on the sportsground to provide shade. That was a great success. All the islanders, who spoke three languages and were brilliant mimics, were also natural musicians and singers. Bill and Anne loved hearing their beautiful singing in the quaint white church, built by the Anglican missionaries with the islanders' help, from pulverised coral. It featured a giant clam shell as a font. On Good Friday, shortly after their arrival, the Ovendens witnessed a miracle. They had been sitting on their verandah, listening to the three-part-harmony hymns wafting across from the church close by, while gazing out to sea. Both were lost in thoughts of their families and friends at Mass, far, far away, and, moved by the circumstances, they knelt to recite prayers. After several minutes they saw a sudden whirling motion in the water that gained in intensity, then began rising in a spout, climbing vertically till it was about 10 metres tall. Then it divided into two, then three – identical spouts in a triangular pattern, mesmerising them for several minutes till they dropped gradually. Bill sincerely believes this phenomenon – to him, a symbol of the Trinity – was more than a coincidence. He has often thought, *Were we being told we were not alone on that tiny speck in the remote Coral Sea?*

They had a fascinating time on Darnley, with enough ups and downs to fill a book. Bill was keen to enthuse some of the children to want to become teachers and return home to educate their own people. With this project in mind, and wanting to see another year of improvement in all the pupils' skills, he asked to stay on in 1964, then again in '65. Towards the end of the couple's stay there, they were visited by Queensland Premier Jack Pizzey, who the locals called Mr Fizzey. On his return to Brisbane, he gave a glowing report to the *Courier-Mail* about Bill's achievements with the island children, how impressed he was with how much he had improved the school, and stated that he wanted to fast-track his promotion to headmaster of a mainland school with a significant Indigenous population.

This article must have got up the nose of one or more of the powers-that-be in the Education Department, for Bill was then sent to another highly undesirable post in the state, which absolutely shocked him. With his experience and background it was a total insult to be relegated to being assistant teacher, and put in charge of no fewer than fifty-five (!) of the lowest achievers of Murgon School. Many of them were rude, undisciplined and badly behaved; most were not at all interested in attending school or learning anything. With no support from above, his considerable talents were wasted there. To make matters worse, the principal, who ran what was in Bill's eyes the worst school he had ever seen, insisted that his huge class of low achievers were subjected to having to take the same Friday weekly test as the high achievers. Then in an exercise of humiliation he'd send their marks, with the class percentages compared to other classes, around to all the other teachers. Most schools at that time were moulded into a certain modus operandi by the district inspectors, and principals wanting to move up the ladder dared not deviate. The Inspector who visited Murgon made a very poor impression on Bill. Apart from their differences of opinion on educating children as opposed to merely following a set regime, he tried to bait Bill into an argument by saying racist remarks about his Darnley Island students.

The only bright spot in the first six months of 1966 was the February arrival of Simon, a little brother for Mark. In June, after many requests for a transfer, he was finally sent as principal to a 'dying school' that was about to shut down. It had to be better than Murgon! Fairney View near Ipswich was a great little school and the children were all keen learners, but it was scheduled to be closed at the end of 1967 due to dropping enrolments. Having been made persona non grata with some jealous powers that-be-following the *Courier-Mail* story, Bill had to restart at the bottom rung of the principal's ladder to prove again that he could run a successful school. His toughest job at Fairney View was the disposal of the contents of the old 'dunny', which he did with a handkerchief wrapped around his face; but the odour of that, and even of his third baby's – Dominic's – nappies, was more pleasant than that of the 'excreta' tipped on him each Friday at his previous appointment.

Bill spent 1968 as head teacher at Peranga School, west of Toowoomba – a time he enjoyed with nice country kids, then he was given the challenge of nearby Evergreen School, where a positive attitude to learning was sadly lacking. Bill burnt a lot of midnight oil there to make up what these children had been missing out on. He encouraged them to set their sights broader than becoming workers on their families' small dairy farms. He made great progress and regards the victories he experienced there as the most fulfilling of his career. During those two years he experienced terrible mice and rat plagues. His house was in the middle of a black-soil plain surrounded by grain fields, and his dog, Prince, a Scotch–border collie cross, was kept very busy. Prince became a hero when he fought a huge king brown snake to the death in the schoolyard. The dog would not allow any of the children or Bill near the snake, which kept rearing up and striking at the dog. Eventually Prince charged in, grabbed it near its head and threw it high in the air, away from the onlookers.

Evergreen was the coldest place Bill ever lived in. Water pipes burst in winter. Perhaps those freezing winters were responsible for yet two more baby boys, Chris and Matt, arriving during their time on the Western Downs?

The District Inspector's reports on Bill's transformation of Evergreen School were highly flattering, and finally, after his disappointments, he was upwardly mobile, spending the next fourteen years as Principal of Marlborough ('72–75), Townsville South ('75–78), Gympie Central ('79–85) and Maryborough West ('86) state schools. In all these places, Bill not only met the challenges each school presented, but extended himself to form or become involved with – as coach or committeeman – local and school sporting organisations, in all sports from rugby league to table tennis, plus musical activities. At Marlborough (the birthplace of tennis great Rod Laver), Bill decided the children should be coached in 'taipan drill' – what to do if they saw one of the deadly, aggressive snakes in the school grounds. On his first morning there, he saw two of the killers peering through a window, standing on their tails in the trough where the children drank water. What a shock! He despatched them with a long piece of twisted wire, then contacted famous snake handler Ram Chandra, who was only too happy to visit the school and talk to the children about taipans.

Townsville South School provided Bill with plenty of 'lively' memories. It was a poor area that the police frequently visited and had many 'latchkey' children. Bill's staff – apart from one male teacher – were very supportive with his efforts to help the neglected children in the school. A wonderful lady, Elsie Cartwright, brought lunches and clean clothes to her classroom to give to the children who needed them. When one of the new teachers complained about the smell of some of the obviously unwashed pupils, Bill took her for a drive around the neighbourhood to show her what sort of background many of them came from. When Bill asked one mother why her five-year-old son hadn't been at school all week, she replied in a don't-care voice, 'I haven't seen 'im for a week!'

When he'd first started straightening the pupils up, he went home one night and was highly amused to hear, then see, one of the most rebellious – a girl called Jenny – jumping up and down on the trampoline in his front yard, yelling in time to her bouncing, 'Oven-den's a ba-sted! Oven-den's a ba-sted!' To her amazement, he called out through the louvres, 'I love you too Jenny!' It was a great feeling to get through to these children, get them learning, and improve their lives.

Gympie Central was a very 'tired' school needing a good shake-up when he took over. Programs and policies were overhauled amid much resistance from an entrenched staff. However, when positive progress was being made, they were won over to his way of doing things. He re-entered the school in the Interschool Sports Comp, organised a school orchestra and many concerts, and, with the help of other principals, a driver training facility. When he moved to Maryborough, the staff of his new school received a large 'missing person' poster from his previous workmates at Gympie, featuring his photo and these words: 'We miss him. Please send him back!' Maryborough West was years behind what he'd left at Gympie. It was back to square one, but he battled on with the energetic enthusiasm of a dedicated soldier. During his first month at Maryborough he was asked to also act as the Inspector of Schools, Wide Bay. Soon afterward he had to face the unpleasant task of handing a male teacher, charged with molestation of pupils, over to police. As a principal it's wise to always expect the unexpected, but this incident was a particularly shocking experience.

In June that year, he was appointed District Inspector of Schools, Emerald, responsible for the North-West and Central Queensland regions – an enormous area. It had taken him twenty years since Fairney View to get to this position of prestige and power – where he should have been at least a decade earlier. At last he could fulfil his ambition to be an inspector regarded as helpful to school communities. Bill had very bad memories of a few destructive ones. His new position was, due to the geographic size of his territory, only suited to someone of great energy and stamina. He regularly drove 800–1000 kilometres in a day, several days a week, often on rough roads, dodging roos, emus and pigs. When he took fresh bread and milk to teachers in remote areas, memories flooded back of how hard he'd done it years before, compared to modern conditions. Setting up networks for isolated children to contact each other was one of his proudest achievements, and the new Distance Ed School in Longreach was one of his favourite institutions. It was always entertaining to hear the station children telling him, or their teacher, their 'news' over the radio. ('We marked calves yesterday, Miss, 'n' Dad knocked the tomcat's pills out too!')

In 1988 he was appointed Supervisor of Studies, Brisbane South region, selecting and transferring teachers state-wide, appraising teachers and principals for promotion, and leading the region's Social Education Program. Tied to a telephone for six days a week, Bill often missed the freedoms and the interaction with the students he had previously enjoyed. The job was productive and professionally rewarding, but at times frustrating. He could see the educational effort in some Brisbane schools was well below that in many of the country areas, where youthful inexperience and exuberance often resulted in exciting educational effort and programs.

A practical bloke with commonsense to match his many other skills, he was right in his element overseeing, from go to whoa, the establishment of Hilliard State School at the Gold Coast. He researched vital information such as the catchment area and population estimates for several years ahead, interacted with the community and the Works Department, then carefully chose the right staff. With that highlight of his career executed to perfection, Bill decided 1991 was a good year to retire. He could see the Education Department was gearing up for a massive restructure that would not suit him. A colleague who'd attended Teachers College with him, back in '55 and '56, had reached the same conclusion. Driving together to the city to formalise their resignations, they were like two kids celebrating break-up day.

Bill credits Anne with having made the often-difficult career he had chosen much easier by being a tremendous support in many ways. To have an intelligent, cheerful and sympathetic person to discuss the day's problems with was worth more than gold. Anne would have many stories herself about the conditions they sometimes lived in. They now live the good life they deserve. In a quiet area on Brisbane's northern outskirts, their comfortable modern home is full of interesting mementoes and has lovely bush views. As always, Bill is fit as a mallee bull and enjoys many physical activities, plus the cultural outings available to people who live in or near cities. He is a man who has made his mark in the world and had a positive influence on literally thousands of children and hundreds of young teachers. Wherever he has been, he's changed things for the better . . . and it hasn't been easy. If ever a man deserved an enjoyable retirement, it's Bill Ovenden.

BONZER

SANDY THORNE

'I was born to make people laugh. Marry that with an impulsive nature, add to the mix an undisciplined childhood, chuck in a psyche that rebels against silly rules and, hey presto, you've produced a bloody ratbag!' – Sandy Thorne

Growing up in Bald Hills near Brisbane in the 1950s and '60s, when dunnies were outside and Sunday roasts were likely to come from you own chook pen, Sandy had a great time making the most of her freedom in the glory days of the Sunshine State. But she also got into more strife than Flash Gordon. With a philandering father drifting in and out of her home life and a collection of very loyal animals as her constant companions, Sandy honed her survival skills and quickly learned how to talk her way out of sticky situations, emerging with an ability to laugh at herself (and to entertain the class in the teacher's absence).

This hilarious memoir is a bonzer adventure through childhood in a bygone era.

NURSES of the
OUTBACK

ANNABELLE BRAYLEY

The work of a nurse is challenging enough, but when you add a remote location, the stakes are so much higher. Meet fifteen courageous people who prove that the outback runs on nurse power.

There's Anna, who is on duty as the fury of Cyclone Yasi tears through inland Queensland; Maureen in outback New South Wales, who faces everything from a snakebite to a helicopter crash; and Catherine, newly graduated and determined to make a difference in the Gulf Country she and her rodeo-riding husband call home.

From some of the most remote places on earth, we witness the harshness and isolation as well as the camaraderie of life in small towns. These intrepid nurses tend to life-threatening emergencies, manage everyday health care and even patch up the local pets. From Bidyadanga to Broken Hill, Mount Isa to Marree, these tales are full of gutsy feats and classic outback spirit.

Annabelle Brayley collected the stories that appeared in the best-selling *Bush Nurses*.